THE DECLINE OF EUROPEAN NAVAL FORCES

THE DECLINE
OF EUROPEAN
NAVAL FORCES

Challenges to Sea Power in an Age of
Fiscal Austerity and Political Uncertainty

JEREMY STÖHS

Naval Institute Press

Annapolis, Maryland

Naval Institute Press
291 Wood Road
Annapolis, MD 21402

Library of Congress cataloging-in-publication data is available.
978-1-68247-308-5 (hardcover)
978-1-68247-309-2 (eBook)

♾ Print editions meet the requirements of ANSI/NISO z39.48-1992 (Permanence of Paper).
Printed in the United States of America.

26 25 24 23 22 21 20 19 18   9 8 7 6 5 4 3 2 1

First printing

To Diana

CONTENTS

ILLUSTRATIONS

FOREWORD

In 1902, in his second annual message to Congress, President Theodore Roosevelt remarked, "A good Navy is not a provocation to war. It is the surest guaranty of peace." A good navy needs sufficient commitment to machines, personnel, manufacturing, management, money, and mentality, as naval historians Jon Sumida, David Rosenberg, and the late Wilfried Stallmann have repeatedly pointed out. But what if peace—or the impression thereof—lures good navies (and their political masters) to scale down on the number of ships and personnel, accept reduced readiness, recruitment and retention, diversify dramatically in absence of a common threat, focus on lower-end missions, and accept naval deindustrialization and a post-heroic, "peace dividend" mentality? How good can these navies still be in peace, crises, and war? How reliable are they for their overseas allies, how much of a force are they to reckon with for others? These are some questions that Jeremy Stöhs tries to answer. His study focuses on allied and partner navies in Europe and their evolution after the Cold War.

It is the first comprehensive book to lay out how European sea power has declined after the termination of the superpower conflict. In that, it is especially timely given recent events. Global developments with maritime and naval implications are numerous: Russia's annexation of Crimea, the hybrid conflict in eastern Ukraine, the rise of Islamic radicals, the brutal civil wars in Syria and Iraq (which are lighting up the entire Middle East), a row of failing and failed states in North Africa and Central Africa, quests for regional hegemony in the Indian Ocean, and proxy wars around the Strait of Hormuz and the Gulf of Aden, to name but a few. This conflagration requires a somber assessment by European policy makers. The question begs an answer just what kind of navies they want and need, and what political ends this seapower should be directed at in particular. Possible turmoil in the Far East—over the South China Sea and the Korea conflict, to name but two—with unclear ramifications for Europe, add to their set of problems. Transnational global challenges of this century such as climate change, demography, the future of international organizations and the rules-based order, and the reliability of deterrence endure. President Donald Trump repeatedly asserts that "America First" is the new normal. This creates a perfect storm for Europeans already scrambling to meet NATO's self-asserted 2 percent of GDP investment in defense, and to contain the fallout of Brexit, the eurozone crisis, and the rise of political disunity on the Continent.

Europe desperately depends on the maritime highways for its trade. To defend itself and its allies, it must also factor in, and make good use of, the sea as a room to maneuver, to project power, to deter enemies, and certainly to fight. Indeed, the systemic relevance of navies rests on unimpaired access to, and use of, the sea lines of communication. This means that Europe will have to shoulder more responsibility, very soon. If one accepts the premise that the U.S. Navy can or will no longer want to serve as a global force-projection navy and inheritor of the trident that is sea control, Europe is faced with relinquishing command of the sea to other powers. It would have to accept the dire consequences of such transfers of power, or finally step up to the plate to do more. Only through this latter measure, by being honest about its own maritime defense, can transatlantic relations be invigorated properly. After all, NATO is a fundamentally maritime Atlantic alliance.

It also holds true that one goes to war with the forces you have, not the ones you want. As Stöhs' book demonstrates, nearly all European naval forces have dramatically reduced their set of forces from their Cold War heyday. In parallel, absent a blue-water challenge, they sought to embrace the littoralization of naval strategy, namely the rise of unconventional, asymmetric, and hybrid challenges in the confined and shallow waters of the world and the corresponding coasts. Traditional warfare areas were often underinvested in—and gradually unlearned. Counter-piracy, embargo operations, humanitarian assistance, disaster relief, and counterterrorism evolved as central tasks, albeit with platforms designed for much more complex and traditional naval missions. In the outgoing continental era of Western interventions—think Balkans, Afghanistan, Iraq, and Mali—naval forces received significantly less attention in European governments. In what has been characterized as "post-heroic societies" unwilling and unable to invest into defense properly, retention and modernization of the force also suffered dramatically.

A conceptual return to high-end naval missions that will also encompass the low end, coupled with a broader appreciation for the costs and benefits of sea power, is in high demand. This must also include harmonization and ultimately widespread integration of procurement, training, operations, and resourcing to form building blocks of a truly European defense. Spending more in military hardware alone will almost certainly not do the trick. Europe also needs more investment in sound academic work on sea power and how its navies can shoulder responsibility properly. Its people, its governments, and even its challengers need to understand the trajectories of sea power. Europe also needs young and intrinsically motivated individuals who can advance the proper understanding of what navies do, and the strategic and historical implications and timelines involved (the fact that Herr Stöhs hails from a landlocked country like Austria is inspiring!). I am glad that the Institute for Security Policy at Kiel University is able to contribute a small part to Mr. Stöhs' endeavor by funding the indexing for this book, providing him with an opportunity to expand on this study as part of his PhD dissertation, and expose his findings in the conferences and workshops of the Kiel Seapower Series. It goes without saying that we hold President Roosevelt's words dear to our heart.

Dr. Sebastian Bruns, Head of Center for Maritime Strategy & Security at the Institute for Security Policy at Kiel University (ISPK|CMSS)

ACKNOWLEDGMENTS

I would like to express my gratitude to Professor Joachim Krause and Stefan Hansen at the Institute for Security Policy at Kiel University, as well as Dr. Sebastian Bruns, head of the adjunct Center for Maritime Strategy and Security, for their support in publishing this book. I am indebted to Astrid Kuhn at the Stiftung Wissenschaft & Demokratie (Foundation for Science & Democracy) for the financial support of my research. I am also grateful to my colleagues at the Austrian Center for Intelligence, Propaganda & Security Studies (University of Graz) for the fruitful collaboration over the years. Above all, I want to thank my parents, family, and friends for their support throughout my life and Diana for her unwavering love.

ACRONYMS AND ABBREVIATIONS

A2/AD: anti-access/area denial

AAW: antiair warfare

ABM: antiballistic missile

AIP: air-independent propulsion

APAR: active phased-array radar, also AESA (active electronically scanned array)

APR: Asia-Pacific region

ASM: anti-ship missile

AsuW: anti-surface warfare

ASW: anti-submarine warfare

CATOBAR: catapult-arrested take-off barrier-arrested recovery

CIWS: close-in weapon system

CODOG: combined diesel or gas

COIN: counterinsurgency

CT: counterterrorism

CTF: combined task force

DOD: U.S. Department of Defense

EEZ: exclusive economic zone

EMI/EMC: electromagnetic interference/electromagnetic compatibility

EMPAR: European multifunction phased array radar

ERAM: Extended-Range Active Missile (RIM-174 Standard Missile 6)

ESSM: Evolved Seasparrow Missile

FREMM: Frégate Européenne Multi-Missions

GDP: gross domestic product

GIN/GIUK: Greenland-Iceland-Norway or Greenland-Iceland-U.K. gap

HADR: human assistance and disaster relief

ISIS: Islamic State in Iraq and Syria (also IS: Islamic State)

ISR: intelligence, surveillance, and reconnaissance

JMSDF: Japan Maritime Self-Defense Force

LCF: Luchtverdedigings en Commandofregat, Dutch air-defense frigate

LCS: littoral combat ship

LHA: landing helicopter, assault (amphibious assault ship)

LHD: landing helicopter dock

LPD: landing platform dock

LSD: landing ship dock

MCM: mine countermeasure

MOD: ministry of defense (general)

MPA: maritime patrol aircraft

MW: mine warfare

NATO: North Atlantic Treaty Organization

NFR: NATO Frigate Replacement for the 1990s

OPV: offshore patrol vessel

OSCE: Organization for Security and Cooperation in Europe

PAAMS: principle antiair missile system

PRC: People's Republic of China

RAM: radar absorbing material

RDN: Royal Danish Navy

RIMPAC: Rim of the Pacific (exercise)

RN: Royal Navy

RNLN: Royal Netherlands Navy

RNoN: Royal Norwegian Navy

SAM: surface-to-air missile

SAR: search and rescue

SCALP/Storm Shadow: Système de Croisière Autonome à Longue Portée (General Purpose Long Range Standoff Cruise Missile)

SDR: Strategic Defense Review (U.K.)

SDSR: *Strategic Defence and Security Review* (U.K.)

SIAF: Spanish-Italian Amphibious Battlegroup

SIGINT: signal intelligence

SLBM: submarine-launched ballistic missile

SLOC: sea lines of communication

SM: standard missile

SMART-L: Signaal multibeam acquisition radar for tracking, L-band

SNMCMG: Standing NATO Mine Countermeasure Group

SNMG: Standing NATO Maritime Group

SSBN: ship, submersible, ballistic missile, nuclear (nuclear-powered ballistic missile submarines)

SSK: ship, submersible, conventional (diesel-electric powered submarine)

SSM: surface-to-surface missile

SSN: ship, submersible, nuclear (nuclear-powered attack submarine)

STANAVFORLANT: Standing Naval Force Atlantic

STANAVFORMED: Standing Naval Force Mediterranean

STOVL: short take-off and vertical landing

SYLVER: Système de Lancement Vertical (vertical-launch system)

TEU: twenty-foot equivalent unit (standard container)

UNIFIL: United Nations Interim Force in Lebanon

UNISOM: United Nations Operation in Somalia

USN: United States Navy

USSR: Union of Soviet Socialist Republics

VLS: vertical-launch system

PART 1

Introduction

There are no trends extant—technological, economic, political, or military—which suggest an imminent diminution in the strategic leverage of sea power.

Colin S. Gray

Over the past five hundred years, every century can be considered a maritime century. Decade after decade, seafaring peoples—from the Portuguese and Spanish to the French, Dutch, and British—ventured farther out into the vast realms of blue water in search of uncharted lands, new trade routes, and vast riches. However, this process was far from being a peaceful endeavor and many wars were fought to decide who was to command the sea. In former days, it was crucial for economic power to be backed by military force and few rulers were foolish enough to underestimate the utility of naval forces in protecting their political and economic interests. It was this competitive nature among the leading European states, and the useful marriage of commercial and military sea power that put the West far ahead of the rest, thus permitting the creation of colonial empires.[1] Consequently, other powers unwilling or unable to follow suit, such as the Chinese Ming Dynasty or the Ottoman Empire, were degraded to second- or even third-rank powers.[2]

Today, naval scholars rejoice at the achievements of those exciting times. Historians marvel at the superb seamanship of Magellan,

3

Vasco da Gama, or Sir Francis Drake and study the military feats of Lord Horatio Nelson, Admiral Tōgō Heihachirō, and Adm. Chester Nimitz. Today, the sea no longer appears to be the great unknown it once was—full of opportunities as well as constant danger. In fact, traditional naval conflict has become a rare sight and only a few people are still alive to tell the tales of the last great war at sea. Yet the underpinning rules of geopolitics—that is to say, how the geography of our planet affects how we interact with each other in politics and international relations—remain constant. In this sense, the oceans of this world will continue to be the most important medium of power distribution on this planet. As Colin S. Gray states: "If the coming of the railroad, internal combustion engine, air, missile, nuclear, and space eras could not demote the strategic value of sea power significantly, it is difficult to see what could emerge to do so over the next several decades."[3]

It may seem somewhat peculiar for a scholar from a small country like Austria to write about a topic concerning naval matters.[4] After all, the end of World War I and the subsequent provisions of the Treaty of Saint-Germain not only stripped Austria of its entire naval fleet but, more importantly, also of its direct access to the sea. Therefore, since 1918 (except for the period of Nazi rule), Austria has been a landlocked country and thus part of roughly 23 percent of the world's states not to have a coastline.[5] However, its prosperity and wealth are inextricably linked to the sea—even if the average Austrian citizen wastes little time pondering this circumstance.

Life on our planet finds its origin in the salty matter we call the ocean. Over two-thirds of the earth's surface is covered by this enormous body of water that, together with the seabed below, provides mankind with a precious source of food, energy, and raw materials. Of equally great importance is the ability to carry these goods in the safest and most cost-effective way—by sea. In fact, 90 percent of global commerce is currently transported by ships, along lines that span the oceans, from continent to continent. One can imagine them as great highways at sea.[6] What many people in Austria, and elsewhere for that matter, forget is that in the globalized world in which we live, every single state relies on the unimpeded flow of maritime commerce. Although Austria does not directly import and export goods by sea, its two largest trading partners, Germany and Italy, certainly do. In fact, both countries have significant stakes in seaborne trade, as do their European neighbors such as Denmark, Great Britain, Spain, and Greece. Were a crisis to arise somewhere in the world, impeding trade via the sea lanes, the global supply chain would quickly be affected and possibly even falter; it would have severe repercussions on industries, economies, and people across the globe.[7] If one of the narrow straits, such as the Strait of Hormuz through which over 17 billion barrels of oil pass every day, were obstructed or closed to shipping by hostile actors, the consequences would quickly be felt across the globe—even in a state as neutral and benign as Austria. Therefore, maintaining the freedom of navigation, also known as the "good order at sea," as well as shared access to the global commons is of utmost importance.[8]

For the past seventy years the United States and its naval forces have protected the international system of maritime trade.[9] As retired Rear Admiral Chris Parry observes, "America [has been] able to protect—and guarantee itself and its friends—access to the world's resources and deny access to an opponent or other disturber of the international peace."[10] However, the tide is turning. We are witnessing fundamental changes in geopolitics the likes of which we have not seen in the last five hundred years. For the first time in modern history, the center of gravity in world affairs is in the process of shifting from the West (the Atlantic and Europe) to the East (the Indian Ocean and Asia-Pacific region). In light of this development, there is the possibility that the United States, like Britain before it, will no longer be willing or able to perform the role as the global guardian of the seas. Yet, security at sea will remain of pivotal importance to guarantee all states free access to a large part of the global commons and the global economy. Hence, it is also in the interest of Europe as a whole to make provisions for this eventuality, something many European states have neglected over the last twenty-five years. Sea power, both of an economic and military nature, "will be critical to the world's future, one way or another," the renowned British naval historian Geoffrey Till concludes. "The only real question," he adds, "is whose seapower it will be?"[11] Over the course of the following chapters, I will provide some answers to this pressing question.

With the USSR relegated to the pages of history in December 1991, many people believed that the threat from maleficent regimes to Europe's security had disappeared once and for all. After almost sixty years of militarization and the looming threat of nuclear war within the heart of Europe, peace had finally come. As an immediate reaction, military funding was cut across the board as the large armies, fashioned for the cataclysmic showdown with the forces of the Warsaw Pact, were no longer needed. Nearly all the European countries reduced their defense spending in the initial aftermath of the Cold War. For the most part, these reductions continued for more than two decades. Unsurprisingly, smaller defense budgets also meant that Europe's armies shrunk in overall size. West Germany's military, for example, had roughly 330,000 active duty personnel and 700,000 reservists in 1990; the current land forces have been reduced to around 60,000 service members. At the same time the number of mechanized units has dropped from 16 panzer brigades to 12 panzer companies.[12] Or put differently, out of the 2,125 Leopard 2 main battle tanks delivered to the Bundeswehr, only 176 were operational in 2014.[13] Similar examples can be found across Europe. Not only had the threat of the Red Army and its large mechanized forces disappeared but, more importantly, the military operations in the Balkans, Iraq, and Afghanistan heralded a paradigmatic shift in how land warfare was fought.[14] Although heavily armored units represented the only credible protection against improvised explosive devices, rocket-propelled grenades, and roadside bombs in these contingencies, the evolution of counterinsurgency and counterterrorism warfare made large numbers of mechanized units seem anachronistic and unnecessary.[15]

Naval warfare, on the other hand, has also witnessed significant—yet far less costly—changes. Many principle functions of naval forces have remained constant over the centuries and navies today conduct very similar missions as they did a quarter of a century ago. However, the conditions of the post–Cold War security environment allowed more traditional naval capabilities, such as sea control and conventional deterrence against peer competitors, to give way to a much broader range of the naval tasks. Although the so-called post–modern navies of today are, in theory, envisioned to fulfill duties running the gamut of the intensity spectrum, in practice, Europe's naval forces increasingly focus on effectively operating in operational environments at the lower end of the intensity scale. These operational environments are markedly different from those of the Cold War.[16] For example, a greater emphasis was placed on expeditionary capabilities, necessary to conduct stability operations, peace enforcement, and crisis management in faraway littoral regions of the world, or using naval assets for human assistance operations.

Notwithstanding this evolution of naval operations and the different interpretations of what navies ought to be able to do,[17] the maritime sphere, by nature, precludes similar developments as those of land-based forces. Asymmetrical warfare, despite being a buzzword in naval quarters, has less impact on naval planning and the shape of naval forces than the unconventional fighting that has become such a common feature of modern land warfare. The "wars among the people"[18] we see on land today cannot be fought at sea. As Sir Julian S. Corbett wrote in his seminal work, *Some Principles of Maritime Strategy,* "You cannot conquer sea because it is not susceptible of ownership [and] you cannot subsist your armed forces upon it as you can upon enemy's territory."[19] Therefore, because the oceans are uninhabited by man, no person can be subjugated to the maritime forces at sea.

While there is a general reluctance among Western states to engage in military ground operations after the experiences in the so-called Global War on Terror, the number of naval operations conducted by European states has continuously grown over the past few decades. Yet the drastic decline of available naval assets, a concomitant downsizing of Europe's armed forces, and the consequent reduction of specific capabilities have left operational gaps and precarious shortfalls in training and readiness. These developments pose grave risks to the future of Europe's ability to protect its interests—and not only at sea. To avoid the possible detriment such a development could have on the prosperity and security of the people living on the continent, the Europeans need to rethink their propensity for saving as much money as possible on defense.

History provides numerous examples in which the rise and fall of great powers was decided by a state's or an alliance's ability to successfully engage in trade by sea, and if challenged, to protect its vital interests by hard power in the form of its naval forces. Four hundred years ago, Sir Walter Raleigh famously stated, "Whoever commands the sea, commands the trade; whosoever commands the trade of the world commands the riches of the world, and consequently the world itself."[20] Despite dramatic changes in the global security environment over the last two decades, there is no indication that the fundamental axioms of sea power will be called into question any time soon.[21] Therefore, it is the responsibility of current and future governments to decide whether Europe will be relegated to the outermost fringes of a world centered on the Pacific Ocean or if Europe can reverse its growing geopolitical and strategic irrelevance by reviving and recommitting to its naval capabilities.

The main aim of this study is to gain insight into the development of Europe's naval forces since the end of the Cold War. A better comprehension of the manifold changes undergone over the past twenty-five years by the most important European navies warrants a thorough analysis of defense policies, fleet structure, and naval operations. We will therefore focus on the effects the post–Cold War security architecture has had on the selected naval organizations. In an increasingly diverse security environment, states and their armed services have had to deal with the emergence of new technology, growing threats, and conflict across all areas. Many European states have reacted to these seismic shifts by transforming their military forces. As a result, most European naval forces today bear little resemblance to the respective fleets at the end of the Cold War.

An analysis of eleven different navies, over the course of twenty-five years, is prone to generalization. This is particularly true when each navy is viewed through different prisms—in this case, strategy, technology, and operations. Historians will find the brief descriptions of past events wanting while strategists might criticize that important capstone documents are not mentioned or insufficiently discussed. Practitioners with years of operational experience are likely to point out the shortcomings in analyzing past naval operations while others might have hoped for a more comprehensive examination of naval technology and its effects on sea power. In truth, every single navy deserves to be discussed at length, filling volumes in the process. But such a detailed study is far beyond the scope of this work. The following chapters provide an overview of selected developments in Europe's naval history. Given these caveats, this book is intended to reach a broad readership (with or without an extensive naval background). It is hoped that it can serve as a stepping stone and an incentive to further pursue the study of European sea power.

CHAPTER 1

Principles of Sea Power

Earth is called the Blue Planet for a reason. From space the shimmering blue orb allows the observer to comprehend the sheer vastness of the world's oceans. Seventy percent of its surface is covered with water and 80 percent of the world's population lives within 100 miles of the coast.[1] Although we neither find shelter nor sanctuary among its waves, we have been able to access the valuable resources it contains and found means to move upon its surface in a most cost efficient manner. Thus, the world's trade is dependent on the waters connecting the continents. In fact, 90 percent of global commerce travels by sea. What's more, the unique characteristics of the continental landmass and demographic factors have led to 75 percent of this trade having to traverse a small number of narrow canals and straits.[2]

The moment man ventured out to sea, the maritime realm became a sphere of conflicting interests. Different parties sought to expand their influence by peaceful means and commercial enterprise as well as by the use of force. Hence, the concept of "sea power" was born. Despite the dramatic evolution of mankind over the ages, many principles that govern this concept remained constant. "Much about sea power is enduring," Rear Admiral Parry offers. "[It] can be best expressed as the combined investment in the sea of the various components and resources of a state or enterprise in the pursuit of favourable outcomes."[3] These investments are neither constant nor can they be strictly categorized, but instead depend on a multitude of factors. In general, a distinction can be made between *hard power* and *soft power*. The former is based on the use or threat of force (economic or military), while the latter is understood to be ruled by the principles of cooperation and consensus, by means of diplomacy, by respectable policies, and other such benign measures.[4] Over the last several centuries, those countries capable of merging hard and soft power—such as Portugal, Spain, France, and Britain—have created vast colonial empires and could make their economic and military presence felt around the world.[5]

From this bipartite approach, sea power can be subdivided into four elements: 1) the business of international commercial trade by sea; 2) the utilization of the ocean's resources, be it the exploitation of oil and gas under the seabed or creating energy from the ocean's continuous tidal flow; 3) using naval forces or economic instruments in support of national interests in time of peace; and 4) naval operations in war.[6] As we can see, sea power cannot be fully understood without considering all these aspects of maritime endeavors. Admiral Parry acknowledged, "In this regard, appearance can be deceptive. The most powerful navy in the world is that of the USA; the largest merchant fleet is held by the Greeks; the largest fishing fleet, by volume and activity, is Chinese; and the biggest commercial shipping company is Danish. In this sense, sea power is diffused."[7]

Trying to address all forms of sea power would be a futile effort. Our main aim therefore is to focus on Europe's naval forces; in other words, the individual states' naval hard power. Although chiefly European naval issues—in peace as well as in crisis and war—will be analyzed, the economic factors of sea power (commerce and the exploitation of natural resources) merit attention and will therefore also be touched upon.

History has shown that the marriage of naval power and commercial maritime power constitutes a principal factor in a state's ability to gain power, wealth, and prosperity. As Alfred Thayer Mahan famously stated: "Control of the sea by maritime commerce and naval supremacy means predominant influence in the world . . . (and) is the chief among the merely material elements in the power and prosperity of the nations."[8] Much has changed since Mahan published his profound writings in 1890. However, his ideas and those of his British contemporary, the naval strategist Julian S. Corbett, remain quintessential for the understanding of sea power. Their insight into maritime strategy remains as timely as ever, as it relates to military as well as economic issues.

From a modern perspective, the two strategists based their presumptions on the somewhat "old fashioned [concept of the] nation-state as the basic unit of concern," Geoffrey Till explains, whereas today we are witnessing a period in which these formally established systems of statehood, society, and civilization are being perforated by the profound changes in the way people engage with each other. Notwithstanding these developments, any scholar concerned with maritime issues needs to indulge in these "seminal and enduring works of maritime strategy."[9] This is, according to Mahan, because the elements of sea power are governed by "the unchangeable, or unchanging, order of things remaining the same in cause and effect, from age to age. . . . They belong as it were, to the Order of Nature, of whose stability so much [was heard of in Mahan's day]; whereas tactics, using as its instruments the weapons made by man, shares in the change and progress of the race from generation to generation. From time to time the superstructure of tactics has to be altered or wholly torn down, but the old foundations of strategy so far remain, as though laid upon a rock."[10]

Therefore, we can assume that the principles of sea power described in this chapter will continue to remain applicable in the decades to come. Where maritime strategy, war on and from the sea, and the utility of sea power in general are concerned, a close reading of history is of paramount importance in forming viable conclusions about the past and making meaningful predictions of the future. As Mahan wrote in the opening pages of his chapter on "Naval Principles," in *On Naval Warfare:* "A study of the military history of the past . . . is enjoined by great military leaders as essential to correct ideas and to the skillful conduct of war in the future."[11] He continues by arguing that throughout time, military tactics have often undergone change due to the evolution of weapon technology, while other aspects of war at sea have remained unaltered and universally applicable, thereby forming general principles.[12]

One of these general principles is the purpose of naval forces. The British scholar Ken Booth argued that the three basic functions of a navy are its military, diplomatic, and policing roles. Of the three elements, the military function represents the foundation of this trinity.[13] Essentially, military force can be utilized to attack an enemy, to defend oneself against attack, or to deter an enemy from attacking.[14] Naval forces are in many cases the best tool to perform these tasks. They are able to react to crisis quickly and can project power over great distances. At the same time, navies have distinct advantages over other military forces because they can operate freely in the vast realms of international waters. As Adm. Carlisle A. H. Trost put it, "Operating in international waters, [navies enjoy] the unique advantage of being able to signal menace without violating sovereignty, and once the need is past, of being able to sail over the horizon without signaling retreat."[15] Ultimately, the sole purpose of navies is "to influence decisions and events on land, because that is where people live."[16]

To have an influence on history, as the title of Mahan's writing indicates, a country's navy must command the sea. However, it would seem obvious that, given the vastness of the oceans, any effort to patrol it in its entirety at all times would be a hopeless undertaking. "You cannot conquer the sea because it is not susceptible of ownership," Corbett rightfully pointed out. "You cannot, as lawyers say, 'reduce it into possession,' because you cannot exclude neutrals from it as you can from territory you conquer [and] you cannot subsist your armed force upon it as you can upon enemy's territory."[17] Therefore, he concludes, its natural state is to be free from possession—or "uncommanded."[18] So how can a naval force exercise sea power if it cannot command the sea as an army can command enemy territory?

According to Mahan the key lies in *communications*. In this sense, the term denotes "the lines of movement by which a military body, army or fleet, is kept in living condition with the national power."[19] However, such lines of communication are not limited to military strategy but rather can be applied more generally to any form of communication between two geographical points of distribution.[20] For example, the great highways at sea upon which 90 percent of global commerce travels represent such strategic lines of communication. A navy capable of controlling this maritime traffic is, in turn, able to greatly influence decisions made on land. Both Mahan and Corbett therefore ascribe to the principle that controlling these strategically important sea lines of communications (SLOCs) is the key to preeminent sea power. According to Corbett,

> By winning command of the sea we remove [a possible] barrier from our own path, thereby placing ourselves in position to exert direct military pressure upon the national life of our enemy ashore, while at the same time we solidify it against him and prevent his exerting direct military pressure upon ourselves. Command of the sea, therefore, means nothing but the control of maritime communications, whether for commercial or military purposes. The object of naval warfare is the control of communications, and not, as in land warfare, the conquest of territory.[21]

Since the end of World War II the U.S. Navy has fashioned a fleet powerful enough to control the global SLOCs. In fact, throughout this period, only the Soviet Union ever seriously challenged U.S. naval supremacy. However, throughout its history Russia has remained a continental land power, and despite its impressive naval buildup during the Cold War, it was never able to overcome Western naval dominance. Ultimately, NATO and its principles of sea power withstood the test.[22] Gray further expands on the superiority of sea powers over land power: "One argument is that modern history has shown the inability of preponderant continental power to fashion potent enough maritime (or air) instruments for the defeat of offshore sea powers. Another, more convincing, is that no land power has been sufficiently preponderant on land as to have the surplus resources necessary for the conduct of successful war against great-power enemies offshore."[23]

Today, the pillars upon which U.S. naval strategy rests are a reiteration of this "maritime narrative."[24] Despite criticism of not having a similarly comprehensive maritime strategy as the one it pursued during the 1980s, the U.S. Navy is making provisions to remain the world's only globally steaming navy, capable of substantial forward presence; maintaining credible nuclear and conventional deterrence; exacting sea control and power projection; providing maritime security; and providing human assistance and disaster relief (HADR).[25]

The conclusion we can reasonably draw from over five hundred years of predominance through sea power is that the European states with direct access to the sea also used to understand the importance of powerful naval fleets as a guarantor of economic wealth and prosperity. Yet it seems that in the wake of the Soviet demise, the Europeans largely considered their own security and that of international system of trade as inviolable. How else can the dramatic decline in the size and capability of Europe's naval forces since the end of the Cold War be explained?

Today, the process of designing and building capital warships and other naval platforms can take decades. By the time a ship, submarine, or aircraft enters service, the security environment in which it will operate might differ greatly from that for which it was originally designed. Similarly, if a government decides to cancel the procurement of a new weapons platform or finds itself under financial pressure to reduce the size of its fleet, it will be faced with profound strategic ramifications down the line. Therefore, eliminating naval capabilities—such as the ability to operate submarines or maritime patrol aircraft due to short-term fiscal restraints—can rightfully be considered dangerously shortsighted. In practice, it strips the country of important political tools of hard power and in most cases the costs to regain such capabilities make such an undertaking difficult, if not impossible.

Modern warships need to be capable of conducting a vast variety of missions. During the greater part of the Cold War, NATO destroyers and frigates were designed to protect resupply convoys from the United States to Europe against the threat of attack by Soviet submarines. Guided-missile cruisers provided the necessary air defense for carrier battle groups engaging the enemy in various theaters around the globe. Nowadays, most surface combatants are no longer classified as cruisers; rather, destroyers and frigates conduct everything from antipiracy operations to fleet air-defense tasks. Therefore, ships need to be designed with sufficient room for incremental upgrades over their service life—which in some cases can be fifty years. In keeping with this dictum, the current trend among all first-rate navies around the world is to operate large, multipurpose surface combatants.

As the size and sophistication of these platforms grow, so does the price of each ship. This development constitutes one of the reasons for the overall decline of ship inventories over the past few decades. For many smaller states, it is no longer feasible to operate a fleet with dozens—and in some cases hundreds—of warships. At the same time, "there is a centuries-long pattern of democratic, or relatively democratic, commercial-minded sea powers choosing to neglect their defenses in peacetime," Gray observes.[26] With dwindling defense budgets, the logical consequence has been the reduction in the number of ships, submarines, and aircraft, along with the requisite crews. As we will see, advanced weapon systems and sensors with far better radar coverage or a greater operational effectiveness can compensate for the decline of a fleet's size to a certain degree.[27] Still, the size of the fleet—the number of ships—determines where it can be at any given point in time. And this is the key to naval power: In order to wield significant naval power, to this day there is no substitute for a relatively large, well-balanced fleet that can exercise sea control (also at great distances from home), and project power into faraway regions, thus (most importantly) representing a credible deterrent force.[28] It can be argued that deterrence has in fact replaced the destruction of the enemy as the principle function of naval forces. Therefore Lord Nelson's famous assertion, "What a country needs is the annihilation of the enemy [and] only numbers can annihilate,"[29] can be translated as: What a country needs is a sufficiently large force, *with the potential capability to inflict unacceptably high losses to the enemy* in the case of belligerence. This is more likely to be achieved with superior forces, both in quality and quantity.

Deterrence is a complex concept. Clearly, a good case can be made that nuclear deterrence has worked over the past six decades. One cannot be as confident in claiming that the same has been the case for conventional deterrence. Recent history has shown otherwise. Neither Saddam Hussein nor the Argentinean junta (the so-called Dirty War of the '70s and '80s) shied away from invading foreign territory, despite their respective opponents possession of far superior firepower.[30] Sam J. Tangredi, a senior American defense planner, makes an excellent point by arguing that even though predictions about another country's intentions and possible actions are difficult, a less credible military capability increases the probability of the other side pursuing a more aggressive course. Moreover, "deterrence is not a physical property—it is a state of mind."[31] Therefore, to achieve credible deterrence, a nation's (or alliance's) military forces have to exhibit powerful capabilities and be deployed in a specific manner so hostile actors will believe they are unlikely to overcome them. The problem inherent to this equation is that it is often based on assumptions. Vast sums of money are spent on military equipment every year to provide countries with the presumed necessary deterrent capabilities. "Yet the forces themselves may never be used," Tangredi surmises. "This is not a standard business model."[32]

Few battles at sea have occurred in the last seventy years and for the foreseeable future large force-on-force engagement remains highly unlikely. Unfortunately, if history teaches us anything, it is that major interstate conflict cannot be entirely ruled out. For that reason, the growing defense procurement in the Asia-Pacific region, for example, must be observed closely. Naval historian Karl Rommetveit suggests that contrary to European developments, "the naval build-up in the Asia-Pacific is significantly focused on war fighting capabilities and . . . Asian navies are better funded and provided with extra resources to perform non-traditional security tasks."[33] In particular, China's military buildup is deeply vexing to U.S. defense planners, many of whom are already predicting the inevitable end of U.S. naval supremacy unless large-scale investments are made.

European leaders have to draw their own conclusions from current geopolitical developments. As Lord Salisbury, the British secretary of state for India and later prime minister under the reign of Queen Victoria, once warned, it would be a mistake to take any assessment—especially that of defense planners—at face value: "No lesson seems to be so deeply inculcated by the experience of life as that you should never trust experts. If you believe the doctors, nothing is wholesome; if you believe the theologians, nothing is innocent; if you believe the soldiers, nothing is safe."[34] However, despite the fact that a healthy degree of skepticism toward overly pessimistic statements from the military and defense establishment is warranted, common sense should nevertheless allow even the most casual observer to see that since the Cold War, European sea power has not fared well.

Based on the principle that it is "better to be master in some trades rather than mediocre at many,"[35] niche specialization ostensibly offers smaller states a way out of the financial conundrum—not least because it is much cheaper to maintain a force specialized in few areas than to operate a multipurpose fleet. However, there are also serious drawbacks to this approach. Specialized fleets find it much more difficult to adapt to new threats, while "a navy that maintains a wide range of skills, is best placed to cope with a variety of expected and perhaps unexpected operational contingencies."[36] Therefore, many European states now rely heavily on the naval forces of friends and allies (in particular the United States) to fill the capability gaps their austerity policies have created.

As we shall see in the course of the discussion, this trend entails considerable strategic risks against the backdrop of current shifts in the geopolitical landscape. Indeed, the western European states often barely manage to conduct basic peacetime duties at the desired rate and have little to no surge capacity in the case of emergency. Rear Admiral Parry laments that "in conflicts not involving the USA, these 'come as you are' navies will have to fight with what they have, or play for time."[37] What makes this situation even more precarious is that there is a growing degree of uncertainty about whether other states—and most importantly, the American "Arsenal of Democracy"—would be willing and able to quickly rush to Europe's assistance.[38]

Over a hundred years ago, "Mahan painted an encouraging picture of the manner in which naval strength underpins and encourages economic prosperity and then feeds from it in a kind of virtuous circle," Till observes.[39] This process is clearly visible in the Asia-Pacific region, where naval power is growing in lockstep with commercial maritime trade. This practice constitutes a core principle of sea power. The more money that is allocated to naval shipbuilding programs, the faster naval sea power can grow, thus providing the beneficial conditions necessary for the seaborne trade industry to expand and vice-versa. However, "the arrows go both ways." When countries are less willing to invest in their naval forces—for example in times of peace or during economic difficulties—the circle can become a vicious one.[40] The British Royal Navy, for example, has not only been truncated by roughly 60 percent since the end of the Cold War, but at the same time the country's merchant marine and shipping industry have experienced years of hardship. Once commanding the largest trading fleet in the world, the island nation is currently only ranked twentieth among the biggest merchant fleets in regard to registration and gross tonnage.[41] In the end, sea power (both in economic and military terms) will continue to underpin economic prosperity and political influence in the world. Although it is often overlooked in the public debate, the mutually reinforcing relationship between commercial and military elements of sea power is well worth the investment.[42]

In the coming decades of the twenty-first century, the principles of sea power outlined in this chapter are likely to remain constant. The current economic and military maritime efforts by the United States, Russia, and many Asian states allow us to infer that sea power will, by all reasonable estimates, remain an essential instrument of foreign policy in an increasingly competitive world.[43] As in centuries past, those actors who are willing and able to utilize the maritime domain to a greater degree than their competitors will likely be able to secure more favorable outcomes for themselves and their clients. The sea lines of communication will continue to be vital for a prosperous global trade regime while well-balanced, general-purpose fleets continue to constitute the most useful policy tools to deter aggression, project power, protect national interests abroad, and, if necessary, secure these interests by the use of force.

CHAPTER 2

The Pivot toward Asia and the Consequences for Europe

Our problem is not that [the Europeans] doubt our commitment.
. . . The allies do about as much as they think they have to do. And
they don't think they have to do too much because the U.S. is there
to bankroll them.

BARRY R. POSEN

Merely two decades after the hallmark moment that saw the
dissolution of the Soviet Union and the Warsaw Pact, the
geopolitical landscape is again undergoing dramatic change, shifting
from a period of Western preponderance to an age of multipolar
power distribution. Consequently, the United States has "come down
from the peak of hegemony that it occupied during the unipolar
era,"[1] ceding some regulatory capabilities along the way. While the
emergence of globally networked, radical Islamic terrorism presents a threat to the spread of democracy and the proliferation of
human rights, an increasing number of states are no longer willing
to find their political decision-making processes at the discretion of
the United States. Regional powers, such as China, Russia, Iran, and
North Korea, which either feel disenfranchised or threatened by the
United States, are resisting the "liberal world order" the Americans
have promoted ever since the Second World War.[2] America's inter-
ference in regional affairs throughout North Africa and the Middle

East has sparked public criticism in many parts of the world, not least within Europe itself, where large parts of the population are deeply troubled by the numerous crises along its southern borders. According to a widely held belief, the U.S. military interventions over the last decades are the root cause of much of the turmoil engulfing Libya, Syria, and Iraq, and are chiefly responsible for the current refugee crisis. Despite this popular protest and contempt, Europe will need the United States as a close ally—politically, economically, as well as militarily. For one, the Europeans continue to be dependent on several key U.S. military capabilities in order to conduct military operations themselves, especially in medium- and high-intensity warfare and in operations over longer periods of time. Moreover, only the United States can provide Europe with a credible conventional and nuclear deterrent. Finally, the leaders in Europe continue to look to the United States for stewardship of the sea, hence for the protection of the freedom of navigation, upon which the health of Europe's economies rests.

As a corollary, the changes in the global order have also affected the intricate system of seaborne trade. Over the past decades, the focus of commercial and maritime activity has moved from the West to the East and from the Atlantic to the Indian Ocean and the Pacific Ocean. By 1984, U.S. trade across the Pacific had eclipsed that with western Europe, laying the foundation for current developments.[3] Thirty years on, a greater value of goods is being imported and exported among developing countries (South–South trade) than between developing countries and developed countries (South–North trade).[4] These developments coincide with the "downwards drift of most Western navies and the growth of others, most obviously in the Asian-Pacific, [which] promises a profound shift in the future world's naval balance in the decades to come."[5]

Of the many naval powers in the Asia-Pacific region (APR),[6] the People's Republic of China has undergone the most profound transformation in recent years. Within Southeast Asia, China has not only become a regional power in its own right, but one that is also directly challenging U.S. influence in the region. Against the backdrop of this growing military presence, the U.S. armed forces are redirecting their focus from previous areas of operations, such as the Atlantic, the Arabian Sea, and the Persian Gulf, to the Asia-Pacific region in order to secure their continued interests in the region.

While many scholars agree that Europe will remain one of three areas in the world that are critical to the United States,[7] there is mounting discontent within the United States over the degree to which Europe provides for its own security. Given the fact that the European continent as a whole is both more populous and has a larger economy than the United States, critics have called upon the Europeans to become far more self-reliant when it comes to defense. Pundits in Washington and elsewhere argue that Europe has been on a long procurement holiday while free-riding on the backs of American taxpayers for years. Political scientist John Mearsheimer, for example, leaves no doubt about his repugnance toward Europe's unwillingness to strengthen its militaries: "When the Cold War ended . . . I'd pull everything out of Europe. The idea that we are spending absurd amounts of money to defend rich Europeans . . . drives me crazy. Let the Europeans defend themselves."[8] Yet despite the election of Donald Trump as president, it remains unclear to what degree the United States will revoke its obligations toward its NATO allies. Given Russia's growing political and military influence (ranging from the Atlantic, along Europe's eastern border, through Ukraine and the Black Sea, all the way to the Syria and the Mediterranean), additional U.S. forces have been redeployed to Germany, Poland, and the Baltic states as well as to the waters along Europe's northern and southern flanks.[9]

Despite these standing commitments, the shift of the geopolitical center of gravity from West to East appears irreversible and will compel the United States to worry less about Europe and more about how to shape events in Asia. As Geoffrey Till explains, "Already much of the US Navy . . . sees the Atlantic merely as an area that must be passed through on the way to somewhere more important. And this perception is more likely to grow than to diminish in the future. [The result will be] a fast developing and historic shift in the naval balance between East and West which is likely to result in substantial but currently unknowable change in the world's security architecture."[10]

At present, China is the main motor behind military buildup currently under way in the Asia-Pacific region. For over fifteen years the PRC has continuously increased its defense expenditure (a 175 percent increase between 2003 and 2013)[11] causing many of its neighbors to hedge against China's growing power. While most of these states are now themselves actively strengthening their military forces, many—such as Australia and Singapore—are also forging closer diplomatic and military ties with the United States. From Washington's point of view, China's actions are largely understood to be specifically designed to prevent U.S. military forces from gaining access to, and operating near, into, or within the South China Sea and the East China Sea—a strategy often referred to as anti-access/area-denial or A2/AD.[12] As a result, the United States views these developments as "primary strategic challenges to [its] international security objectives"[13] and in 2012 announced that it would "out of necessity rebalance towards the Asia-Pacific region."[14]

So far, diplomatic efforts have shown mixed results in easing the tension among the conflicting parties in the APR. The United States therefore also seeks to apply pressure on China, while providing reassurance to its allies and friends by increasing its military presence in the theater of operation. Given the distinct littoral features that govern this region of the world and limit the mobility of land-based troops, mainly naval and aerial assets have been redeployed to the APR. More than half of U.S. naval vessels, most notably its carrier strike groups, and 60 percent of the Air Force's oversea-based assets have already been allocated to the Asia-Pacific region.[15] As Øystein Tunsjø, an East Asia expert at the Norwegian Institute for Defence Studies, points out, "[In] 2007, for the first time in 60 years, more [U.S.] ships were based in the Pacific than in the Atlantic. Two-thirds of the U.S. Navy used to be located on the East coast and deployed in the Atlantic, but about two-thirds are now located on the West coast and operate in the Pacific. Newly commissioned ships [such as the littoral combat ship and *Zumwalt*-class destroyers] will largely be deployed to Asian waters."[16]

Meanwhile, the Chinese have successfully modernized their own armed forces, replacing a Cold War–era mass peasant army, with a modern fighting force that uses the entire spectrum of twenty-first-century warfighting technologies. Furthermore, China's defense industry has developed a number of weapon and sensor systems that have not only gained much attention among Western defense analysts but have also lead to a widespread public debate over the extent to which the military balance of power in the APR has already shifted in Beijing's favor. Despite being criticized in the past for obtaining many of these capabilities through reverse engineering, espionage, cyber attacks, and other such dubious measures, China has been able to produce a range of sophisticated combat aircraft, long-range ballistic missiles, and state-of-the-art warships.

The U.S. government, keeping a close eye on these developments, remains highly suspicious of China's publicly announced plan to expand its "comprehensive national power" and "[secure] China's status as a great power."[17] American officials point out that although "Chinese leaders express a desire to maintain peace and stability along their country's periphery [and] avoid direct confrontation with the United States and other countries,"[18] the Chinese government remains unwilling to be more transparent regarding its military and security policies. Consequently, Chinese actions could, in the words of the U.S. Department of Defense, "[pose] risks to stability by creating uncertainty and [by] increasing the potential for misunderstanding and miscalculation."[19]

In particular, the PRC's latest efforts to forcefully expand its sphere of influence, laying claim to islands in the South China Sea and East China Sea and using these as military bases, have caused much alarm among the stakeholders in the region. Over the past few years, China has engaged in territorial disputes with its neighbors over a number of islands, reefs, and rocks, ranging from the Korean Peninsula and Japan, and southward to Taiwan, the Philippines, and

Indonesia. These islands, would not only increase China's exclusive economic zone but in strategic terms would constitute part of an imagined first line of defense against possible foreign intervention. In addition to these pending disputes, the historic rivalry with Japan as well as the unresolved issues concerning Taiwan are being closely monitored by the United States as China's A2/AD networks within the aforementioned first island chain are becoming increasingly formidable. China's actions suggest that it is aiming to gain military superiority over all its adversaries within the region, thus enjoying escalatory dominance should Beijing resort to the use of force in pursuit of its political objectives.

In addition to the defense of the waters within the imagined first island chain, the leadership of the Communist Party also wants to establish what is called "Far Sea Defense."[20] In general terms, this second line of defense stretches farther out into the Pacific, well beyond the first line of defense. The strategic necessity for these two lines of defense can be understood in both military as well as economic terms. Apart from geographical characteristics of the Asia-Pacific theater, which make an amphibious landing on the Chinese mainland highly improbable, the country's nuclear arsenal can be considered a sufficient deterrent to dissuade an opponent from attempting an invasion. A naval blockade, on the other hand, presents a much more viable military scenario. Such a campaign could have a crippling effect on the China's ability to wage war, given its economy's dependency on foreign oil and other resources. Although China still relies on coal as its primary source of energy, it has already surpassed Japan as the second largest oil importer in the world—most of it from the Middle East and Africa. Therefore, China is keen on securing these SLOCs, particularly the numerous critical straits between the Middle East and Southeast Asia, which in the case of war could be closed by the U.S. Navy.[21]

The United States will for a number of reasons continue to rely on its naval forces to deter aggression and maintain its influence in the region. First, since the Second World War, the United States has been able to maintain a naval fleet that has been, and will continue to be, unchallenged in a fleet-on-fleet engagement for the foreseeable future. The current global geographical and political parameters allow Alfred Thayer Mahan's principles of controlling the SLOCs to ensure economic, political, and military dominance to be applied.[22] Further, while U.S. ground capabilities have been put to the test in asymmetrical conflicts such as those in Afghanistan and Iraq, this paradigmatic change of warfare does not affect the realm of blue-water operations to the same extent. Therefore, the United States Navy can continue to rely on its ability to deter by presence.

America's naval presence, however, is growing somewhat thin. Given its numerous commitments across the globe, even a military behemoth like the United States military finds itself facing a dilemma. The U.S. Navy is still by far the largest and most powerful naval fleet in the world, operating more than 280 ships, including 10 aircraft carriers, 100 cruisers, destroyers, and frigates (littoral combat ships), more than 50 attack submarines, and in excess of 30 amphibious warships. However, under the new Optimized Fleet Response Plan (2014) the United States will not be able to increase its globally deployed naval presence of around 95 ships. As one retired naval officer claims, "The lethality inherent in this presence, based on the ship types deployed, [will] be less than today's 95-ship presence."[23] In fact, only two carriers were intended to be forward-deployed at any given moment in time—down from three or four carriers.[24] Moreover, it is questionable which European nation would come to the assistance of the United States in case naval conflict erupted with China, and despite claims to the contrary, any such assistance would be rather insignificant, given the small number of assets available to Europe's navies.

So where does this fundamental shift leave Europe? The following case studies aim to provide some answer to this question.

PART 2

CHAPTER

Case Studies
Europe's Naval Forces

Over the course of the following chapters, the development of European sea power—the military element, that is—since the end of the Cold War will be examined. Throughout this book, the terms "Europe" and "European sea power" are used frequently. In a broad sense, Europe is understood to signify a relatively unified body of like-minded states with similar domestic interests and common foreign policy goals located on the European continent. But Europe is far from being a cohesive political and cultural entity, united by shared goals and visions. On the contrary, in the 1970s, Secretary of State Henry Kissinger highlighted Europe's *disunity*: "Who do I call if I want to call Europe?" he is supposed to have asked.[1] Indeed, a case can be made that Europe's heterogeneity is the principle reason for its strategic weakness. Europe's power remains diffused and divided. The amalgamate of strikingly different states (take Finland and Turkey for example) with distinct cultural, religious, and social backgrounds have made the pursuit of common foreign policy objectives and a joint defense and security strategy a painstaking matter.[2]

In theory, the concept of "European sea power" would therefore have to be broadly understood to encompass all European states and their assets actively invested in the maritime domain. Even if a narrower definition of the term—that is, "maritime security assets," or in other words, "naval power"—were to be applied, one would strictly speaking also have to discuss the contributions of landlocked states such as Austria, which has for the first time embarked a special forces unit on a German navy vessel in support of the European Union's naval operations in the Mediterranean,[3] not to mention the navies of other European states, such as of Portugal, Croatia, or Finland. The capabilities of all add or detract from Europe's ability as a collective entity to protect and promote common interests at and from the sea—at home as well as abroad.

Notwithstanding these incongruities, the present study will limit itself to European states that have direct access to the sea and make rather sizeable investments toward maintaining and operating naval forces—eleven countries in total.[4] All European states under discussion are either NATO members, part of the European Union, or both. The principle aim of each case study is to gain insight into the evolution of the respective naval forces over the course of a quarter century. For that reason, the focus of this analysis will be threefold.

First, the study takes a platform-centric point of view, with the composition of each force as well as the range of their capabilities and their important technical features receiving particular attention. To make the steep decline in both military expenditure and overall size of Europe's naval forces more tangible, two separate graphs provide an outline of each country's annual defcnse spending (share of gross domestic product) and the number of major warships in service. It is safe to say that throughout history the principle criterion of any naval force (and any military force for that matter) has been its size. Although size—in other words, the number of naval platforms—does not necessarily reflect a fleet's capabilities, it does represent the most important unit of measuring naval power. Given the limitations of this study, not every type of naval platform qualifies to be taken into consideration. Despite their importance, not every training craft, transport ship, and helicopter will be listed. Rather, this analysis focuses on the backbone of modern naval fleets, namely aircraft carriers, large surface combatants (such as destroyers and frigates), submarines, and ships designed for amphibious warfare. Smaller surface combatants, such as guided-missile attack craft, and mine countermeasure vessels, are not included in the graphs. Although these platforms will also be discussed (with the exception of offshore patrol vessels, or OPVs), they play a less important role in today's European naval planning than they did during much of the twentieth century.

For the last twenty-five years, many navies around the world have undergone profound transformation. In light of a steadily evolving security environment, countries that had been primarily focused on defending their littoral waters today operate "blue-water" navies. While fast attack craft, small diesel-electric submarines, and mine warfare vessels used to be the preferred tools for territorial defense in the relatively confined, littoral "green waters" (often also referred to as "brown waters"), today much larger, more sophisticated warships are being built to conduct a multitude of operations over long periods of time and over great distances.

The classification of naval ships can be at least as misleading as simply comparing the number of warships between two navies. For example, throughout the last century, cruisers (nominally the second-largest surface combatants after battleships/battlecruisers)[5] displaced anywhere between five thousand and ten thousand tons of water. Modern ships of similar size, such as the British Type 45 *Daring* class, with a displacement of nearly nine thousand tons, are designated as destroyers (generally ranked one tier lower). To make things even more complicated, the new German *Baden-Württemberg*–class (F-125) combatant will displace more than seven thousand tons once she enters service, but is referred to as a "stabilization frigate." Only two decades ago, many frigates in service with Europe's navies were small warships (one thousand to three thousand tons), primarily designed for escort duties and anti-submarine warfare. Nevertheless, "the possession of given numbers of large surface combatants is often regarded as rough indication of relative strength and purpose."[6] Therefore, the listing of all larger surface combatants in one category not only provides us with better means of comparison between the different navies, but also illustrates the rapid numerical decline of platforms across Europe's fleets over the last twenty-five years.

Apart from quantity, quality obviously plays a significant role in assessing naval strength. However, evaluating a ship's capabilities and operational performance is a somewhat more difficult undertaking than counting grey hulls. First of all, we have not witnessed any major military confrontations at sea in more than thirty years from which we could draw meaningful conclusions. In fact, the last war to provide insight into major naval warfare dates back to the Falklands War in 1982.[7] And even in that case, it was mainly a contest between the British surface forces, their carrier air wing, and the Argentinean air force. In absence of large fleet-on-fleet engagements, much of the debate regarding the ostensible capabilities of naval forces is theoretical (particularly in the case of high-intensity warfare at sea). However, recent military interventions (Iraq, Bosnia, Afghanistan, Libya, and Syria), ongoing maritime security operations, and technical analyses allow for some insights into past, current, and future capabilities of the ships and crews of Europe's navies. For that reason, a good part of each chapter will be devoted to the examination of the technical aspects of modern warships.

Second, a further source of analysis is the strategic framework in which each navy operates. All European states under scrutiny are either part of the European Union or NATO and thus share common security interests. However, the variety of historical, political, and geographical circumstances have resulted in each country identifying a number of key security demands that they deem essential to their safety and prosperity. Accordingly, many European naval forces are on the one hand assigned to multinational operations, such as fighting piracy off the Horn of Africa, but also pursue their own—sometimes conflicting—strategic aims at sea.

Norway, for example, will remain vigilant toward Russia's growing naval posture in the High North and therefore is in the process of strengthening traditional naval capabilities.[8] Italy, on the other hand, will likely waste far less thought on the possible reemergence of Russian sea bastions around the Kola Peninsula. Rather, the Italian navy and coast guard are confronted with a human catastrophe unfolding right before their eyes. Smaller offshore patrol vessels are needed to rescue refugees from drowning as they seek to escape the horrors of war and poverty across North Africa and the Middle East. Larger warships remain critical in protecting Italy's interests in the greater Mediterranean region over the long term. To the East, neighboring Greece remains deeply vexed about Turkey's growing military posture despite both countries formally being NATO allies. As a consequence—and contrary to the general trend toward expeditionary capabilities and blue-water navies—Greece's military strategy largely remains focused on territorial defense. Further, the British Royal Navy is trying to reassert itself as a first-rate naval power with global power-projection capabilities by reshaping its fleet around two new aircraft carriers.

As we can see, there are numerous diverging and opposing strategic requirements among (and within) the European armed forces, notwithstanding common security goals spelled out by NATO and the EU. Additionally, continuous reduction in defense expenditures over the last two decades has only complicated the already difficult balancing act of how to best allocate military funding toward national as well as collective defense. By taking a closer look at the aims and provisions stipulated in each country's defense white papers and other public statements over the last two decades, valuable insight can be gained regarding the core missions of the navies as well as the degree of trust they enjoy within their respective country's defense and security strategy.

Third, and finally, a comparison of each navy's responsibilities—assigned to them by their political and military leadership—and actual capabilities as they present themselves in operational environments provides evidence that many naval forces have found it difficult to fulfill their assigned duties in times of relative peace. Overstretched and underfunded, most navies have little to no means to effectively deal with emerging threats without diverting assets from other standing commitments. Moreover, in light of the United States' rebalance toward the Asia-Pacific region the studies illustrate that strategic foresight among Europe's policymakers and defense planners to address these pressing issues has been sorely lacking. As a consequence, the following analysis will give little solace to those who are concerned that Europe might have become increasingly marginalized in a maritime century in which the center of gravity is likely to have shifted away from the Atlantic and toward the Pacific.

CHAPTER 4

United Kingdom

Keep Calm and Get Those Carriers Operational

Volumes could be written about the dramatic decline of
British maritime power over the course of the last hundred years. Once the world's preeminent sea power (Britannia,
rule the waves!), the British Royal Navy (RN) today can barely be
considered Europe's most capable naval power. As Figure 5-1
indicates, the size of the British[1] fleet has been reduced by roughly
60 percent since the end of the Cold War. Although the RN continues to operate a balanced fleet, declining defense spending over
the last two decades has caused a considerable reduction in platforms and personnel. Generally speaking, the RN is much smaller
and less capable now than it was in 1990 when compared to other
naval powers of each era. This development is likely to undermine
Britain's role in world affairs and runs the risk of the country
forfeiting its ability to defend core national interests near home as
well as abroad.

Within less than twenty-five years, the Royal Navy has been
forced to cede a number of important capabilities. Without question,
the most noticeable among these cuts has been the decision to

decommission all the navy's aircraft carriers. After almost seventy years of successful carrier operations, the RN has lost its entire fleet of Harrier combat jets while its last aircraft carrier was withdrawn from service in 2014. Since then, the United Kingdom has been awaiting the commissioning of the new *Queen Elizabeth*–class carriers, scheduled to enter service in the early 2020s. Meanwhile, the fleet of escorting large surface combatants has been reduced from forty-eight ships in 1990 to a mere nineteen destroyers and frigates in 2017, and the number of attack submarines has been halved.

Apart from making due without its fixed-wing strike asset, the Royal Navy has found itself in serious trouble in other areas as well. Faced with the highest rate of deployment of Russian submarines since the Cold War, the RN's anti-submarine warfare (ASW) capability, formerly a forte of the red ensign not least due to its vast experience fighting the German U-boats during both World Wars and keeping a close eye on Soviet subs—has proven insufficient to track Russian movements across the North Atlantic. Ongoing cutbacks and cost-saving measures, such as the cancellation of the Nimrod MRA.4 maritime patrol aircraft (MPA) program and decommissioning of ASW platforms, has atrophied the navy's ability to conduct such important tasks. Even the highly anticipated order of nine Boeing P-8 Poseidon MPAs will only partly fill the capability gap. The only area not to be truncated to such a significant degree is the RN's amphibious forces. And yet Britain's armed forces would find it difficult to deploy a brigade, let alone a division, over greater distances, as a report by the Atlantic Council in 2016 emphasized.[2] To make matters worse, the shortage in sufficiently trained crews as well as the difficulty to attract young men and women add gravity to the challenging situation the Royal Navy finds itself in. In many cases the manpower shortage has left the navy unable to put to sea at the desired rate and to effectively conduct the widening range of naval missions included in its portfolio. Similar developments have become apparent among all but a few European countries.

With the end of the Cold War, the enormous provisions for a cataclysmic showdown between East and West were no longer

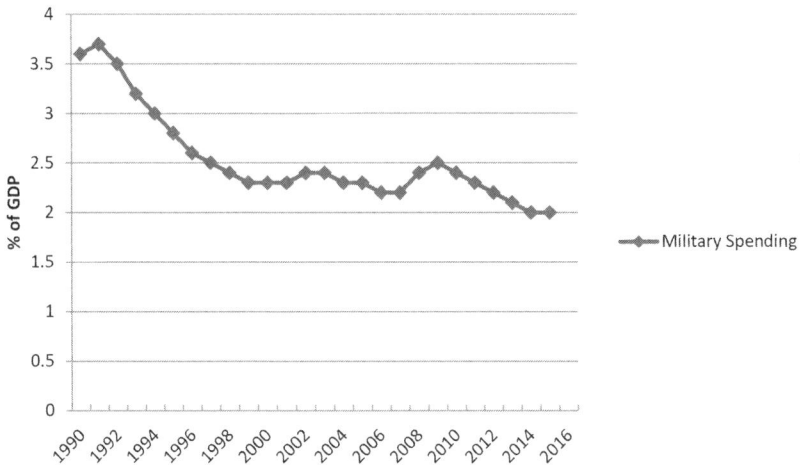

Figure 5-1. U.K.: Defense Spending in % of GDP, 1990–2015
Source: SIPRI Military Expenditure Database.

considered warranted. In the case of the Royal Navy, this meant that "its own Cold War mission of hunting Soviet submarines had vanished, and along with it the chief justification for large chunks of the Fleet."[3] The emergence of new forms of conflict, which ranged across the gamut of the intensity spectrum, led many European countries to make substantial adjustments to their national defense strategy. However, the most pressing question that needed answering was to what extent Europe's governments would reduce their armed forces as part of the "peace dividend."[4]

The United Kingdom presents us with a somewhat ambiguous case study. On the one hand, the U.K. remains one of the few European NATO members committed to spending a significant share of its gross domestic product (GDP) on defense (around the 2 percent margin), and has actively participated in numerous UN, NATO, and U.S.-led military operations around the globe over the last two decades. On the other hand, since the end of the Cold War, it has been unable (or rather unwilling) to maintain its military capabilities in relation to the armed forces of similarly powerful states in the world. Critics have argued that as a direct consequence of this strategic shortsightedness, the RN has lost much of its former might and no longer qualifies as the great naval power it once was.[5]

At the height of the Cold War, only the two superpowers (the United States and the Soviet Union) had more capable naval forces than Great Britain. Twenty-five years after the fall of the Iron Curtain, a brief comparison with other naval powers should suffice to comprehend the dire state in which the Royal Navy currently finds itself. Clearly, the U.S. Navy remains the undisputed naval leviathan and despite recent discussions about its ostensible decline, it will continue to operate the most powerful naval force for the foreseeable future.[6] In addition, depending on one's locus of analysis, a number of other navies can be considered on par with, if not superior to the RN in terms of size and capability.

Russia, for example, is currently making a concerted effort to regain its former glory by modernizing its fleet of Soviet-era warships as well as building new submarines and surface combatants. As a result, Russia commands both substantial nuclear as well as conventional naval forces.[7] China's process of "national rejuvenation"[8] has led to the construction of a sizable fleet of modern vessels within a very short period of time. The Chinese fleet is steadily becoming a more effective force in blue-water operations, causing the Americans to shift their strategic focus from the Atlantic to the Asia-Pacific region.

Similarly, the Indian navy is also undergoing a significant modernization process and currently deploys 2 aircraft carriers, 13 submarines, as well as 31 destroyers and frigates. Commodore Manohar K. Banger therefore questions why "the Indian Navy is now a 100-ship navy yet [is] still considered by the major powers to be a brown-water force," when Great Britain only has 25 surface combatants but remains adamant that it operates a credible blue-water navy.[9] While it can be argued that the Indian navy still suffers from frequent setbacks and shortcomings with construction and maintenance processes as well as operational effectiveness that in turn prevent it from achieving parity with the former colonial power, Japan is often understood to operate a larger and more capable navy than the RN. In fact, despite the JMSDF's (officially the Japan Maritime Self-Defense Force) lack of power-projection capabilities, some naval analysts consider the Japanese navy to be the world's second-most effective conventional naval power apart from the U.S. Navy.[10]

Even among the European navies, a case can be made that the French navy would deserve to be put in the spotlight of any study on European naval power; a proposition that is surely loathed by many Britons. Both the British and the French navies operate a similar number of frigates and destroyers. They each possess four strategic ballistic missile submarines (SSBN), which form their strategic nuclear deterrent, as well as six nuclear-powered attack submarines (SSN). Both navies are also able to conduct relatively sizable amphibious operations. What puts the French ahead of the British (at least until the early 2020s) is the ability to deploy its naval air arm from the *Charles de Gaulle* aircraft carrier. Apart from the United States, no other nation can project power to the same degree or conduct air strikes from the sea with similar effectiveness as the French navy's air wing—the Aéronavale. However, there is a silver lining on the horizon for the British Royal Navy. Notwithstanding its recent decline, there is reason to believe that it will again become Europe's most effective naval fighting force, a position it firmly held throughout the twentieth century.

The dramatic events at the end of the 1980s and early 1990s marked the beginning of a new era—even if subliminal tensions between Russia and the West persisted. Great Britain was quick to interpret the fall of the Berlin Wall and the breakup of the Soviet Union as the harbingers of a drastic change in the global security environment. In light of these changes, the U.K.'s armed forces were considered to be too large and too expensive. Based on these conclusions, naval writer John Roberts explains, "The MoD [Ministry of Defence] commenced a far-reaching study into future defense requirements and policy titled 'Option for Change.' . . . The fundamental aim of the study was to find large-scale savings to fund the expected 'Post-Cold War Peace Dividend' whilst preserving as much of the front line as possible."[11]

Saddam Hussein's invasion of Kuwait and the consequent military operation under the auspices of the United States put a brief halt to the planned defense cuts. The military success of the coalition vindicated the widely shared concept of conventional combined-arms warfare, despite the increasing relevance of asymmetric forms of conflict.[12] However, regardless of their success in the liberation of Kuwait, the British army and air force suffered most under the directive of the defense review. In an official document, the British government reflected, "The most significant cuts fell on the Army, which was reduced in strength by one third, from 160,000 to 120,000. The largest cuts were in the ground forces based in Germany which were reduced by over half. Tactical air power based in Germany was significantly reduced with the closure of two out of four RAF bases and the withdrawal of six RAF squadrons."[13]

These decisions were met with heavy criticism, mostly for the study having been written without carefully assessing the "exact nature of the [evolving] strategic security environment."[14] The RN fared somewhat better than its sister services. Only a small number of older warships were initially to be taken from service while the number of personnel was to be reduced from almost 69,000 (including the Royal Marines) to 55,000 by the mid-1990s. Despite these cuts, the Royal Navy's future looked promising. All three 20,000-ton *Invincible*-class aircraft carriers and their respective rotary- and fixed-wing detachments remained in service, providing significant operational flexibility to Western interventions in the Balkans, Iraq, and Afghanistan over the coming years. By this time, the United Kingdom's new nuclear deterrent, in the form of the 16,000-ton *Vanguard*-class SSBN, was also entering service, replacing the older *Resolution* class. Close cooperation with the United States during the design and construction phase provided the British boats with the American Trident II submarine-launched ballistic missile (SLBM). Each missile could be fitted with up to 12 nuclear warheads. Four of these boats were built, allowing the RN to continuously have at least one submarine with a maximum of 192 nuclear warheads at sea.[15]

With regard to the RN's attack submarine force, an important decision was made: namely, to withdraw all of its conventionally powered submarines. Being subject to financial restrictions, the Royal Navy's leaders concluded that operating a mixed fleet of nuclear and conventional diesel-electric submarines had become unfeasible. The first sea lord, Admiral Sir Benjamin Bathurst, noted at the time:

> The judgment we made to withdraw the Upholder class [conventional submarines] was the toughest decision the Navy Board has had to make for many years. I would like to emphasize that . . . we had a hard choice to make, and we decided to consolidate around SSNs because by retaining support for two types there came a point where we wouldn't be able to afford to run both classes given the other resource needs within the Navy.[16]

On the other hand, experience from Operation Desert Storm had convinced the British of the utility of sea-launched cruise missiles. As two senior British analysts note, "The hunter-killer submarine force, originally designed to search for and attack its Russian counterparts in the North Atlantic and Arctic, was rerolled for land attack with the inclusion of Tomahawk missiles in its arsenal."[17] An initial order for sixty-five American-built land-attack missiles was made in 1995, adding significant long-range kinetic striking power to the RN's silent service.[18]

Meanwhile, the large escort fleet was undergoing constant modernization. Both the destroyers and frigates had shown significant vulnerabilities during the Falklands War where the ships' air-defense systems had been unable to effectively engage low-flying targets. In total, six ships were lost to enemy air attacks. As a result of this costly experience, the Royal Navy quickly reacted and introduced significant upgrades to its SAM (surface-to-air

missile) systems as well as improving its damage-control procedures. Like many other navies in the world, the RN fitted their
warships with close-in weapon systems (CIWS) such as the
American Phalanx. [19]

The creeping reduction of surface forces during the later years
of the decade was largely compensated for by the introduction of
more capable units. In particular, the Type 23 *Duke*-class frigates
represented one of the finest multipurpose frigates in the world,
despite having been specifically designed for ASW missions in the
North Atlantic.[20] In total, sixteen of these ships were built between
1990 and 2003 and all but three remain in service as one of the RN's
most versatile assets. Despite the somewhat more capable Sea Wolf
SAM system on board the Type 23 frigates, the Royal Navy exerted
itself in finding a suitable replacement for the obsolescent Type 42
Sheffield-class destroyers, two of which were sunk by Argentinean
forces in 1982. "Particular weaknesses identified were the Type 42
destroyer's inability to illuminate—and therefore engage—more
than two targets simultaneously."[21] Fortunately, previous cooperation within NATO had laid the foundation for the RN's successor
to the unfortunate Type 42. During the 1980s, plans of a common
frigate design for most NATO allies were drawn to alleviate the
pressing need for a capable surface combatant. Insurmountable
differences over the respective capabilities and features of the ship
ultimately led to the cancellation of the so-called NFR-90 program.[22]
However, the idea of a joint venture between the European treaty
members persisted, not least because of immense costs of designing
and building a class of warships packed with sophisticated weapon
systems and electronics.

In 1992, the project called "Horizon" was brought to life. A trilateral cooperation between the United Kingdom, France, and Italy
set out to build a new class of destroyers that could provide a credible multitiered fleet air defense against even the most advanced
aerial threats. Despite the U.K. abandoning the joint venture in
1999, substantial progress had been made regarding the ship's
general layout as well as the radar and SAM systems and the

British shipbuilders went on to incorporate many design features also found in the Italo-French *Horizon* class. In the end, Italy and France each commissioned a pair of nearly identical ships, while the British Royal Navy received six Type 45 destroyers, known as the *Daring* class. Apart from some smaller differences in the ships' appearances, the main point of distinction between the *Daring* and her "cousins" concerns the radar system. All ships are fitted with the SMART-L long-range volume search and track radar as part of their principle antiair missile system (PAAMS). However, while Italy and France have chosen to install the somewhat less capable EMPAR (European multi-function phased array radar) for target search, acquisition, and tracking, the *Daring* class is fitted with the BAE Systems Sampson multifunction radar, located on top of the ship's main mast, thus providing an increased search radius.

The intransigence on the part of the Royal Navy in incorporating the highly capable Sampson radar, in spite of its costs, was, for the most part, founded in the navy's operational requirements toward the planned vessel. They were designed to provide fleet air defense for the RN's carriers against a sophisticated opponent upon the high seas (ergo, without air-defense coverage from land-based assets). The RN's planning envisioned "a much more demanding operational scenario than either the [French navy or the Italian navy]."[23] However, some defense insiders believe to have spotted some shortcomings as a result of the *Daring*'s general antiair warfare (AAW) layout. "[The focus] of the Type 45's air-defense role has resulted in the remaining [basic] weapon fit being somewhat sparse for a ship of the *Daring*'s size,"[24] (that is, a single BAE Systems 4.5-inch (113-mm) Mk. 8 naval gun, a Lynx or Merlin helicopter, and two single 30-mm guns[25]). In addition, increasing costs and the austere fiscal environment in recent years have led to the program being truncated after the completion of six vessels. Instead of replacing the twelve *Sheffield*-class destroyers on a one-to-one basis as initially planned, at the end of the day the RN will have to make do with only six ships.

In contrast to shrinking escort fleet, the RN's amphibious capabilities were strengthened as part of the U.K.'s strategic reorientation towards joint expeditionary operations.[26] As mentioned previously, the majority of European states made substantial adjustments to their naval doctrines, shifting from the previous prevalent concept of territorial defense and sea control in the North Atlantic and approaches to the European shores to crisis prevention and conflict resolution farther away from home. Projecting power from the sea onto land, therefore, became a desirable capability for most of today's larger navies. The 1998 *Strategic Defence Review* (SDR) substantiates these aspirations:

> In the post–Cold War world, we must be prepared to go to the crisis, rather than have the crisis come to us. . . . Against this background, the SDR suggested a continuing shift in focus away from large-scale open-ocean warfare toward a wide range of operations in littoral areas. This reflects changes in the potential maritime threat, especially relative to NATO, the missions of our forces and the likely geographic location of future operations. These changes are a continuation of trends since the end of the Cold War. They include a decline in the likelihood of an open-ocean anti-submarine or anti-surface threat on the scale previously envisaged.[27]

The helicopter assault ship HMS *Ocean* was the first ship to epitomize this strategic reorientation. By 2007 two *Albion*-class assault landing ships (LPD)[28] and three *Bay*-class dock landing ships (LSD) had been added to the fleet, replacing the much less capable *Fearless* class and elderly tank landing ships. Although the new warships represented a considerable financial burden, they gave the Royal Navy hitherto unprecedented capabilities to project power over great distances, and more importantly, into the littoral waters and onto distant shores.

The most important procurement decision made by the British government since the end of the Cold War, however, has been the construction of two *Queen Elizabeth*–class aircraft carriers. Although this process has elicited considerable debate among politicians, military brass, and the broader public, the recent decision to commission both carriers can be considered a hallmark moment for the Royal Navy. Having experienced some operational limitations with the *Invincible*-class carriers, such as the difficulty to launch Harrier jump jets from their short decks in hot weather conditions,[29] the SDR in 1998 announced that the three ships would be replaced by two new aircraft carriers. These new ships would be designed to "[deliver] increased offensive air power, and . . . to operate the largest possible range of aircraft in the widest possible range of roles."[30] Initially planned to displace between 30,000 and 40,000 tons and embark up to 50 aircraft, the total tonnage was increased significantly over time, while acquiring such a number of jets no longer seems financially feasible.

Apart from the aircraft carriers, further promising provisions were stipulated in the SDR. For example, many observers at the time believed that the procurement decision regarding the carriers necessitated all twelve air-defense destroyers to be built.[31] As it turned out, this was wishful thinking. On the other hand, the successor program to the venerable *Trafalgar*-class and *Swiftsure*-class attack submarines was expanded and by 2016, three boats of the new *Astute* class have entered service while an additional three hulls are under construction. Construction of the seventh and final boat has been confirmed and tentative plans see her entering service in 2024.[32]

According to the white paper, only minor adjustments had to be made in other areas. The mine countermeasure (MCM) force was to be strengthened by five instead of ten ships, while the existing Nimrod MR.2 maritime patrol aircraft were to undergo modernization with work on the Nimrod MRA.4 already under way. Finally, the air force's land-based Harrier GR7s were merged with the navy's Sea Harriers and put under joint command, "enabling them to operate equally effectively from both land and sea."[33]

In summary, "the *Strategic Defence Review* is an impressive document," one commentator wrote at the time, "which seems to indicate that the Ministry of Defence has taken a cold, hard look at British defence policy for the next century in the light of diplomacy and industrial capability."[34] These upbeat remarks regarding the SDR were quite justifiable, considering that its provisions were made in a "time of relative plenty."[35] The Royal Navy can be thankful for the prudence and strategic vision the political and military leadership displayed at the time. "It may not have seemed like it at the time but, with the benefit of hindsight, the SDR probably marked [the] modern high-point for the Royal Navy."[36] Had the foundation for a well-balanced and capable fleet not been set during these critical years it is likely that by now the once-proud British Royal Navy would have been reduced to a small regional force with limited power-projection capabilities, considering the years of stringent defense cuts that followed.

Over the last two decades, the British armed forces have conducted a vast number of operations, ranging from large-scale mechanized warfare during Operation Desert Storm to current antipiracy operations around the Horn of Africa.[37] Moreover, the Royal Navy regularly participates in naval maneuvers and also hosts international exercises, such as the annual Cougar exercises[38] in the Mediterranean, the Middle East, and Indian Ocean. "The UK still has expeditionary capabilities to join US-led operations [to the] East of Malacca" an analyst notes, adding, "disaster relief after Typhoon Haiyan by the destroyer HMS Daring and the helicopter carrier HMS Illustrious prove that British capability [albeit limited]."[39]

However, the costliest deployments, both in terms of money and lives lost, have been the wars in Iraq and Afghanistan. As a key ally to the United States, the United Kingdom has suffered considerable casualties in the various actions associated with the war on terrorism. In addition to the painful sacrifices the country has made in the last decade, the strategic focus on counterinsurgency (COIN) and counterterrorism (CT) operations has also promoted what critics refer to as sea blindness: "[Many] countries in NATO are transfixed at the moment by the problems in Afghanistan [Syria, Iraq, and

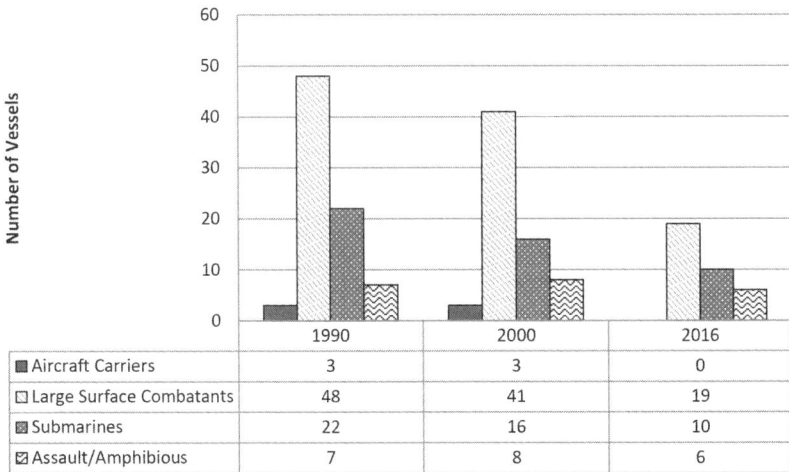

	1990	2000	2016
■ Aircraft Carriers	3	3	0
□ Large Surface Combatants	48	41	19
▨ Submarines	22	16	10
☑ Assault/Amphibious	7	8	6

Figure 5-2. U.K.: Number of Major Vessels

Sources: *The Naval Institute Guide to Combat Fleets of the World, Military Technology Almanac, World Naval Review.*

North Africa] and the threat from transnational actors. In doing this they have developed a sea blindness that appears to forget and marginalize their maritime heritage," defense analyst Dave Sloggett laments.[40] In the case of Britain, over the course of the last decade the armed services were hard pressed to come up with new strategies and tactics of how to prevail in the land wars of the twenty-first century, which looked nothing like the conventional conflicts the military had trained for during the Cold War.

With its combat missions in Iraq and Afghanistan having come to an end, Britain must now look beyond Basra and Helmand Province. Still, much controversy remains regarding what future conflicts will look like. Some argue that if Western powers again decide to intervene militarily, it will be in Afghanistan-like stabilization operations, fighting insurgencies with so-called Joint Rapid Reaction Forces and large expeditionary contingents—in other words: "boots on the ground." Some proponents of air power have disagreed with this notion, and opine that air power alone, be it land or sea based—manned or unmanned—would suffice when the ground war is fought by special operations units, or some sort of indigenous fighting forces, such as rebels or militia groups.[41] This argument is often backed by the NATO-led air campaign in Libya, in which interdiction bombing gave the disjointed rebel units a chance to overthrow the Gaddafi regime. Still others argue that a potential interstate conflict is likely to occur in the next decades. In such a case, the counterinsurgency (COIN) strategy—which has affected all military branches by replacing high-performance and heavy military assets with lighter but cheaper systems designed for COIN operations—has left armies vulnerable in high-intensity conflicts.[42] While considerable adjustments have been made to the force structure, enabling the British Army and Royal Marines to become far more effective in fighting asymmetric wars on land, the Royal Navy of today cannot be considered more capable in dealing with various threats than it used to be.

By the end of the last decade, the RN's large-scale procurement plans were causing additional strain on the defense budget, already considerably burdened by the growing costs of the wars overseas. Although defense spending remained at a comparatively high level (over 2 percent of GDP), it came as little surprise that after the 9/11 attacks, large and expensive programs such as the *Daring*-class destroyers were cut in order to reallocate funds toward combating the "increased threat from international terrorism," as the *Delivering Security in a Changing World* white paper in 2003 highlighted.[43] That such measures would have severe ramifications for the Royal Navy in the long term seem not to have been fully appreciated or were conveniently overlooked. At the time, even a senior defense journalist dismissed the cuts to the destroyer force as "no surprise and in indeed not a 'real' loss."[44] To those in charge, it should at least have occurred that the surface fleet would eventually be reduced to a little over twenty vessels—and that this number represented a rather optimistic estimate.

In 2010, the British government published the infamous *Strategic Defence and Security Review* (SDSR) under the descriptive title of *Securing Britain in an Age of Uncertainty*.[45] In the light of the global economic downturn, the European debt crisis, and the ongoing war in Afghanistan, the entire armed forces were to become the victim of a "draconian downsizing."[46] The Royal Navy's combat air fleet was disbanded and in the process the aircraft carrier fleet was eliminated. Of the three *Invincible*-class carriers, the lead vessel had already been decommissioned in 2005, but was kept in reserve. In 2011, the ship was towed to Turkey and scrapped. The second ship, the *Illustrious,* remained in service until 2014, albeit its capability was limited due to the absence of fixed-wing aircraft. The third, the *Ark Royal,* had joined the fleet in 1985 and was previously scheduled to be withdrawn once the new class of aircraft carriers became operational. In accordance with the SDSR, the British government decided to "decommission HMS *Ark Royal* immediately,"[47] after only twenty-five years of service, thus creating a capability gap until the *Queen Elizabeth* enters service around 2020. By comparison, the USS *Enterprise,* decommissioned in early 2017, was in service for over fifty years.

The lack of naval air power was clearly visible during the NATO-led air campaign against Libya in the summer of 2011. After axing the *Ark Royal,* Britain had to rely on the Royal Air Force's Tornados and Typhoons to conduct strike missions from the British air bases, whereas French Rafale combat aircraft flew sorties from the *Charles de Gaulle* carrier off the coast of Libya, as did the Italian and U.S. Harriers from the *Giuseppe Garibaldi* and the USS *Kearsage.* Having an aircraft carrier in the theater of operations would have made a crucial difference for the British forces, both in terms of cost reduction and mission effectiveness.[48] Moreover, the current hiatus will also result in considerable challenges in restoring such capabilities. Fortunately, close ties with the United States have provided opportunities for British personnel to train on the U.S. Navy's aircraft carriers in order to maintain their flying and flight-deck handling skills.[49]

Today, the surface fleet has been consolidated around the 6 Type 45 destroyers and 13 Type 23 *Duke*-class frigates, with its successor, the Type 26 and Type 31, scheduled to replace the *Dukes* in the course of the next decade. Cost overruns and delays in the Nimrod

MRA.4 program ultimately led to the cancellation of the maritime patrol aircraft and with it the loss of an integral element of the U.K.'s ASW and maritime situational awareness capabilities. These capabilities have been sorely missed, particularly in the more recent past, when Russian submarines were allegedly sighted in the waters off Scotland. In a somewhat embarrassing move, the Royal Navy had to ask its allies for assistance in the search for these submarines.[50] What is more, a further round of cuts to manpower levels has left the Royal Navy with a force of roughly 30,000 military personnel, less than half of that at the end of the Cold War.

To sum up these developments, a recent RAND study comes to the conclusion that "reduced manpower levels, curtailed equipment procurement, and [subsequent] capability gaps [have] direct consequences for the U.K.'s ability to carry out current and future missions."[51] Although the Royal Navy is making investments to maintain a balanced naval force—deciding to commission both new *Queen Elizabeth*–class carriers and planning a new class of ballistic missile submarines—some analysts ask if the British Navy is not backing the wrong horse. "A key question . . . is whether a balanced force is ultimately in the strategic interests of the United Kingdom, or whether such a force should be abandoned in favor of a 'cruising' navy requiring a greater number of frigates and destroyers and providing more naval presence in a greater number of places than the current fleet plan can accomplish."[52] In fact, "considering the United Kingdom's global economic interests and its desire to remain closely aligned with the [U.S.] Navy, a force of less than 20 combatants might not suffice."[53]

Over the past decade the Royal Navy, by and large, has tried to trade quantity for quality. By pursuing a strategy of "leapfrogging," or "cutting defense expenditure heavily today while investing in new types of capabilities,"[54] the Royal Navy hopes to profit down the line, or in other words accept "that there will be some significant long-term gain, but also some significant short-term pain."[55] This practice cannot be seriously considered an appropriate solution to the problem, especially if national security and collective defense is at stake. Furthermore, the need for readily available surface combatants is unlikely to become any less critical in the future. At any given moment in time, British destroyers and frigates are conducting numerous tasks, in different parts of the world, as the former first sea lord, Sir Mark Stanhope, describes:

> Standing commitments [at the time included]: Protecting Iraqi oil infrastructure, anti-piracy, counter-terrorism, counter-drugs, safeguarding overseas territories and Crown Dependencies including the Falklands. Those missions require at least five or six ships at any one time and the wisdom is that you need three or four ships for each commitment, in order to guarantee having one on station. That means one out there, one, possibly two, in refit or maintenance and another training to deploy. In frigate and destroyer terms there is not a lot, if anything left over for emergencies such as war or for training with allies to underpin alliances that prevent wars.[56]

Clearly, such a high frequency of deployments also increases the wear and tear on the warships and their crews, thus increasing the likelihood of miscalculations and accidents. As recent collisions involving U.S. warships have painfully demonstrated, fatigue not only takes its toll on the ships but also becomes visible among the men and women who do their utmost to protect their country's interests at sea.

In order to alleviate the strain on the a navies' principle surface combatants, many European states now operate flotillas of small corvettes and off-shore patrol vessels (OPVs), specifically designed for the increasing number of low intensity antipiracy, drug interdiction, fishery protection, and search and rescue (SAR) operations. Currently, the Royal Navy has only four such vessels (called the *River* class) in service, of which only one is assigned to operations outside of Britain's exclusive economic zone (EEZ).[57] As a consequence, the more capable frigates and air-defense destroyers also have to conduct all other operations, in which their multimillion dollar electronics and weapons suites are rarely needed. General Sir David Richards points out this paradox: "You get to this ridiculous situation where in Operation 'Atalanta,' off the Somali coast, we have £1 bn. (Type 45) destroyers trying to sort out pirates in a little dhow with RPGs . . . costing $50. . . . That can't be good."[58]

The SDSR in 2010 caused considerable capability gaps among all branches of the armed forces. However, there is cautious optimism in naval quarters, concerning the future of the Royal Navy. After years of defense cuts, military expenditure was slightly increased from 2015 onward.[59] In light of a somewhat better economic situation, Prime Minister David Cameron announced that instead of selling or mothballing the second carrier, the *Prince of Wales* would join the fleet early in the next decade. "The second carrier will be brought into service. [This] means the Royal Navy will be able deploy a carrier 100 percent of the time," Cameron stated.[60] Britain is likely to once again deploy fast jets, in the form of the Lockheed Martin F-35B, from the decks of its aircraft carriers and thus regain substantial power-projection and deterrent capabilities.

Moreover, it is likely that the teething problems the new *Astute*-class SSNs have encountered will have been sorted out by the time the carriers arrive, making them some of the most capable hunter-killer submarines in the world. The design phase of the replacement for the four *Vanguard* ballistic missile submarines is well under way and while only eight Type 26 ASW frigates are to be built, the remaining funding will be spent on a new class of lighter, multi-purpose frigates, with greater export potential.[61]

In the long run, the RN might benefit from this adroit decision in a number of ways. First, the new, smaller Type 31 frigate could conceivably become an attractive competitor on the booming global market for small surface combatants, whereas the Type 26 seems to promise little success. Second, the vessels would be mainly used for lower-intensity operations and constabulary duties, allowing the RN's principle surface combatants to focus on their designated roles. And third, it less likely that the ships will fall victim to a renewed round of budget cuts, were Britain's economy to tank as a result of the U.K.'s withdrawal from the European Union. In any case, anything short of the construction of thirteen new frigates and four SSBNs would only exacerbate the already critical state in which the RN finds itself.[62]

Aside from the possible negative impact the popular vote to leave the European Union might have on the U.K.'s defense industry (and the state of its national security on a whole), the British Royal Navy will likely operate a multipurpose navy with increased power-projection capabilities by the beginning of the next decade. Notably, the RN will have emulated the United States' naval forces with which it arguably shares the closest military-to-military cooperation of any two countries in the world. As one naval analyst notes, the British navy "looks strikingly like the US Navy, except [at] a fraction of its size." However, "the resources necessary to achieve these goals are to some degree harvested from savings gained from a significantly smaller escort and combatant fleet."[63] Notwithstanding this predicament, operating a balanced naval force gives the political and military leadership the most effective tool in order to deal with the changing security environment and a myriad of emerging threats. "The general tendency [in the twenty-first century]," Till observes, "is to guard against the difficulty of prediction by building general purpose fleet capabilities that can be adapted to respond to unexpected events and trends."[64]

After having reached its nadir since the end of the Cold War, the British Royal Navy is now slowly recovering from the severe retrenchment that had befallen all branches of the armed forces. With numerous high-profile procurement projects under way, the Royal Navy can look forward to a somewhat brighter future. However, the reduction in the size of the fleet over the last twenty-five years has been very costly in strategic terms. To many observers, "a decline in the RN's global footprint still seems inevitable given the decline in the number of its ships and people."[65] Such a development is likely to accelerate the already ongoing shift in the global naval balance from West to East.[66] Against the backdrop of the latest SDSR and pending negotiation on "Brexit," some of the findings in this chapter regarding Britain's naval forces might need to be qualified in the months to come. In the end, the Royal Navy still has a long way to go before it regains the status it enjoyed at the end of the Cold War.

CHAPTER 5

France

Stretched, but Willing—Europe's Most Capable Naval Force?

Over the centuries, the British and the French fought heroic naval battles to decide who was to rule the sea, and thus the world. In the end, French aspirations for global dominance ended in 1805, with the crippling defeat at the Battle of Trafalgar against Lord Horatio Nelson and the concentrated might of the Royal Navy. From that point on, Great Britain would rule supreme for more than a hundred years. Finally, its power was eclipsed by that of the United States and its navy. During the Cold War the British naval forces were a critical element of NATO defense planning against the Soviet threat. Consequently, the British slowly shifted their naval focus from a global power-projection capability to anti-submarine warfare in the North Atlantic, relying on the American carrier battle groups to take the fight to the enemy in the case of war. France, on the other hand, for both political and geographical reasons, had to build and maintain a balanced multipurpose fleet, able to shoulder the burden of every conceivable maritime task.

The French navy, the Marine Nationale, developed under very different strategic preconditions. In 1966, as a result of insurmountable differences between France and the United States regarding the former's status within NATO, President Charles de Gaulle displayed his Gallic pride by announcing the country's withdrawal from the alliance.[1] Therefore, the French navy not only had to provide a credible nuclear deterrence in the form of its ballistic missile submarines (referred to as the *Force océanique stratégique*) but also needed to be capable of conducting naval operations ranging across the intensity spectrum—from fleet air defense to fishery protection.

The second defining factor that has shaped the French navy over the centuries, is the unique nature of the country's geography. While other European states such as Italy or Norway have maintained relatively confined geographical spheres of interest—the greater Mediterranean region and High North respectively—France has enjoyed (or suffered from) access to the Mediterranean, the Atlantic, and the English Channel (and thereby, the North Sea). The security of the numerous sea lines of communication that run through these waters are of vital interest to France, which like so many other nations is heavily dependent on seaborne trade. Furthermore, France still retains numerous oversea territories, including French Guiana in South America (home to Europe's spaceport); Guadalupe and Martinique in the Caribbean; Réunion in the Indian Ocean; Adélie Land in Antarctica; and French Polynesia in the middle of the Pacific Ocean. Apart from the United States, France is the only country to have its naval forces continuously deployed to all three major oceans of the world[2] and possesses the second largest exclusive economic zone (EEZ),[3] which stretches more than 4.2 million square miles. Accordingly, over the past few decades the French navy has operated a mix of "first-rate" warships, as well as patrol vessels designed for low-risk sea surveillance, fishery protection, and constabulary duties more generally.

Sustained military expenditure in excess of 3.5 percent of the nation's GDP throughout the Cold War allowed the French fleet to evolve into one of the most capable naval forces by the time the global confrontation between East and West had drawn to a close. Although its surface fleet comprised thirty-eight large surface combatants, compared to Royal Navy's forty-eight, the Marine Nationale had one distinct advantage over the RN—and most other large naval forces of the time. Instead of relying on small cruiser-sized aircraft carriers that could only deploy the Harrier jump jets (such as the British *Invincible* class, the Italian *Giuseppe Garibaldi,* or the Spanish *Principe de Asturias*), the French operated two flat-deck carriers using a CATOBAR system (catapult assisted take-off barrier arrested recovery). This system allowed heavier aircraft such as the Dassault Étendard IVPs, Grumman F-8E Crusaders, and the Alizé maritime patrol planes to safely operate from the carrier, thus increasing the naval air wing's combat radius and payload. In essence, the French carrier battle groups around the *Clemenceau* and *Foch* represented Europe's most powerful conventional naval assets.

In addition, the *Jeanne d'Arc* helicopter carrier, somewhat similar in design to the Soviet *Moskva* class, provided the fleet with ASW and amphibious capabilities. At the time, the escort fleet consisted of eighteen cruisers and destroyers, as well as twenty-four smaller frigates. Although a considerable force, many of these ships had already been in service for nearly thirty years and were becoming increasingly expensive to maintain. Other units, such as those of the *Cassard* class, belonged to the most capable air-defense destroyers while the new class of *George Leygues* ASW destroyers represented the core of the navy's multipurpose surface capabilities.[4]

Like Britain, the French navy used to operate a mix of domestically built nuclear-propelled and conventional diesel-electric submarines during the Cold War. Akin to Britain's decision to abandon its fleet of diesel-electric submarines, the French navy began to decommission its flotilla of *Daphné* SSKs in 1997. Domestic shipbuilding also remained a key element of the nation's naval power. A new class of strategic ballistic missile submarine had already been laid down at the national shipyards at Cherbourg[5] and progressively entered service over the following years. Four nuclear-powered attack submarines of the *Améthyste* class were also ordered to augment the existing *Rubis* class, but in the end only two units were built, bringing the number of nuclear attack submarines to a total of six. Interestingly, these boats were relatively small compared to other SSNs and displaced less than the Japanese *Soryu*-class and *Oyashio*-class conventional submarines.[6] As noted, the French DCN shipbuilders has also constructed the highly capable *Agosta* and *Daphné* SSKs, which were particularly useful in confined and shallow waters closer to shore. The vessels' qualities are underscored by their considerable commercial success.[7]

The need for offshore patrol vessels, formally referred to as surveillance frigates, has already been briefly addressed. Warships, such as the *D'Estienne D'Orves* class, in service with the French navy in 1991, would not qualify as credible surface combatants today, given their shortcomings in size, speed, and armament (1,140 tons, 23 knots, 1 100-mm gun, 4 Exocet missiles, and an ASW rocket launcher). Yet, at the end of the Cold War they provided an indispensable element of the Marine Nationale's fleet, in particular because they could be built in great numbers. Interestingly, compared to the British, France has always sought to maintain a sizable fleet of such OPVs. However, their design features and nature of deployment often blur the line between the various classes of warship. (Offshore patrol vessels now have reached the size and in some cases the capabilities of ships classified as frigates twenty-five years ago.)

In terms of amphibious capabilities and auxiliaries, France had already made respectable investments by the time other European countries only began to fully appreciate the utility of such forces. One large, 9,300-ton dock landing ship (LSD), a smaller 3,310-ton LSD, 2 older *Ouragan*-class ships and 5 medium-sized landing ships provided comparatively robust power-projection capabilities, despite some critics arguing at the time that the "amphibious assault capabilities [were] dangerously reduced."[8] With 5 large fleet replenishment ships and a sizable fleet of mine hunters, the French navy could generally consider itself on par with the British navy, outclassed only by the U.S. Navy and the Soviet naval behemoth.[9]

The drastic geopolitical transformation that occurred at the end of the twentieth century also had far-reaching repercussions on the French armed forces. Military spending was quickly reduced and the entire defense structure underwent extensive reorganization. The so-called Optimar 95 plan, issued only a year after the Cold War had come to an end, called for numerous changes to be made—including the reform of all previous naval command structures. In short, the naval squadron and flotillas were to be dissolved and the "bulk of the surface fleet [was] subdivided into three large specialized formations, which could be looked at as coherent 'force pools.'"[10] Somewhat similar to the development of the *Alpha* and *Delta* groups in Spain "the Joint Chief of Staff [would] be able to 'pick up' at will the naval assets he [needed] to face a given crisis situation," Jean-Louis Promé explains.[11]

It can be said that the foundation for the current force structure was laid during this period of time. The aircraft carriers and the majority of the surface fleet (including air-defense and ASW frigates, the amphibious forces and fleet replenishment tankers) as well as the nuclear attack submarines were henceforth stationed at Toulon in southern France. The rest of the French fleet is homeported at Brest on the Atlantic coast. The primary mission of the frigates and OPVs stationed at Brest is to protect the SSBNs on their way to and from their nearby base at Île Longue. The larger part of the mine countermeasure force also operates from its base in the Bretagne and is supported by various replenishment vessels.[12]

Despite serious efforts being made to modernize the fleet during the 1990s, it would not be long before the French navy found itself facing numerous challenges. During the early years of the decade, the defense budget had remained remarkably stable (around 3.3 percent of GPD), but began to shrink dramatically midway through the 1990s. By the year 2000, the defense expenditure had decreased by more than 20 percent, to 2.5 percent of GDP. Apart from the aforementioned structural streamlining measures, these fiscal limitations forced the navy to make a number of concessions.

By the late 1990s the navy had "opted to abandon the conventional submarine component,"[13] thus ceding some underwater warfare capabilities. Unlike Britain, however, France has retained

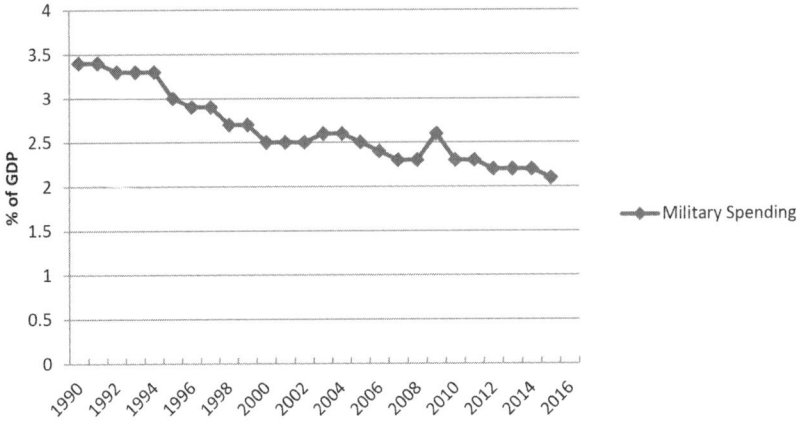

Figure 6-1. France: Defense Spending in % of GDP, 1990–2015
Source: SIPRI Military Expenditure Database.

its industrial capacity to develop state-of-the-art conventional submarines. To this day, French shipbuilders are held in high regard, winning a number of lucrative defense acquisition deals.[14] The surface fleet, built around two carrier strike groups, also took a big hit. The aircraft carrier *Clemenceau* was taken from service in 1997, with her sister ship, the *Foch,* awaiting the arrival of its nuclear-powered successor before being decommissioned and sold to Brazil in 2000. Since then, the French navy has had to make do with a single aircraft carrier—the *Charles de Gaulle.*

While some procurement projects were cut, such as the second pair of *Cassard* air-defense frigates,[15] others were postponed or underwent "programme stretching measures"[16] in order to avoid rash decisions coming back to haunt the navy. As a French analyst stated at the time, "Given the very long delay between the launching of a modern weapon system and its eventual entry into service, a wrong decision today could compromise the credibility and effectiveness of the French defense posture as a whole in the 2000–2010 timeframe."[17] On a more positive note, French naval architects had conceived a revolutionary ship design in the meantime, allowing a glimpse of what could be expected in twenty-first century naval development. When the *La Fayette* frigate entered service it exhibited groundbreaking design features, not seen before in any warship.[18] The public interest in the ship was heightened when it was featured in the 1995 James Bond movie *GoldenEye*.

Stealth technology had become a buzzword in the post–Cold War era as American radar-evading strike aircraft penetrated enemy air-defense networks with seeming impunity. In the maritime realm, "The best way to protect a ship is still to avoid detection," one commentator observed.[19] Designed to drastically reduce the ship's radar cross section, the hull and superstructure of the *La Fayette* were slanted to "control radar reflectivity"[20] and were covered with radar absorbing material (RAM). The usual openings found on a ship's hull and superstructure was all masked with retractable screens to enhance stealth. Apart from their groundbreaking features, the ships provide a reasonable amount of firepower, despite having been designed for long-range missions, overseas possessions control, and defensive operations closer to home.[21] A single 100-mm/55 gun can be used against air, surface, and land targets while the eight Exocet SSMs and Crotale CN2 SAM systems provide additional protection in medium-threat environments. Further, a helicopter can be embarked, able to operate in rough weather conditions owing to the ship's sophisticated stabilization system.[22]

On the international market the *La Fayette* design has enjoyed considerable success. Modified versions of the vessel have been sold to Singapore, Taiwan, and Saudi Arabia. However, for the French navy, the frigate has become something of a double-edged sword. On the one hand, the *La Fayette* class pioneered naval ship design and had significant influence on later surface combatants, such as the *Horizon*-class destroyer and FREMM-class frigate (FREMM stands for *FRégate Européenne Multi-Missions*). Moreover, the *La Fayette* gave the Marine Nationale exactly what it needed at the time, namely a state-of-the-art warship and a technology testbed, which could fill the gap between the fleet's OPVs and first-rank ships.[23] On the other hand, it is safe to say that very few people in the naval service at the time would have imagined the five units of the class, referred to as second-rank ships,[24] to someday assume the role of front-line combatants, constituting nearly a third of France's escort fleet as is the case today.[25] Inherently slow, arguably too lightly armed for high-intensity conflict (although the ships are currently receiving upgrades to their combat systems and weapon systems), the *La Fayette* exemplifies how important it is to build multipurpose surface combatants, capable of conducting a wide variety of missions and with room to grow, in order to quickly adapt to an ever changing security environment. In hindsight, one can question the decision to invest so heavily in signature reduction, instead of building more powerful and heavily armed warships. Even at the time, it was not reasonable to believe that the stealth frigate would ever have to avoid sophisticated anti-ship missile (ASM) fired by an angry local fisherman, while on station off the shores of Martinique or Tahiti.

For more than two centuries, France has been able to rely on a powerful military industry. In more recent years, the French defense sector has provided cutting-edge designs in many areas of military research and development. In terms of shipbuilding, the partially state-owned Direction des Constructions Navales (DCNS—now Naval Group) industrial group can rightfully be considered one of the most experienced and successful manufacturers of naval weapon systems in the world. Indeed, it is one of the few companies able to design and build nearly every kind of warship—from conventional and nuclear-powered submarines, to patrol vessels, frigates, assault ships, and even aircraft carriers. More importantly, over the last two decades, the French naval industry has successfully teamed up with other European shipbuilders to develop some of the most capable naval vessels in service today. These experiences and the continued cooperation with Italy's Fincantieri shipbuilding company has led to the construction of the versatile FREMM frigates (*Aquitaine* class), eight of which have been ordered by the French navy.[26]

Many design features of both the *Horizon*-class destroyer as well as the *La Fayette* become evident in the navy's new warship. Most notably, the FREMM frigates incorporate signature reduction measures to make them arguably the stealthiest warships in service today.[27] Despite its radar system being somewhat less sophisticated than on the Italian version of the FREMMs (operating the Herakles radar instead of the more capable Selex EMPAR radar), it nonetheless provides robust air-defense capabilities. Besides its AAW weapons, Exocet anti-ship missiles, and SCALP/Storm Shadow land attack cruise missiles, the ship's anti-submarine warfare capabilities merit attention. Apart from the obligatory torpedo launchers, the ship has a Thales low frequency, active and passive sonar mounted on the ship's bow. "Providing long-range detection irrespective of environmental conditions, it is particularly effective at detecting targets above the thermal layer and has been influenced by Mediterranean anti-submarine conditions."[28] A second variable-depth sonar is deployed from underneath the flight deck and is designed to find submarines even at very great distances beneath the thermal layer. Once a submarine has been located, the *Aquitaine*'s helicopter is responsible for its pursuit. The Westland Lynx model currently in service is being replaced by the more capable French version of the NH90.[29]

This brief description clearly shows that many French warships rely heavily on European defense technology. As defense spending and with it the demand for defense procurement orders among European states decreased in the wake of the Soviet collapse, France fought hard to maintain its military industrial capacity, thereby also ensuring that Europe's defense industry remained competitive on the international market.[30] Successive French defense white papers underscored the necessity to strengthen the common European defense sector. They urged that the "industry must be European," and made their case by stating that "individual European countries can no longer master every technology and capability at national level. . . . As regards the other technologies and capacities that it may wish to acquire, France believes that the European framework must be privileged: combat aircraft, drones, cruise missiles, satellites, electronic components etc."[31]

While many European surface combatants had relied on American sensors and armament, such as the Tartar and Standard

Missile (SM) 1ER for upper-tier fleet air defense during the later years of the Cold War, the French were adamant that their future warships should be fitted with European weapon systems. In order to create their own air-defense capability—a primary element of modern warships—a Franco-Italian defense consortium set out to develop the Aster missile series. Both the short-range Aster 15, for point and local air defense, as well as the larger Aster 30, for long-range air defense, have been successfully tested against a variety of targets. Due to their active seeker and thrust vectoring control, they are considered superior to all but the latest U.S. air-defense missiles.[32] Currently, several warships are fitted with the DCNS SYLVER vertical launch system, capable of firing both Aster and SCALP cruise missiles. These include the four French and Italian *Horizon*-class destroyers, the British Type 45 (which evolved from the *Horizon* project), the export versions of the *La Fayette* frigate, the Italian aircraft carrier *Cavour,* as well as all new FREMM-class frigates. However, the first ship to carry the Aster air-defense missile system was the nuclear-powered *Charles de Gaulle* aircraft carrier— the backbone of the Marine Nationale.

For many years the aircraft carrier program appeared to be ill-fated. While the keel of the *Charles de Gaulle* was laid down in 1989, five years would pass before the ship was launched. It took another seven years for her builders to overcome various technical deficiencies before she finally joined the fleet. Despite the challenges the development of such a complex ship entails, it is important to note that since her introduction she has provided successive French governments with an invaluable instrument to project power abroad. At a displacement in excess of 37,000 tons and a length of 261 meters, the French carrier will not only remain Europe's largest warship until the *Queen Elizabeth* joins the British fleet in the 2020s, but is also considered the most powerful aircraft carrier in service today, save the American supercarriers.[33] Despite almost two decades of continuous discussion regarding the construction of a second carrier (a possible cooperation with the British seemed to be the most cost-effective solution), the topic has now been dropped

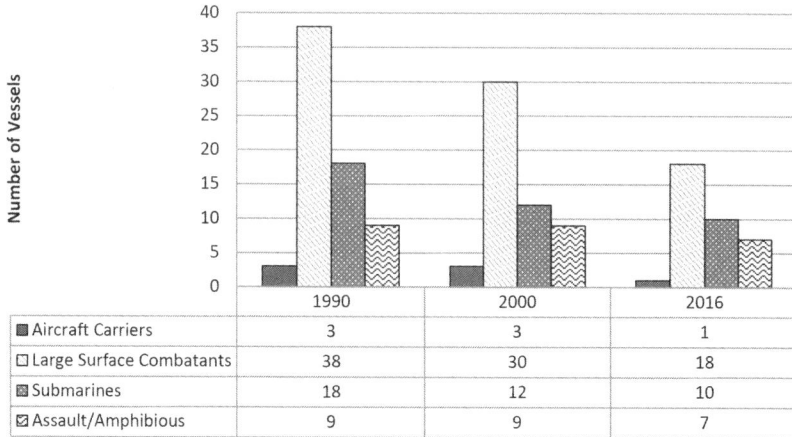

	1990	2000	2016
▣ Aircraft Carriers	3	3	1
▢ Large Surface Combatants	38	30	18
▤ Submarines	18	12	10
☑ Assault/Amphibious	9	9	7

Figure 6-2. France: Number of Major Vessels

Sources: *The Naval Institute Guide to Combat Fleets of the World, Military Technology Almanac, World Naval Review.*

indefinitely. Consequently, not a single European large-deck aircraft carrier will be operational between 2017 and 2018, during which period the French ship undergoes her mid-life refueling and overhaul. Only the Spanish and Italian naval forces will be able to deploy a very limited number of combat aircraft from their carriers during this time period.

Halfway around the world, in an area of growing geopolitical importance, rising powers are making great strides in developing their own aircraft carrier capabilities. India, for example, is in the process of deploying Russian-designed MiG-29K jets from the deck of its refurbished Soviet–era *Admiral Gorshkov,* while the obsolete *Viraat* will be replaced by India's first domestically built aircraft carrier around 2019. Similarly, China has also begun to deploy aircraft from its first "flat-deck," the *Liaoning,* and its own domestically built carrier is undergoing sea trials. While experts note that these efforts do not amount to a credible aircraft carrier capability, both China and India have made tentative provisions to build fleets around numerous carrier battle groups. Moreover, considering the current naval arms buildup that is under way in the Asia-Pacific region, these developments clearly highlight the opposite trajectories that European and Asian sea power are on.

While China, India, and other states in the APR might have caught up to France in terms of available naval platforms, the French navy has a clear advantage when it comes to operating aircraft from the decks of its carriers. Apart from the *Charles de Gaulle*'s nuclear propulsion, the most striking difference to other carriers is the installation of catapults and arresting wires rather than a so-called ski jump. French naval aviation has greatly profited from the American's experience in CATOBAR carrier operations, acquiring large parts of the catapult and arresting system from the United States.[34] The Aéronavale, the French navy's fleet air arm, has also worked closely with its U.S. counterparts, regularly deploying from U.S. Navy carriers. "The goal of [these efforts is] to demonstrate, on a large scale, our ability to integrate with US forces," the commander of a French air group explains,[35] while a senior U.S. pilot adds that "integrating with the French did not pose any major problem. . . . Basically, we have the same mentality and all French pilots have been trained by the US Navy."[36]

In recent years, shared security needs, such as fighting radical Islamic terrorism, have led to closer diplomatic and military-to-military cooperation between France and its Westerns allies. In 2009, under President Nicolas Sarkozy, France formally rejoined NATO, leading a RAND study to conclude that "France today is much more integrated in NATO planning and operations than at any time since the mid-1960s."[37] Such measures have enhanced the ability of the various European militaries to effectively deploy together as well as with their most important ally, the United States.

As it turns out, the French armed forces, and the Marine Nationale in particular, have proven to be an indispensable tool of French foreign policy and a major factor in international affairs. Within the country's sphere of influence, running along a "geographical axis from the Atlantic to the Mediterranean, the Arab-Persian Gulf and the Indian Ocean,"[38] the Marine Nationale has enabled the French government to quickly react to crises, or any situation in which it sees its national interests at stake. Despite increased political and economic headwinds, to date it is considered a strategic priority that the French armed forces maintain a "full spectrum"[39] force and sufficient military means to conduct large-scale, high-intensity interventions globally, whereby a priority is given to the above-mentioned geographical sphere of interest. However, given the structural limitation of its armed forces, the French defense white paper of 2008 qualifies these aspirations by acknowledging that for "significant" and "major" operations, assets from other countries would be needed.[40] In other words, France will remain dependent on the United States' heavy sealift and airlift capabilities, its naval replenishment and aerial refueling platforms, its large stock of precision ammunition, and American command and control facilities, as well as its intelligence, surveillance, and reconnaissance (ISR) assets.[41]

Since the end of the Cold War, France has nonetheless proven to entertain a credible fighting force. The French navy has participated in numerous military operations, from enforcing the embargo against Serbia during the 1990s, to conducting air strikes with its Super-Étendard and Rafale fighter-bombers against al-Qaeda and Taliban hideouts in Afghanistan as part of Operation Enduring Freedom (the French military operation was called Operation Herakles). In 2011, the French carrier strike group played a key role in the air campaign against the regime of Libya's longtime ruler Muammar Gaddafi, while in 2015 and 2016 the *Charles de Gaulle* was redeployed to the Middle East to join U.S.-led air strikes against the so-called Islamic State (IS) in Syria and Iraq. In light of the latest terrorist attacks on French soil, the French government has repeatedly emphasized that it is determined to continue the fight against IS and other terrorist networks. Under these political circumstances, the French navy will need to be prepared for a further increase in operational tempo in order to meet the growing demand of naval strike assets.

Unfortunately, between 2008 and 2016, the size of the French navy continued on its previous trajectory. Even the initial plan to operate an escort fleet of 18 vessels was considered too costly in light of an 11 percent cut to the navy's budget.[42] Consequently, instead of 11 FREMM-class frigates (18 were initially planned) only 8 will be procured, bringing the number of "front-line" frigates down to the aforementioned 15 ships by the end of the decade. Six of these warships will be designed for ASW tasks (i.e., to protect the sea-based leg of the France's nuclear deterrent) while the last two units will be upgraded to provide fleet air defense. The number of ballistic missile and attack submarines remained untouched.[43]

In accordance with its defense strategy which underscores France's continued global ambitions, the countries amphibious forces have been strengthened considerably over the years. Three *Mistral*-class landing helicopter dock (LHD) ships were built between 2003 and 2012[44] and together with the *Siroco* LHD provide more than "just limited crisis response and humanitarian intervention," as one analyst critically remarked.[45] Frankly, apart from Britain, France has the largest amphibious force in Europe, both of which are part of the Combined Joint Expeditionary Force, established in 2010/2011 as part of the Lancaster House Treaties.[46]

The aforementioned *Mistral* has also been the ship to attract the most attention in the media over the past years. In 2010, after more than two years of secret negotiations, France and Russia signed a contract for four of these highly capable assault ships to be built in both French and Russian naval yards. The decision, however, was not well received by a number of NATO members who feared that these ships would give the Russian fleet the amphibious capabilities it had so sorely lacked during the war against Georgia in 2008. Given the renewed confrontation between East and West, the French government ultimately had to submit to the pressure from its allies, first postponing and then ultimately canceling the delivery of the *Vladivostok,* which had already embarked a Russian crew for training at sea.[47]

The dispute over the *Mistral*s for the Russian navy offers two important insights into current naval issues. First, regardless of sensationalist claims that Russia's naval industrial capacity will soon be back in full swing, the country remains unable to build large surface warships. As Mikhail Tsypkin puts it, "the Russian defense industry is not dead by any means, but Russia is no longer an autarkic defense industrial power."[48] The difficulty to find a substitute for Ukrainian-built ship turbines is but one example for the problems that plague the Russian shipbuilding sector. Second, France will have to pay back the money it has already received from Russia. More importantly, by pulling out of the deal, Paris ran the risk of becoming stigmatized as an unreliable partner, potentially having detrimental consequences on securing future defense acquisition bids. Fortunately, the latter has not been the case. In the meantime, Egypt has placed an order for twenty-four Rafale jets, as well as two FREMM frigates, and has bought both *Mistrals* built for Russia (with financial aid from Saudi Arabia) whereas DCNS has also been awarded the construction of Australia's future submarine fleet.[49]

Among the European states, France currently operates arguably the most capable naval force. For the most part, it has maintained a well-balanced fleet, including carrier strike power and a nuclear deterrent. Assets, such as the *Mistral,* which deployed French forces to Mali in 2013, will become increasingly important if the United States continues to slowly shift its priorities away from Europe. Therefore, the French effort to create synergies by cooperating more closely with its friends and allies in Europe, not only in operational terms, but also in defense procurement projects has to be considered particularly praiseworthy. The defense agreement between the United Kingdom and France (The Lancaster House Treaties) "could provide a roadmap to more effective European defense cooperation, based on deeper capability planning and mutual dependency."[50] Although, as a British defense analyst continues to insist, "[the Franco-British cooperation] side-steps the strategic question of the role of NATO and the United States in European defense and security [and does not] address concerns among some European states over the long-term disengagement of the US from Europe," it has nevertheless "set the 'gold standard' for defense cooperation [in Europe]."[51]

According to official sources, France is likely to remain actively engaged along its "geographical axis of interest," which currently includes the Sahel, the European periphery, Sub-Saharan Africa, the Persian Gulf, the Horn of Africa, and the Indian Ocean.[52] Moreover, the French navy will continue to commit naval forces to policing duties in its overseas territories and across France's huge exclusive economic zones. However, as a result of the most recent austerity measures, the size of the naval fleet has been significantly reduced and former "second-rate" vessels, assigned to the aforementioned tasks, are now part of the Marine Nationale's "first-line" of surface combatants. Jean Moulin somberly concludes that "the Marine Nationale finds itself in a difficult position, with no reduction in its commitment but fewer resources."[53] The future of the French armed forces will be largely dependent on the nation's economic health and continued investments toward its defense industry. Only in 2015 has "France's GDP, along with that of the Eurozone in the aggregate, recovered to the pre-crisis level of late 2007," a study by the Atlantic Council points out. "Substantial structural reforms in the short and medium terms are the prerequisites for sustainable [economic] growth."[54]

For now, the French navy will continue to rely on its mixed fleet of both aging, second-rate as well as of state-of-the-art warships. The Marine Nationale will remain Europe's most powerful naval force until the early 2020s, after which it will rank a close second to Britain's strengthened navy. It will continue to be looked to when crises occur and in support of both French and allied interests abroad. It will be willing—but it will be stretched.

Italy

Between Global Interest and Regional Necessities

*The strategic space where Italy feels herself involved has its centre
of gravity in the Mediterranean Sea. It starts from Gibraltar
and moves along two main lines[,] one reaching the Black Sea
and the Middle East through the Balkans and the Aegean Sea; the
latter moving southward through the Red Sea down to the Indian
Ocean, the Gulf, and including the Horn of Africa.*

ADMIRAL ANGELO MARIANI,
CHIEF OF THE ITALIAN NAVY

For millennia the denizens of the Italian peninsula have looked
toward the sea in hope of prosperity and wealth. Throughout
history its geographical position has proved expedient to those
prudent enough to take advantage of the surrounding waters. The
adjacent shores and the hinterland of the Mediterranean basin used
to be some of the most fertile and prosperous lands in the known
world. Economies and cultural exchange flourished as merchants
transported and traded goods from near and far. Some gained for-
tunes exchanging goods on the brisk markets that connected the
Levant with the Spanish peninsula and the North African shores
with the ports of what is now the Turkish coastline.

Had the Phoenicians, Greeks, Carthaginians, and Romans commanded the seas throughout antiquity, a millennium later, Italian
military and commercial sea power again shaped events in the
Mediterranean. Throughout the thirteenth, fourteenth, and fif-
teenth centuries, Italy's princely states were able to fashion large
navies and merchant fleets, thus reaching hitherto unseen cultural
heights. However, given their geographic position, which confined
them to Mediterranean waters, city states such as Florence, Genoa,
and Venice were not able to maintain their power once the New
World was discovered in the late fifteen hundreds. Ultimately,
Italy's states were "maritime state[s] with too narrow and geotrop-
ically too exposed a base of resources at home to compete with
the emerging much larger sea and land powers,"[1] such as Spain,
France, and Britain. Nonetheless, the Mediterranean would remain
an important region of the world and as of late has regained much
of its former strategic relevance.

Looking back on the more recent past, the Italian naval forces
have lived through challenging times. After centuries of gradual
decline, Italy's naval power reached its nadir at the end of the Second
World War. Due to its role during the war as part of the Axis, the
navy was reduced to less than a third-rate sea power by the provisos
of the Paris Peace Treaty. However, over the course of following
decades Italy's Marina Militare, as the navy is called, underwent its
own renaissance. The primary reason for this development lay in the
Soviet Union's vigorous attempt to challenge NATO's naval supremacy in the 1970s and 1980s. The unprecedented Soviet naval buildup
during this period necessitated a capable Italian fleet to secure
NATO's southern flank. As one analyst explains, "After a period of
low-key performance," the Soviets' large-scale naval deployments
to the Mediterranean elicited "a renewed *Marina Militare* [to
abandon] its previous 'silent service' policy [and] become, almost
overnight, a more overt player on the world stage."[2]

Italy's new vision for its national defense was developed between
1975 and 1985 and a raft of major defense documents and procurement programs constituted a watershed for the Marina Militare.

Based on Italy's aspirations to take on a more assertive role in international affairs, the new doctrine underscored the importance of Italy's armed forces in defending the country's national interests. Multinational missions farther away from home (such as the peacekeeping effort in Lebanon, 1982–84) were considered an important element of Italy's foreign policy. In essence, Italy's new foreign policy objectives represented a major stepping stone for the country's strategic reorientation and the modernization of its military, as Admiral Giampaolo di Paolo stated: "The White Paper of 1985 contained some important guidelines, aiming at restructuring defense towards a better integration of the forces at both operational planning and management of resources levels; from the definition of missions, the unification of the line of command, to the organization of the industry and procurement policy."[3]

Italy's transition from a strategy of static defense to a more active engagement, either alone or as part of a multinational operation, continued throughout the 1990s. These changes were also heavily influenced by extrinsic political events, such as the dissolution of the Soviet Union and the Gulf War. The resulting evolution of Italian defense, promulgated in the Modello di Difesa in 1991, highlighted the increasing challenges of the post–Cold War era and the utility of military force in support of the government's agenda. Cooperation within NATO, the European Union, and United Nations was to be expanded in order to legitimize the use of force.[4] A scholar of European defense policy summarizes these tenets as follows: "The key point of the whole document seems to be the identification between security and the safeguarding of political and economic interests abroad, by means of new power projection capabilities of the military instrument, as the heart of the country's foreign policy."[5]

Although the Modello di Difesa also included a general reduction of Italy's force structure, Admiral Umberto Guarnieri was certain that at the time, the navy was well equipped to fulfill these tasks. The force of the 1990s, he pointed out, was "composed of elements of better quality, able to preserve the security and national interest of Italy, wherever necessary be it alone or in cooperation with its allies."[6] Over the past twenty-five years, the following basic "strategic functions" listed by Guarnieri have remained largely unchanged. In fact, the Marina Militare's primary tasks are now much the same as at the time of their inception:

- During peacetime, presence and surveillance in the areas of strategic national interest;
- during times of tensions and crisis, protection of national interest and cooperation with international security organizations; and
- during war, contribution to the combined defense of national and allied homelands.[7]

Based on Italy's doctrinal continuity, the navy's fleet structure has also undergone little alteration since the end of the Cold War. Numerous vessels currently in service were commissioned during the modernization process in the 1980s, laying the foundation for the Italian navy of today. Despite the declining numbers and growing age of its warships, the Marina Militare continues to field a balanced fleet that can conduct operations over a wide range of contingencies. In concordance with its defense policy it has been able to deploy naval air power, maintain power-projection capabilities, deploy naval forces—both alone and with its NATO allies—and promote maritime security. However, similar to other European countries, continued cuts to Italy's defense budget have reduced the size of the fleet to such an extent that the navy runs the risk of losing some of the aforementioned capabilities.

To make matters worse, the Italian navy—arguably more than any other—is confronted with the problem of having to maintain both high-intensity war-fighting capabilities as well as extensive naval provisions for low-intensity conflicts and humanitarian aid operations. Maritime search and rescue (SAR) operations are not new to the Italian navy and coast guard. However, the recent influx of refugees trying to make their way from North Africa and the Levant to the shores of Europe has caused unprecedented strain on the Italian sea services.[8] Migration, as Parry stresses, "is particularly acute in the Mediterranean where there is a marked disparity in wealth, opportunity and social provision between the northern and southern shores."[9] In these operations, which occur on a daily basis, the Marina Militare and Guardia Costiera have saved thousands of people from certain death as they flee the war-torn regions of Africa and the Middle East. These missions require both resources and outstanding seamanship in humanitarian assistance and disaster response (HADR), qualities that often come at the cost of more traditional capabilities of naval forces. "[The] *Marina Militare's* activities in this regard make it stand out in terms of its compliance with the duties imposed by treaty—and by humanity—in respect of the safeguarding of lives at sea."[10]

Fortunately, Italy has been able to rely on its substantial defense industry to develop state-of-the-art warships and weapon systems. This powerful industrial base includes the Fincantieri shipyards, which are among the largest and most important shipbuilders in Europe, Agusta and OtoBreda as part of the Finmeccanica group, and the naval propulsion specialists of FIAT Avio. Italy's ship designs are considered among the best in the world and Bernard Prézelin went so far as to state that "Italian naval architects are artists."[11] Italian ships and weapon systems have also had considerable success on the export market. Although the "heyday [of] the Italian naval shipbuilding industry" dates back to the 1970s and 1980s, the country remains at the forefront in the field of naval technology.[12] In part, this can be ascribed to Italy's ability to make smart choices when it comes to balancing "indigenous development, offshore procurement and license production."[13] Moreover, the Marina Militare does not simply rely on its naval vessels to exact its strategic interests, but in fact pays as much attention to utilizing the latest technology as it does to manning platforms with highly professional crews.[14] This approach has had a lasting effect on the fleet's ability to perform its duties but also comes at a considerable cost.

By the time the confrontation between East and West drew to a close, Italy's Marina Militare fashioned a sizeable fleet, capable of

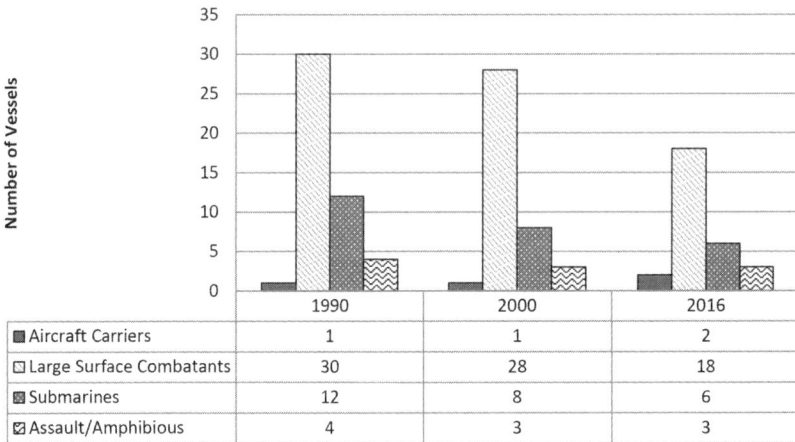

Figure 7-1. Italy: Number of Major Vessels

Sources: *The Naval Institute Guide to Combat Fleets of the World, Military Technology Almanac, World Naval Review.*

conducting a broad range of naval operations. In 1989, after a hard-fought battle against stiff political opposition as well as her sister service, the more prestigious Aeronautica Militare, the Italian navy finally acquired its first batch of AV-8B+ Harrier II, short take-off or vertical landing (STOVL) jets. With one move, the navy was not only able to replace its increasingly obsolete helicopter carriers with the *Giuseppe Garibaldi* aircraft carrier (launched in 1983) but, more importantly, joined an exclusive club of navies with an organic fixed-wing aviation capability.[15] Unlike Australia, Canada, and the Netherlands, who all lost their carrier forces throughout the Cold War, the Italian navy was able to operate two naval groups, each with an aerial detachment.[16]

To consolidate the "naval force [around] a nucleus of 18 combatant ships of the first echelon, of which two are flat deck aircraft carriers,"[17] as the naval doctrine demanded, Italy's surface fleet was extensively modernized. Notably, in 1991 its ships had only been in service for an average of eight years,[18] with a pair of new air-defense destroyers (*Animoso* class) already under construction. Together with the two *Audace*-class destroyers and the larger helicopter-carrying cruiser *Vittorio Veneto,* these ships provided the fleet with the necessary protection against enemy aircraft and missiles throughout the 1990s. Smaller frigates and corvettes, such as the eight *Maestrale*-class, four *Lupo*-class, and the eight *Minerva*-class ships were all designed to have substantial AAW, ASW, and ASuW capabilities. All cruisers, destroyers and frigates also had an aviation detachment and helicopters embarked, providing additional ability to find and track underwater threats.

What stands out when one compares Europe's navies at the time of the Soviet dissolution with today's naval forces, is that their fleets also included a number of small and often obsolete vessels. The Greek navy, for example, still retained the *Cannon*-class gun frigate (commissioned in 1944) as part of its fleet in 1990. Norway operated the *Sleipner* class (1965) and the Spanish navy was phasing out its *Atravida* class (1953). Italy, for its part, had both the *Albatros* (not to be confused with the SAM system) and the *De Cristoforo* corvettes.[19] While some of the older vessels had been used for training, patrol, and constabulary operations in the fragile security environment of the Cold War, a much more austere financial environment has made these maintenance-intensive platforms unfeasible. Instead of keeping these obsolete ships afloat, more funds and personnel were allocated to modern platforms. The flipside inherent to any reduction in the number of surface combatants lies within the geographic realties of the sea. Technology can make up for some of the losses in physical presence. However, the ability to operate numerous vessels at sea is an advantage difficult to substitute. Even the introduction of longer-range and more powerful maritime surveillance assets and the rapid developments in the area of sensor-fusion and shared information networks can only partially compensate for the lack in numbers. This is particularly the case in constabulary operations such as "fishery protection, pollution control, drug interdiction, and control of illegal immigration,"[20] tasks the Marina Militare is only too familiar with.

For more than two decades Italy's naval ambitions have remained largely unchanged—deploying a well-balanced blue-water navy designed around two aircraft carrier groups and their escort fleet. Its amphibious forces are designed to provide the Italian government with the ability to project power over long periods of time and into regions at a considerable distance from home. These efforts hinged upon two principle tenets: First, on Italy's function as a founding member of NATO and its role in achieving sea control in the Mediterranean Sea; and, second, on Italy's own strategic interests in the region. As Admiral Mariani explained, "[During the Cold War] a great deal of the NATO navies' efforts were devoted to preparing for the battle for control of the sea."[21] With the end of the Warsaw Pact, new challenges emerged. The shift within "the global strategic environment," said Mariani, "[has] contributed to the birth of a new idea which draws attention to the coastal water, stirring up the interest in operations conducted in the littoral environment."[22] Unlike Germany, which had comparably few multipurpose platforms capable of adapting to the new conditions, Italy's naval forces demonstrably proved they were both capable and willing to take a leading role in safeguarding the waters surrounding the European continent. Cernuschi and O'Hara provide an excellent summary of Italy's global presence since its reemergence as a medium-sized naval power:

> [This has] included naval and air confrontations with Libya off Malta in 1980 and 1986; constant naval patrol activities in the Red Sea since 1982; missions off Lebanon between 1982 and 1984 and, again, since 2006; international minesweeping operations in the Red Sea in 1983; Persian Gulf operations in 1987–88; the war against Iraq in 1991; Yugoslavia from 1991–97; Mozambique in 1993; Somalia from 1991–95; Albania in 1997; Eritrea in 1998; the conflict against Serbia in Kossovo [*sic*] from 1999 (where the AV-8Bs from Garibaldi conducted their first bombing missions); Timor in 1999; Afghanistan since 2001 (here again the Garibaldi's air wing participated in combat); Iraq peacekeeping since 2003; and continuous anti-piracy patrols in the Indian Ocean. On 22 November

2011, for example, the new "Horizon" class destroyer Andrea Doria exchanged gunfire with a motorboat suspected of pirate activities eight miles off the Somali coast.[23]

In addition, Italy also participated, if somewhat hesitantly, in the NATO-led air campaign against Libya in 2011, again demonstrating the utility of naval air power as well as the need for a balanced fleet in modern combat operations.

Italy's powerful defense industry has played a central role in enabling the navy to conduct all of the aforementioned operations. However, it also wields considerable political leverage, which not necessarily serves Italy's interest. Apart from being a heavyweight among European shipbuilders, the maritime defense industry has had considerable success in collaborating with other countries in order to offset the costs of designing and constructing warships. Among the most successful bilateral efforts has been the Franco/Italian development of the *Horizon* class and FREMM class, and the French/Spanish *Scorpène*-class submarines. These efforts have shown that, despite different operational requirements and the numerous hurdles such large-scale projects entail, Europe's military industries are able to jointly build highly sophisticated naval vessels, while sharing the costs among the contributing project partners. The *Horizon* project, however, also lends itself to explain the various problems that have plagued Europe's navies in the post–Cold War environment.

After the idea of a common frigate for all NATO partners, the NFR-90, had finally been laid to rest, not least due to the conflicting views regarding its specific capabilities, Italy, France, and the U.K. joined forces in 1992 to further pursue the concept. Largely unaware of the future trajectory of defense spending, the initial plan envisioned a class of twenty-two ships; twelve for the Royal Navy, six for France, and four for the Italian navy. It was soon realized that these calculations where entirely unrealistic and that the military budgets of the respective countries could stomach far fewer ships. "In all likelihood, the RN will eventually have to be contented with six–eight ships, and both the [Marine Nationale] and [Marina Militare] will each procure two to four,"[24] a project insider observed in 1995. Furthermore, due to their strategic incongruence of the states involved, there was considerable risk of the entire project failing before a single ship was built: ["While] the Royal Navy was looking for a large (6,000+ tons) ship, featuring extended range for North Atlantic operations and offering quite considerable surface-to-air missile capabilities; the French, on the other hand, had more 'modest' aims, and were thinking in terms of a substantially smaller ship with reduced range and half the missile battery as called for by the UK."[25] In the same vein, Italy's requirements were more limited due to its fleet being able to operate in the Mediterranean (its primary theater of operations) under the aegis of land-based air power. Continued differences between the U.K. and its two partners finally resulted in the British withdrawing from the *Horizon* project in 1999.[26] Notwithstanding these setbacks, Italy and France brought the venture to a positive conclusion. The Marine Nationale and Marina Militare each received two identical ships which continue to form the mainstay of their fleets' air defense. Displaying considerable stealth features, highly sophisticated electronics, including the PAAMS (principal antiair missile system) with its Alenia EMPAR radar, DCNS SYLVER vertical launch system and Aster-15/30 short- and long-range missiles, the *Horizon*-class ships are among the most capable air-defense destroyers in the world.

Initially, however, the *Horizon* project was also criticized for committing to the tri-national PAAMS system instead of choosing the American Aegis combat system and SPY-1D radar fitted in the Dutch and Spanish frigates of the same era.[27] Regardless of the advantages the U.S. design could bring to the table, the Italians and French have to be commended for upholding a large part of the European defense sector and thus ensuring a competitive position on the naval market, even if in the face of their overbearing American competitors.

> Adopting a US shipborne air-defense system, or even only the surface-to-air missile, would have meant the end of credible

European alternative in many high-technology fields. To this [it] could be replied that maintaining these alternatives makes little sense, given that the chances of ever achieving export sales for PAAMS against the more mature US solutions are exceedingly faint.[28]

Notwithstanding the enormous effort invested in the *Horizon* project, the Italian and French cooperation has proved that such multinational programs can have substantial cost saving benefits if conducted in a prudent fashion. More importantly, they constitute the "only way for European countries to remain present on the international market as designers and producers [of] major weapons systems."[29]

In addition to the two air-defense destroyers, the *Andrea Doria* and *Caio Dulio,* launched in 2005 and 2007 respectively, the Italian navy was also able to commission its first batch of air-independent propulsion Type-212A submarines in 2006–7. Teaming up with Germany's Howaldtswerke-Deutsche Werft, arguably the most experienced conventional submarine builder, proved to be a smart choice in order to effectively modernize Italy's underwater flotilla.[30] Currently the largest European naval project, with an estimated investment of over 10 billion euros, however, is the Franco/Italian FREMM-class frigate program.[31]

Planned as the successors to both countries' principle surface combatants, the FREMM project was able to capitalize on the experiences gained during the development of the previously described *Horizon* class. Further, the new frigates' design was based on features of both the air-defense destroyers and French *La Fayette* stealth vessels.[32] As opposed to their previous collaboration, the two countries decided to facilitate the process by allowing each navy to design major elements of the ship according to their specific requirements. The French needed a rather large number of ASW and AAW frigates to replace the majority of its escort forces built in the 1970s and which could provide sufficient defensive capabilities for its most vital assets: its aircraft carrier and ballistic missile submarines.[33] Moreover, France also has territorial interests in all three major oceanic regions of the world, so it has to cover far more space with its only slightly larger fleet. French planners therefore chose to "select equipment sufficient to meet role requirements over more capable but costly alternatives" in order to "maintain its first-line surface fleet at roughly current strength [15 ships]."[34]

Italy's FREMM frigates, or *Rinascimento* as they are sometimes called, look distinctively different than the French version.[35] Ultimately, the difficulties of finding common ground led the two types to be "closely-related cousins"[36] rather than sister ships, sharing a common hull, similar propulsion arrangement, as well as some of the same equipment, electronics, and weapon systems. Nevertheless, "a key attraction of the FREMM concept," as Waters argues, is "the ability to configure a common design to different roles through limited changes to new equipment outfit."[37] So far, the Marina Militare has received five vessels comprising the general-purpose *Carlo Bergamini* and four ASW variants. The construction of all ten of these highly capable frigates has been approved by the Italian government and they will form the mainstay of Italy's future surface fleet. By the beginning of the next decade they will be joined by a class of small multipurpose surface combatants, the PPA (Pattugliatore Polivalente d'Altura).[38]

While the European debt crisis that started in 2007 has posed a true litmus test for the Marina Militare, Italy's two-carrier doctrine has only complicated the navy's ongoing procurement and appropriation plans. At a displacement of over 22,000 tons, Italy's second carrier, the *Cavour*, is the largest and most expensive warship to be built in Italy since the end of World War II. In addition, its complement of nearly 750 sailors contributes to the navy's considerable personnel costs, which are "one of the highest overhead in any of the developed nation's fleets."[39] On the other hand, the *Cavour* satisfies Italy's demand for a flexible power-projection platform.[40] The vessel showcases significant amphibious capabilities (it can carry a force in excess of 300 marines and can deploy heavy equipment such as tanks into theaters of operations), has medical facilities for HADR, substantial electronic warfare measures, and a sophisticated air-defense system, relying on the same EMPAR radar and Aster 15 missiles as the FREMM frigates. Last but not least, it can operate a mixed aviation detachment of helicopters and STOVL aircraft. As a result, the *Cavour* offers the Marina Militare an essential tool to execute the country's national strategy.[41] Once the license-built Lockheed Martin F-35B is embarked on the carrier (mid-2020s), this fifth-generation combat aircraft will provide the Italian navy with "unprecedented hitting power and protection."[42]

Somewhat surprisingly the *Cavour* did not take part in the NATO-led air campaign against Libya's long-time ruler, Muammar Gaddafi, in the spring and summer of 2011. Nonetheless, Italy's AV-8B Harriers from the carrier *Giuseppe Garibaldi* flew 560 sorties against targets in Libya. Many observers have criticized NATO for interpreting the UN mandate to establish a no-fly zone as a green light for regime change in Libya, creating an environment in which radical Islamic factions have thrived. The following short summary of Italy's participation merely aims to illustrate the extent of its ability to deploy forces in such multinational operations without entering into the debate regarding the legitimacy of the campaign.

Starting in March 2011, ships assigned to NATO's Standing Maritime Groups commenced their strike missions and a naval blockade against the Gaddafi regime as part of Operation Unified Protector. Italy's performance during the campaign has received mixed reviews. For example, one analyst emphasized the Italian navy's contribution to the naval blockade and the ability to deploy its aircraft carrier in the vicinity of Libya's coast. Despite accounting for Italy's initial reluctance to take action—due, in part, to its economic interests in Libya—and its later restraint when it came to striking high-risk targets, he concludes that "by the time the operation finally wound down the *Marina Militare* could take satisfaction in its performance."[43] On the other hand, naval specialist Bryan McGrath, who sets his analysis in a somewhat larger strategic frame, identifies a lack of resolve and commitment among the country's political leadership: "Britain and France proved both highly capable and highly committed," whereas Italy provided only partial support.[44] Indeed, when the financial crisis finally began taking an even greater toll on Italy's economy in the summer of 2011, the newly appointed government showed little interest in continuing the expensive deployment of its principle strike assets and withdrew the *Giuseppe Garibaldi,* leaving the NATO coalition without a considerable part of its much-needed naval aviation.[45]

Over the past few years, Italy's defense white papers have largely reiterated the nation's grand strategy, first postulated in the 1980s.[46] In fact, in his article in the *Naval Institute Proceedings* in 2012, Admiral Bruno Branciforte made a point of stressing that "the navy will be guided by the operational experience gained in the past decade[s]," remaining dedicated to its expeditionary and amphibious capabilities, its fleet air arm, and its multirole platforms, designed to cope with the entire spectrum of possible conflict. It will continue to underpin Italy's national defense and maritime security.[47] "The Italian Navy, in coming years," the admiral said with assurance, "will boast the capabilities needed to fulfill its national and international commitments."[48] Gary J. Schmitt, of the Marilyn Ware Center for Security Studies, has voiced his doubts about this claim: "Like other European states that are reducing number of people and platforms, the pledge is that Italy's military will be 'of smaller dimension but with higher quality.' Whether that will happen, remains to be seen."[49] If, in fact, Italy is to continue to participate in large-scale multinational combat operations, various peacekeeping missions, and ongoing HADR efforts in the Mediterranean, any further decrease in defense spending (as a result of economic difficulties) is likely to cause some serious shortcomings among its armed forces and the navy in particular.

In the future, the Marina Militare will undoubtedly remain under constant strain. As Figure 7-1 shows, in 1990 the navy operated a fleet of 47 large vessels, not counting the smaller, yet crucial, offshore patrol vessels and auxiliaries.[50] By the year 2000 this number had dropped to 40, and has now been further reduced to a total of 31. Italy's maritime surveillance and ASW capability has also waned in lockstep with that of its European neighbors. In 2008, Alenia Aernoautica was awarded a contract to supply the Italian air force with

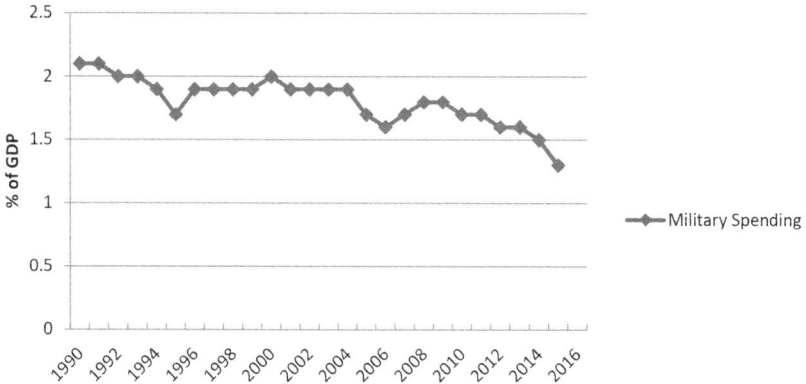

Figure 7-2. Italy: Defense Spending in % of GDP, 1990–2015
Source: SIPRI Military Expenditure Database.

four ATR-72MP (maritime patrol) aircraft, all of which have now been delivered. However, unlike the 18 Breguet Atlantic maritime patrol aircraft that were replaced, the ATR-72MP is not able to conduct ASW warfare. If Italy intends to regain these capabilities, it will either have to upgrade its existing MPAs, or buy a platform such as the P-8 Poseidon. While the U.K. has identified the procurement of MPAs as a key priority in its latest defense review, it is questionable if Italy's defense budget will permit such an investment.

Fortunately, in other areas, the Marina Militare has been able to make improvements. New vessels, such as the *Horizon* destroyer and FREMM frigates, the *Cavour,* Type 212A submarines, and *Commandanti* OPVs, are far more versatile than their predecessors. They have also been able to compensate, at least partially, for their relatively limited numbers by having longer endurance, reduced maintenance and crew requirements, as well as more sophisticated sensor and weapons systems. More broadly, over the last two-and-a-half decades the naval forces have been restructured and modernized in accordance with Italy's transition to an all-volunteer force. From a platform-centric point of view, and considering Italian shipbuilding prowess, as well as its leading position in naval gun technology, electronics, and other areas, there is little reason to believe that the Marina Militare cannot operate a well-balanced fleet of state-of-the-art warships in the future. However, a somewhat larger defense budget will be needed in order to protect Italy's interests both at home and abroad.

As the humanitarian catastrophe continues to evolve opposite Europe's southern and eastern shores, Italy will need to invest in SAR assets and HADR capabilities over the coming years. The Mare Nostrum humanitarian assistance mission alone, which was conducted by the Italian navy under the auspices of the European Union between October 2013 and 2014, cost over 9 million euros a month.[51] Paradoxically, the subsequent Operation Triton, conducted by the EU's Frontex border security agency, was less well funded and far more limited in its scope. Only after hundreds of refugees had drowned did the European Union react to growing public criticism and expand its efforts.

If these circumstances alone are not enough to persuade Italy's ministers to raise defense spending, then the United States' shift toward the Asia-Pacific region should, by all means, be a compelling reason to do so. As the U.S. Navy gradually redeploys its forces from the Atlantic to the Pacific in response to China's emergence as a formidable competitor, "[it] seems to be a reasonable assumption [that] the *Cavour* and the Italian fleet are effectively going to be a substitute [for the] American carrier battle group in the larger Mediterranean as the reduced US Navy carrier line-up is increasingly concentrated on the Pacific and Indian Ocean."[52]

In 1990, the well-known Italian naval analyst Giorgio Giorgerini offered the following assessment of the future operational scenario of the Italian navy:

> It would indeed be difficult to foresee, with a reasonable degree of accuracy, what future situations may demand the intervention of the Italian Armed Forces, and particularly the Marina Militare. One point can, however, be taken for granted. Due to its geographical and political characteristics, the

Mediterranean will remain what it has always been throughout the centuries—namely, an extremely sensitive basin from
both the strategic and the political point of view, an area where
tension and crisis can stream in from all cardinal points and
criss-cross with each other.[53]

Nearly three decades later, this assessment is as timely as ever.
No matter if for humanitarian reasons or out of strategic interest, Italy's Marina Militare will continue to be a most useful tool
in Italy's foreign policy toolkit. However, remedial actions have to
be taken to ameliorate the increasingly difficult situation the navy
finds itself in. It will be necessary to guarantee that these tools do
not suffer from neglect to an extent that will cause them to lose
their utility. Like France and Britain, Italy's fleet has reached a point
at which continued reductions to its force level (both in personnel
and matériel) cannot be compensated for by superior ship design
and better training. Unless the problems of overstretch and the
overhead costs for personnel are not comprehensively addressed,
Italy's future governments will likely have to accept limitations in
the operational capability of the Marina Militare. As a result, the
country's grand strategy, which for decades has relied on the navy
as a principle pillar of the nation's vision of being an indispensable
power in the greater Mediterranean region and the world, could
become unattainable.

CHAPTER 7

Spain

Creating a Well-Balanced Fleet and Maintaining It

For over five hundred years the Spanish navy has left its mark in the annals of history: from the discovery of the New World by Christopher Columbus, to Hernán Cortés' campaign against the Aztecs and the creation of a colonial empire. During much of this time, both naval and merchant fleets provided the Spanish Crown with an indispensable instrument to pursue the *conquista* of new territories and allowed transporting the vast riches gained overseas back to Europe. Spanish power grew along with its expansion across the globe, while its military campaigns were largely funded by precious metals from its colonies.

The Spanish navy, however, is also known for suffering some of the most devastating defeats in history. One of the greatest calamities took place during the Anglo-Spanish War (1585–1604). In 1588, Spain's "Invincible Armada" set sail in support of the planned invasion of England but found its doom in the form of the English galleons and the merciless nature of the sea. After having suffered damage in the battle at Calais, the Spanish commander, Alonso Pérez de Guzmán, 7th Duke of Medina Sidonia, chose to take a route around the north of Scotland and then down the Irish west coast to reach Spanish waters.[1] "Freak storms turned their voyage home into a naval catastrophe. Scattered ships disappeared without trace in the Atlantic Ocean or were wrecked upon the wild north and west coast of Ireland.... Just 67 ships out of the original fleet of 130 managed to reach Spanish shores."[2]

Although the Spanish were able to reassert themselves as a naval power after the events of 1588, their maritime dominance was increasingly challenged by other powers—the English, the Dutch, and most importantly, the French under the reign of King Louis XIV. Throughout the seventeenth century, Spain commanded a fleet of the first order and, for the most part, was able to protect its interests at sea. However, the Spanish War of Succession and the Utrecht settlements in 1713 largely curtailed Spain's ambitions.[3] The country was essentially "stripped of all of its non-contiguous European territories, its succession was determined by outside powers, and it remained diplomatically isolated."[4] Any effort to undo these decisions was effectively cut short by British sea power and the French, who occupied Spain in 1719.[5] Thereafter, for almost a century, the Spanish and French naval forces would fight the growing British naval dominance (Spain's fleet ranked third largest behind the two other great powers) but the alliance was ultimately defeated in the famous Battle of Cape St. Vincent, the Battle of the Nile, and the climactic Battle of Trafalgar in 1805. When the largest warship at the time, the Spanish flagship *Santísima Trinidad*—having lost all three of its masts as well as many of its men—surrendered to the British forces, the ground was set for the Royal Navy's dominance, which lasted for more than a century. Throughout the course of the nineteenth century, Spain's naval power continued to decline and subsequently it lost many of its colonies in South America. Yet it still retained some important territories in the Caribbean, South America, and the Asia-Pacific region. It is somewhat remarkable that Spain's demise would be decided by one of its closest military allies today, namely the United States.

The war in 1898, between the United States and Spain, effectively put an end to Spain's status as a great power. By the late nineteenth century the two nations had been on entirely opposite trajectories: On the one side of the Atlantic, the rising naval power under President McKinley, willing to use force in support of its national interests in the Caribbean and the Pacific—by itself a Copernican revolution in U.S. foreign policy. On the other side, Spain, whose fleet had been annihilated by the superior American warships and, as a consequence, lost all but a small number of its colonial possessions. In effect, the Battle of Santiago de Cuba and Commodore George Dewey's victory at Manila Bay relegated the Spanish naval power to the footnotes of naval history for decades to come.

Today, the Royal Spanish Navy, the Royal Armada Española, has reestablished itself among the world's medium-sized sea powers, albeit not attaining the glory of former days. To a significant extent, Spain owes its naval resurrection to the United States' support during the Cold War. Despite the Franco regime being largely isolated from Europe's ongoing reconciliation efforts after the horrors of the Second World War, strategic imperatives of the evolving confrontation between East and West persuaded the United States to provide Spain with substantial military aid. This included several warships from its large World War II surplus. For example, both Italy and Spain received light aircraft carriers in the late 1960s. While the Italian Marina Militare was not able to operate fixed-wing aircraft from their carriers due to a law dating back to the days of Mussolini that granted the air force the sole right to maintain combat aircraft, the Spanish pioneered the use of STOVL jets from its carriers.[6] Today, despite closer cooperation with other European defense industries in more recent years, Spain's close ties to the United States remain clearly visible within the Armada Española.

Since the end of the Cold War, Spain has been able to make some prudent choices in its procurement policies as well as in regard to its national defense strategy. This is one reason why the Spanish navy has undergone less drastic changes in its fleet than the British navy or the German navy. An adroit apportionment of its defense funding has enabled the country to build and, thus far, maintain a small but modern multipurpose fleet. Because of its configuration,

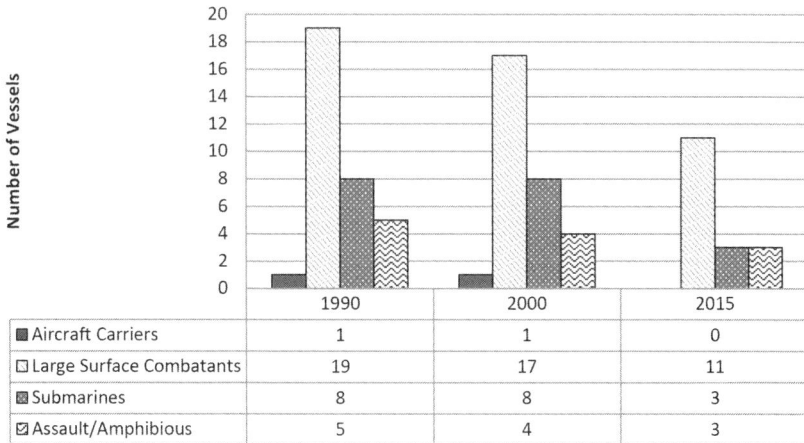

	1990	2000	2015
■ Aircraft Carriers	1	1	0
□ Large Surface Combatants	19	17	11
▨ Submarines	8	8	3
☑ Assault/Amphibious	5	4	3

Figure 8-1. Spain: Number of Major Vessels

Sources: *The Naval Institute Guide to Combat Fleets of the World, Military Technology Almanac, World Naval Review.*

the Armada Española is often compared to Italy's navy and, in fact, shares many similarities, despite being only two-thirds the size.

Like the Marina Militare, the Armada Española is considered to be a relatively well-balanced fleet, capable of conducting missions across a wide range of contingencies, both alone and in conjunction with friends and allies. Further, the Spanish navy has undergone a strategic reorientation from a sea control navy to an expedition-ary force that can "[exert] influence from the sea over coastal areas [in out-of-area operations]."[7] Although the graph above indicates a reduction in amphibious power-projection platforms, the navy's expeditionary capabilities have in fact increased substantially since 1990. While Italy can deploy fast jets from its new *Cavour* aircraft carrier, Spain, likewise, has expanded its ability to deploy naval air power in the form of a dozen AV-8Bs Harrier/Matador aircraft from its new amphibious assault ship, the *Juan Carlos I.* However, Spain's strategic framework differs from that of Italy, thus requiring the Armada Española to provide fewer capabilities. This is mainly due to the varying roles the respective countries seek to play in world affairs. Italy is not only a member of the economic powerhouse known as the Group of 7 (G-7, formally G-8)[8] and a founding member of NATO, but it also intends to remain a regional power in the greater Mediterranean region and an active player in world politics. In order to achieve these ends, its navy also needs to remain a sizeable force—an undertaking that has become increasingly difficult. Spain, on the other hand, has somewhat more limited ambitions abroad and fittingly refers to itself as a "medium power" with its main sphere of interests limited to the western Mediterranean and the Atlantic waters between the Iberian Peninsula and the Canary Islands.[9] Consequently, its navy is the smallest of Europe's four major naval powers.

From this brief description, one might conclude that the last twenty years have been smooth sailing for Spain's naval forces. Unfortunately, this has not been the case. For nearly a decade, Spain has made incremental cuts in its defense spending. These austerity measures are compounded by Spain's struggling economy and high rate of unemployment. The most recent financial crisis has taken a heavy toll on Spain's economy and it is unlikely that the country will be able to recover as quickly as some of its European partners.[10] Consequently, the Armada Española is once again threatening to wither away as it did over a hundred years ago. This time, however, its fate will not be decided by the guns of the U.S. Navy but by political myopia and the fiscal restrictions of the post–Cold War era.

Only twenty-five years ago, there was little indication that the Armada Española would be faced with such challenges. For the Royal Spanish Navy the post–Cold War era undoubtedly began on a high note:

> The day of 31 May 1989 was auspicious for the Royal Spanish Navy. It was on that date that King Juan Carlos handed over to the Armada its new aircraft carrier *Principe de Asturias* in an imposing ceremony attended by a number of foreign warships, including the French aircraft carrier *Foch* and the antiaircraft frigate *Cassard,* assembled in the roads of Barcelona. With the

commissioning of the new carrier, the glorious Royal Spanish Navy has reached today a level of power of which one must go far back into its history to find equivalent.[11]

Not only had the new aircraft carrier been put into service, but the entire naval force was in the process of undergoing substantial modernization and restructuring. In 1990, the navy was not only given a hitherto unprecedented strike capability, in the form of the *Príncipe de Asturias,* it also constituted a watershed moment in Spain's force structure and long-term naval planning. The Alta Mar Plan, presented to the public in March of the same year, outlined the procurement plan for the next fifteen years and took first steps toward the fleet's reorganization into the Grupo Alfa and Grupo Delta.[12] The Grupo Alfa was formed around Spain's capital ship (the carrier and air wing) and included both fleet escort and fleet support vessels. The Grupo Delta was later created in light of the increasing need for amphibious forces in the progressively diverse security environment.

Perhaps most importantly, the Alta Mar Plan was based on the premise that the navy should operate fifteen frigates at any given time and therefore needed a concerted shipbuilding plan to mitigate the capability gaps the decommissioning of its older fleet escort would create.[13] Given the upbeat economic situation at the turn of the decade, this was by no means an unrealistic proposition. As it happened, the escort fleet at the time consisted of fifteen major surface combatants, if one excludes the obsolete World War II (former) U.S. *Gearing* FRAM-I–class destroyers.

The *Gearing* class was not the only U.S. design in service with the Spanish navy. As part of the greater Cold War picture, Spain played an important role in the United States' strategic planning. During General Franco's rule, the United States had provided the Armada Española with second-rate warships. After Franco's death, the reestablished Spanish monarchy was quick to officially align itself with the Western allies, becoming a NATO member in 1982 and a member of the European Union in 1986. In return for U.S.

economic and military support, the Spanish navy provided the alliance with ASW and ASuW capabilities in the Atlantic and Western Mediterranean vis-à-vis the Soviet Union's naval forces.[14] The principle task of the navy (together with its Portuguese allies) was, therefore, to exercise sea control and to protect the SLOCs around the Iberian Peninsula.[15] In 1990, this requirement was reflected in the Spanish navy's fleet structure, which consisted of five *Baleares*-class frigates and four *Santa Maria*–class frigates and a half-dozen of the somewhat smaller *Descubierta*-class surface combatants.

The *Baleares* class was an improved version of the American *Knox*-class frigate. Constructed in the late 1960s and early 1970s, these capable seagoing platforms had relatively modern weapons and sensor suites and were continuously upgraded throughout their service lives.[16] Nevertheless, the Royal Spanish Navy was hard-pressed for a class of new frigates. Although a decision to build new warships was made as early as 1977, the construction of the carrier *Principe de Asturias* had taken precedence over the frigate program. It was not until 1986 that the first of six modified *Oliver Hazard Perry*–class frigates was handed over to the Royal Armada Española. The *Perry* class was originally intended to be part of the U.S. Navy's maritime strategy of SLOC protection, assigned to safeguard American transport vessels from Soviet air and underwater threats, much the same as the Allies had done during the Second World War. Despite the subsequent strategic reorientation under President Reagan, the *Perry* class was built in larger numbers than any other major Western surface warship (72 units in total) and was particularly successful on the international market.[17] The Spanish variant of the frigate, the *Santa Maria* class, has similar capabilities, including the Mk 13 Mod 4 launcher for both Standard SM-1 MR and Harpoon missiles, the ubiquitous 76-mm OTO Melara gun, 6 torpedo tubes, and a CIWS.[18] As noted, the frigate's design allowed substantial upgrades and the 6 ships remain a vital asset in the country's current fleet structure.

Interestingly, the *Principe de Asturias* was the second type of warship derived from the United States' vision of a sea-control navy.

As Bernard Prézelin explains, the "design is essentially that of the final version of the U.S. Navy's Sea Control Ship concept, with a 12-degree ski-jump bow added."[19] He continued:

> Inspired by the "Sea Control Ship," that modern version of the last war's escort carrier of which the U.S. Navy wanted to build several units when Admiral [Elmo] Zumwalt was at its head and which it renounced after his departure, the *Principe de Asturias* is now benefiting from all the progress that has since been achieved in naval architecture. . . . Her very well conceived aviation installations enable her to house on her hangar deck seventeen aircraft. . . . Counting aircraft parked on the flight deck, she can embark and put into action up to thirty aircraft, or roughly twice as many as the British *Invincible,* despite her inferior tonnage.[20]

Having outlined some of Spain's naval air and surface capabilities at the end of the Cold War, it is worth noting that her submarine flotilla was equally effective. With eight submarines—four older but modernized French S60 *Daphné* and four highly capable S70 *Agosta* diesel-electric submarines, built in Spain with French technical assistance, "the situation of the Submarine Flotilla . . . was superb, the best, certainly since the advent of the Second Republic in 1931 (and possibly the best in its history)," Íñigo Puente concluded.[21]

In line with most other European countries, the Spanish armed forces did their best to adapt and restructure their standing forces and to align their procurement plans with the shift within the global security environment. In many ways, today's naval force is a testament to this vigorous effort to maintain a balanced fleet while at the same time addressing the need for larger amphibious forces. Successfully striking a balance between the ability to conduct traditional forms of naval warfare and conducting more novel naval tasks (such as peacekeeping and HADR) is an impressive feat—even more so when one compares Spain's approach toward the growing need for expeditionary capabilities with that of Germany. Unlike

Spain, Germany's political and military leadership has decided to largely (if not solely) rely on multipurpose frigates to satisfy the need for out-of-area capable platforms. The F-125 *Baden-Württemberg* frigate represents the latest evidence of this approach. Regardless of their size and sophistication, none of the German frigates built since the end of the Cold War can be considered on par with even the smallest modern amphibious assault ships when it comes to projecting power from sea onto land. It is therefore not surprising that the German defense white paper remains vague on how exactly the German navy intends to support ground operations on the shores of far-off regions.[22]

The Spanish naval strategy, on the other hand, clearly describes why amphibious forces are essential to the nation's security. Even before the 9/11 terrorist attacks and the subsequent shift toward counterterrorism, stability operations, and littoral combat, the Spanish Ministry of Defense published a white paper clearly stating that amphibious operations represented a cornerstone of Spain's defense policy. It also provides evidence for the general shift among most European states from the idea of sea control toward expeditionary warfare:

> The chief mission of the Navy is to ensure the free use of the maritime routes, which are a particularly significant interest in the case of Spain, as it is a country with vast coastline, archipelagoes and enclaves, heavily depended on trade and on the exploitation of marine resources. However, the strategic environment does not pose great risks for navigation. Therefore, the navies of the allied countries—particularly that of Spain—currently gear their capabilities to exerting influence from the sea over coastal areas of operations far from national territory in what is also a characteristic mission of the Navy.[23]

In 2003, the Spanish *Strategic Defence Review* added that "the very presence of an amphibious force has a deterring effect, obliging the enemy to carry out defensive deployment and distracting a disproportionate number of forces. Therefore it is important to acquire a greater capability for naval power projection over land, a fundamental capability that the Navy can contribute to joint and combined strategy."[24]

The Grupo Alfa and Grupo Delta have already been briefly mentioned. They represent a stepping stone, if but an important one, toward the Armada Española attaining a broader set of capabilities in a time marked by declining defense budgets but increasing needs. Only shortly after the aforementioned white paper had been published, a new directive unified the two groups under a single command.[25]

Meanwhile, the Spanish navy secured the funds for two *Galicia*-class dock landing ships. Capitalizing on the shipbuilding experience of the Dutch Royal Schelde and Spain's Empresa Nacional Bazán (now Navantia), both countries received two units each, providing their respective naval forces with greater power-projection and HADR capabilities.[26] Along with two U.S. tank landing ships, transferred in 1994 and 1995, and the construction of a replenishment oiler, the Royal Armada Española was able to substantially expand its expeditionary capabilities.

Despite growing financial restrictions, the Spanish government continued the development and procurement process of a new fleet escort. Four F-100 Álvaro de Bazán–class frigates were ordered in 1997 and the first of these highly capable, domestically designed and constructed ships joined the Armada Española in 2002. Featuring American-designed Aegis combat system (SPY-1D and SM-2 Block IIIA missile), these ships will constitute the backbone of the fleet's air defense for the coming decades.

Like many other frigate programs across Europe, the F-100 was a consequence of the failed NATO frigate project of the 1980s. Spain joined Germany and the Netherlands in an effort to develop a new class of air-defense warships.[27] Up until that point in time, all large surface combatants in service with the Armada Española had been designed and built in America. However, the only ship the United States had to offer was the *Arleigh Burke*–class destroyer, which, despite being considered the most capable air-defense destroyer in the world, was far too expensive for Spain. Consequently, the state-owned Navantia shipbuilder incorporated some general design features provided by its Dutch and German partners while relying on the American combat and air-defense system. "The selection of the Aegis/SPY-1D/VLS Mk 41 is a good decision given that it is sufficiently proven," an analyst noted. "Its large series production allows one to count on effective technical support incorporating without difficulty the successive improvements."[28] Since then, Spain has proven that its ship designs can compete with the best in the world, in spite of the country's comparatively smaller industrial base. In 2007, Australia decided to procure three *Hobart*-class air-defense frigates, based on the F-100 design. The blocks for these ships are produced in both Spanish and Australian shipyards while the final assembly is currently taking place in Adelaide. In addition, Navantia was awarded the construction of two 27,000 ton, *Juan Carlos I*–type, amphibious assault ships for the Australian navy and one for the Turkish navy (license-built in Turkey).[29]

Laid down in 2005, the *Juan Carlos I* LHDs are truly remarkable ships. Initially called the BPE, the Buque de Proyección Estratégica (Strategic Projection Ship), this is the largest warship ever to be built in Spain. Sometimes mistaken for an aircraft carrier like the Italian *Cavour*, the "BPE . . . comes to very close dimension of the [Italian ship], and indeed she appears having been designed through a rather similar process based on the same operational considerations."[30] However, in addition to operating STOVL aircraft and helicopters from its deck, the *Juan Carlos* also has a large stern well dock to deploy landing craft and other small vessels. Furthermore, she can carry up to 46 main battle tanks and 925 troops. However, the ships have one major drawback. Like most other small carriers, LHAs, and LHDs, they are much slower than the American nuclear supercarriers, largely because of the less powerful propulsion and different hull form.[31] Nevertheless, the *Juan Carlos* is "the very first and only aviation-capable amphibious assault platform to be fitted with a ski-jump . . . for a dramatic increase in the payload/range of fixed-wing STOVL aircraft" such as Spain's AV-8B Harriers.[32]

Unfortunately, the navy's submarine force has not fared as well over the last two decades. As Figure 8.1 indicates, the total number of submarines has fallen to only three *Galerna*-class submarines, all of which are at the end of their service lives. This shortfall in subsurface capabilities are a direct result of the numerous technical hurdles Spain's first air-independent propulsion (AIP) submarine, the S-80, has encountered during her development.[33] It has taken technicians more than three years to rectify major buoyancy deficiencies of the S-80 design and it is unlikely that the lead unit will be ready for launch before 2018. To make matters worse, these circumstances will hardly convince foreign buyers to choose the S-80 over other, more proven designs, such as Germany's Type 214 submarines.

Having outlined the modernization of the Spanish fleet over the course of the last twenty-five years, the Armada Española's deployments during this period also merit examination. "Spain's contributions to NATO's maritime roles, while not in the class of the United Kingdom or France, [have] remained relatively strong in what is admittedly an increasingly weak field,"[34] a senior naval analyst recapitulates. Between 1994 and 1996 the *Asturias* and *Reina Sofía* frigates took part in NATO Operation Sharp Guard, enforcing the embargo against former Yugoslavia.[35] Spanish naval forces have routinely contributed to NATO's standing naval forces in the Mediterranean and the Atlantic—known since 2006 as the Standing NATO Maritime Group (SNMG 1+2) and Standing NATO Mine Countermeasure Group (SNMCMG 1+2)—and, at the time of writing, the frigate *Méndez Núñez* was being deployed as part of the SNMG 1 in the North Atlantic. At the same time, the *Perry*-class *Reina Sofía* was taking action against human trafficking in the Mediterranean as part of the European Union Naval Force, a multinational force created in October 2015 in response to the refugee crisis. Spanish warships have also been conducting antipiracy operations as part of NATO's Operation Active Endeavour and the

EU's Operation Atalanta, off the Horn of Africa. Although there is considerable question regarding the effectiveness of these naval antiterrorism operations, for the time being most European states view their gains of "deterrence and collective defence, crisis management; cooperative security; and maritime security" to be worth the costs.[36]

Over the years, however, Spain's participation in military campaigns (or rather lack therefore) has attracted criticism. The war in Afghanistan illustrates the various degrees of willingness among Europe's armed forces to contribute to military interventions abroad. On paper, Spain remained committed to supporting the Afghan government in fighting al Qaeda and the Taliban, in spite of the steep learning curve all NATO allies faced during their deployment. In reality, not only did Spain deploy a relatively small number of forces, but "NATO troop contingents became divided into those who fought (the Americans, the British, the Canadians, and the Italians) and those who did not fight."[37] Along with France, Germany, and the Netherlands, the Spanish largely belonged to the latter category, according to a group of U.S. defense analysts. This was "mainly due to restrictions or 'national caveats' imposed by their political leadership," and did not necessarily reflect the respective army's actual capabilities.[38]

The U.S.-led invasion of Iraq in 2003 would underscore the deep rifts within NATO. Initially, the Spanish government under Prime Minister José María Aznar, a conservative, provided roughly 1,300 military personnel to the so-called Coalition of the Willing. However, after the devastating terrorist attacks in Madrid in March 2004, the deeply dissatisfied Spanish population voted the Aznar government out of office. Only days later, the newly elected prime minister, José Zapatero, and his center-left cabinet fulfilled one of their campaign promises and ordered the withdrawal of all Spanish forces from Iraq, reaffirming the notion that Europe had become increasingly inconsistent and discordant when it came to collective security issues.

Spain's maritime contribution to multinational operations has been both more consistent and more robust, owing to the country's geographic position and economic dependency on seaborne trade, as well as the far smaller risk involved.[39] Sadly, the brief period of economic growth during the first years of the twenty-first century granted the navy only temporary respite. "When the global economic crisis began rippling across Europe in 2008, Spain took a bigger hit than other Western European states, and its defense budget was cut three separate times."[40] Over the following years, the Ministerio de Defensa tried to compensate for the lack of funding by stretching out procurement plans from fifteen to twenty years. After having decided to acquire a fifth ship of the *Bazán* class during a more favorable budgetary environment, plans for a sixth vessel had to be dropped.

In a second step, troop levels were cut across all services, creating gaps in readiness and the ability to quickly deploy large numbers of forces.[41] Within a period of less than 6 years, from 2010 to 2016, the overall number of military personnel dropped from 32,000 (including 6,200 marines) to 22,000 (including 5,836 marines). This shortage has been amplified by the fact that Spain's defense planners have decided that preserving its general-purpose fleet takes precedence over all other matters. A study conducted by the RAND Corporation warned, "One of the ways the Spanish have ensured continuity of capabilities in the face of spending constraints has been to reduce overall training levels.... All units are no longer required to undergo training to reach an established standard."[42] The overhead costs of manning ships as well as training naval personnel have affected Europe's naval forces across the board. As noted, Italy's navy is hard-pressed to reduce the number of sailors in order to decrease their impact on the navy's budget, yet the naval leadership has remained adamant that highly trained crews are of paramount importance.[43] The Spanish navy, so it appears, was more willing to risk a greater loss of professionalism in order to preserve its fleet.

Simply put, the problems the Spanish navy faces stem from years of a shrinking military budget, which has been constrained further by a struggling national economy. According to the study mentioned above, "[By 2012, the] very low percentage of GDP spent

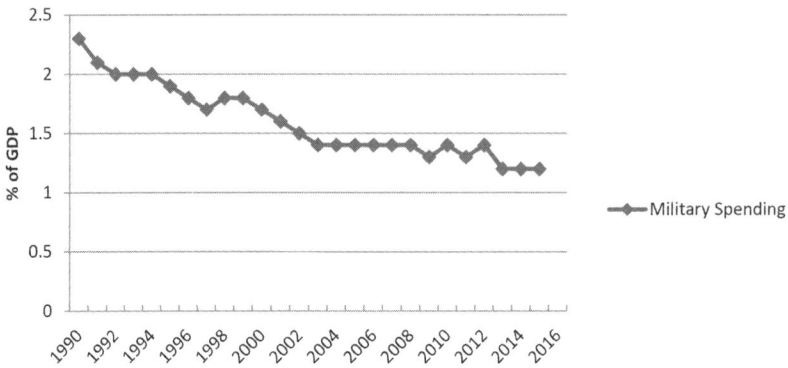

Figure 8-2. Spain: Defense Spending in % of GDP, 1990–2015
Source: SIPRI Military Expenditure Database.

on defense [made] Spain one of the worst performers in terms of defense spending in Europe."[44] However, with the economy slowly recovering, there is a sense of cautious optimism. For first time in several years, the government increased its military budget for two years in a row.[45] Although encouraging, these figures are far from the benchmark set by NATO. Further, the slight budget increases will not amend the shortfalls suffered by the naval forces over the last several years. Quite frankly, much of the damage to the Armada Española has already been done and will continue to plague the navy for years to come.

As Conrad Waters states, "Previous rumors that the aircraft carrier *Principe de Asturias* would be decommissioned were proven correct and the former fleet flagship was withdrawn from service in February 2013."[46] The *Juan Carlos I* now remains the sole platform for the reduced naval air arm. Moreover, the lack of funding for the S-80 submarines and the inability to quickly resolve their technical shortcomings has left the submarine force at its lowest level since the end of the Cold War. In fact, to permit the fleet to operate a minimum of two submarines while the third is undergoing an overhaul, the fourth unit of the *Galerna* class (S-70) was cannibalized for spare parts.[47]

For Spanish naval commanders the growing gap between the number of small surface combatants or offshore patrolling vessels (OPVs) and the number of incidents regarding unlawful or criminal activities is equally vexing. As the *National Maritime Security Strategy 2013* pointed out, "Illicit trafficking is [particularly] common at sea [and] in a broad sense is one of the most serious risks and threats to National Security."[48] In line with many other European states, Spain is therefore participating in the U.S.-led "Africa Partnership Station" operations, providing maritime security along the African shores and thereby extending the cooperation between the numerous states and agencies in the region.[49] However, these additional tasks will continue to put increased strain on the few ships in the Spanish fleet. Only four new OPVs have been built with an additional two under construction. Originally a class of fourteen was planned.

Given the increasing scope and frequency of maritime operations since the conclusion of the Cold War, Spain's effort to maintain a modern and well-balanced fleet is laudable—all the more so if one considers the increasingly austere environment the naval forces have found themselves in over the last decade. Unfortunately, operating such a fleet has a number of tradeoffs. When the financial situation turned sour as a result of Europe's debt crisis, the severe cuts to military spending left the force's training and readiness levels wanting.

Notwithstanding these shortcomings, for the time being the Royal Armada Española remains the fourth-largest naval force in Europe. Despite the country's continuing economic woes, Spain actively participates in numerous international maritime operations. What is more, the country's naval industrial base has grown substantially over the last twenty-five years and its shipyards have secured several high-profile export deals. Given the country's unique geopolitical position on Europe's southern flank and its close political ties to its European, African, and American partners, Spain will likely want to continue to play an active role in world affairs. However, with increased importance being given to the maritime realm over the coming decades, the Spanish navy will be forced to make some substantial investments midterm, in order to maintain a fleet capable of fulfilling the country's strategic goals over the long-term. These investments would include the F-110 successor for its *Perry*-class frigates, a larger number of OPVs, as well as purchasing the Lockheed/Martin F-35 Lighting II, to retain a capable naval air arm. Yet all these projects come with a significant price tag. Given the large number of naval missions that are under way, as well as the need to recruit and train the necessary crews and support personnel, it is hardly possible that this feat can be achieved under the current budgetary levels.

It is therefore possible that within the coming decades the Spanish fleet might have to slowly abandon its multipurpose capabilities, ultimately arriving at a smaller, less powerful force, similar to that of Germany or possibly the Netherlands. In any case, such a development would have adverse effects on Europe's naval power, adding to its overall decline.

Turkey and Greece

Allies and Yet Not Friends—Diverging Naval Powers

Turkey and Greece represent the last two European states to have strategic interest in the Mediterranean theater. Unfortunately, the two countries share a long history of mutual animosity and distrust, tracing all the way back to the Greco-Persian Wars during the fifth century BC. Over much of their history the two states have remained regional competitors, often resolving their differences by military means. Even today, Turkey and Greece "are widely considered to be major antagonistic powers in the region" as Christos Kollias and Gülay Günlük-Şenesen state.[1] Paradoxically, they remain in an unstable limbo between being NATO allies, yet entertaining the possibility of going to war against each other to protect their individual national interests. Despite this strained relationship, the two countries' geostrategic positions as well as their influence in the Mediterranean, the Aegean Sea, and the Black Sea, are worthy of analysis.

Unlike many of their European partners, Turkey and Greece have made substantial investments toward their national defense. A major factor that has kept tension—and defense spending—high has been what a Turkish defense white paper calls the "nonexistence of an agreement determining the sea boundaries between Turkey and Greece on the Aegean Sea."[2] This and other conflicting political views have led to a plethora of unresolved issues ranging from the occupation of Cyprus by the Turkish army and the legal quarrel regarding the status of a number of small islands and rocks in the Aegean Sea to opposing claims relating to the exploration of the vast natural resources of the eastern Mediterranean basin. Unsurprisingly, both actors operate somewhat similar naval forces, though the Turkish navy is somewhat larger. Both countries' defense spending has exceeded that of their European neighbors and has remained well over the 2 percent mark of their national GDP since the end of the Cold War. This seems even more remarkable given the austerity measures that have been undertaken elsewhere over the past decade. Despite economic woes and a somewhat more amicable relationship between the two countries, Turkey and Greece still account for the highest percentage of defense spending of all European NATO members.

Decades, if not centuries, of hostilities between the two states have had profound influence on Turkish and Hellenic military strategies and their respective naval doctrines. During the 1990s, many European countries sought to attain a wider range of maritime capabilities, slowly shifting from the parochial tasks of ASW and ASuW against the Soviet navy toward power projection, out-of-area operations, and littoral warfare far from home. However, given the geopolitical position of Turkey and Greece, their naval operations missions have largely been dictated by the principles of sea control and protection of the sea lines of communication.[3] To that end, both navies largely consist of platforms capable of conducting sea control and sea denial, while expeditionary capabilities, have until very recently only played a secondary role.

The ongoing tensions in the Aegean Sea could set the stage for further conflict in the future. While much attention is currently given to China's territorial claims in the South China Sea and the East China Sea and possible ramifications these actions might have for regional security, little attention is given to the continued enmity between Greece and Turkey and their territorial feuds over various archipelagos of the Aegean Sea.[4] It also goes to show how difficult these conflicts are to resolve, particularly in times of growing nationalism and antagonism in many regions of the world. The situation between the two neighbors remains volatile, and a crisis like the imminent war over the Imia/Kardak islet in 1996 cannot be ruled out entirely. Additionally, the failed coup d'état aimed at overthrowing President Recep Tayyip Erdoğan in July 2016, as well as the ongoing stream of refugees trying to reach Europe's shores via Turkey, could have a potentially destabilizing effect. Still, despite public criticism directed toward NATO and America's foreign policy agenda, mutual NATO membership as well as the moderating role of the United States and its European allies have possibly prevented outright war between the two countries.

As noted, the Turkish and Greek fleets bear some resemblance and have also undergone a similar development since the end of the Cold War. Both states have designed their naval forces around the concept of sea control and the safeguarding of their SLOCs.[5] Therefore, territorial defense operations have taken precedence over other forms of naval capabilities. Compared to the four major European navies already discussed, both the Turkish navy and the Hellenic navy lack large warships necessary to conduct large-scale, out-of-area missions; they have little capability to project naval power over great distances. Neither navy operates warships capable of embarking numerous aircraft or a larger contingent of amphibious forces—in other words, small aircraft carriers, LHAs, or LPDs. For that reason, the number of amphibious forces shown in Figure 9-4 is somewhat misleading. While Greece retains seven ships capable of amphibious operations (including two Soviet-era air cushion craft),[6] the aggregated power of these units does not compare to, say, Spain's two *Galicia*-class LPDs or a single French *Mistral* LHD. On the other hand, the Hellenic and Turkish navies possess a substantial number of smaller warships, ranging from frigates and corvettes to guided-missile craft and patrol craft.

Moreover, both maintain the ability to conduct sea-denial operations by fielding capable submarine flotillas of German design as well as mine warfare vessels. This comes as no surprise. The geopolitical realities of the region have persuaded both states to invest heavily in these aforementioned capabilities, not least due to the significance of the Bosporus, the Aegean Sea, and the Eastern Mediterranean.

Turkey

Between the Turkish navy and Hellenic navy, the former is both somewhat larger and more capable. This goes hand in hand with Turkey being a larger, more populous state that also enjoys the benefits of a more powerful economy. Over the past twenty-five years, the country's industrial base has grown considerably and Turkey's armed forces have greatly profited from this development.[7] While the state has been able to expand its domestic shipbuilding capacity, launching its first domestically designed and built frigate in 2008, Greece remains largely dependent on foreign sales. For more than two decades the Turkish leadership has made a concerted effort to modernize and strengthen its military and has in turn created one of Europe's most powerful armies. In 2009, American defense analyst George Friedman pointed out that by his estimate, Turkey's conventional capabilities had surpassed those of France and Germany—also providing evidence of the general decline in military power among the aforementioned European states. "[Turkey] has one of the most substantial armies, not only in the region, but in Europe. Except for the British army—and it would be an interesting fight, I wish I could stage it . . . there is no European army that could face Turkey. . . . And this is important, because Turkey was historically the dominant power in the region."[8] Since then, from a purely material standpoint, the Turkish military has arguably strengthened its conventional military forces. However, its armed services have suffered a great psychological blow when thousands of soldiers and officers were arrested and detained for their alleged involvement in the failed coup. "The Turkish military is now a broken force and it will take years for it to heal," an analyst from the Atlantic Council opined.[9] It remains unclear if internal factionalism and mistrust will, in fact, put an end to Turkey's aspirations of becoming the most powerful regional actor, a vision it has successfully pursued since the end of the Cold War.

In line with the seismic shift that occurred at the beginning of the 1990s, Turkey's security environment also changed drastically. For the larger part of the Cold War, Turkey had been subject to the constant threat of a Soviet military thrust southward, aimed at taking the Turkish Straits.[10] In the case of war, the Turkish fleet would be assigned to fight the Soviet Black Sea Fleet as it moved to secure the exit to open waters (similar to Germany's role in the Baltic Sea).[11] It is not by chance that the Turkish government purchased and license-produced many warships of German design. The similar geographical constraints of the Baltic Sea and the Black Sea,[12] as well as the similar size of the Soviet Forces deployed to the respective theaters demanded similar naval strategies and capabilities. As a result, in 1990 the Turkish fleet consisted of 16 submarines (including 6 German Type 209), 22 surface destroyers and frigates (mostly older American designs augmented by 4 newer German MEKO 200 class), 22 German fast-attack craft, as well as numerous smaller vessels solely designed for territorial defense.[13]

Unlike many European countries that reduced their naval forces as part of the post–Cold War peace dividend, Turkey gradually increased its naval power over the following years. Owing to a hike in its defense budget—reaching over 4 percent of GDP in the mid- to late-1990s—the country was able "to maintain [its] ambitious growth programme and strengthen NATO's southern flank."[14] Numerous warships were commissioned into the fleet, more than half of which were of American origin.[15] As part of U.S. military assistance to many NATO allies, a total of six *Oliver Hazard Perry*-class and eight *Knox*-class frigates were transferred to the Turkish navy under "grant-in-aid" programs during the later years of the Cold War.

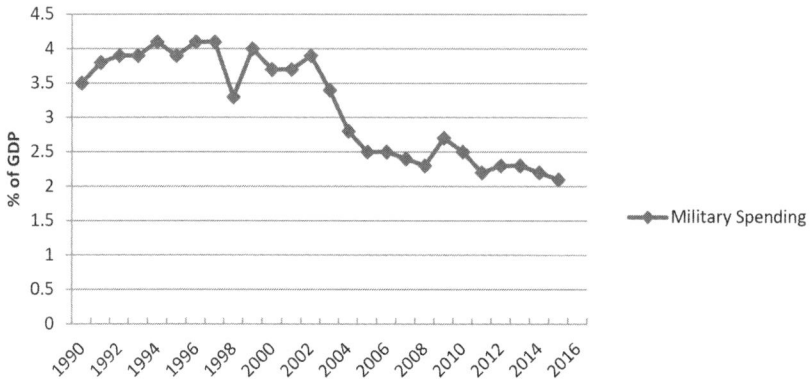

Figure 9-1. Turkey: Defense Spending in % of GDP, 1990–2015
Source: SIPRI Military Expenditure Database.

Also, the Gölcük shipyards, located on the southern coast of the Sea of Marmara, were awarded the shared production of four improved MEKO 200TN–class frigates.[16] These frigates provide impressive capabilities for such relatively small vessels (3,100 tons). All Turkish MEKOs have a hangar for a single helicopter, hull-mounted sonar, air and surface search and track radars, Harpoon missile launchers, the widely used and powerful 127-mm/54 caliber Mk 45 guns, Sea Sparrow air-defense systems, and Sea Guard CIWS. Torpedoes, jammers, and decoys complete the ships' offensive and defensive capabilities. In addition, the navy can capitalize on the ships' modular design, which greatly facilitates the installation of new weapon and combat systems. The octuple launcher module atop the hangar area has been exchanged for the Mk 41 vertical-launch system firing the more advanced folding-wing Evolved Seasparrow Missile (ESSM) in the last two units of the class (F 246 and F 247). By the year 2000 the submarine force was also making great strides in expanding its capabilities. Most of the older U.S. submarines, dating all the way back to World War II, had reached block obsolescence and were being retired, while license-built Type 209/1400[17] started entering service at a rate of one ship per year.[18] Although by this time the total number of submarines had decreased, Turkey's underwater fleet was in a much better state than it had ever been.

Despite this progress (and claims to the contrary) the military's power-projection capabilities remained regionally limited and the navy was largely confined to its defensive-minded doctrine. While the Turkish Naval Strategy of 1997 with the telling title "Toward the Open Seas" promoted greater naval power projection, the national defense white paper published in 2000 mostly reiterated the same naval tasks that had been expected of the Turkish navy in the early 1990s, namely: territorial defense (of the Turkish Straits in particular); protecting the SLOCs; participating in multinational operations; as well as humanitarian aid, and search and rescue.[19] Therefore, "the operational requirements of the Turkish Naval Forces [dictated] owning modern platforms having the capacity and capability of undertaking Above Water Warfare, Anti Submarine Warfare and Air Defense Warfare. Reconnaissance, surveillance and submarine warfare for preserving and protecting maritime transport in the surrounding seas has an important place among the duties of the Navy."[20]

Again, amphibious operations and power projection over greater distances was not considered a primary concern. In fact there is not a word of either concept in the 107-page document.[21] It is also somewhat surprising that it would take another decade before the Turkish leadership decided to make substantial naval investments in these areas.

In part, of course, the country's military doctrine has to be ascribed to its unaltered geographical position and historical experiences. Surrounded by regions of instability and conflict—the Balkans to its northwest; the current war in the Ukraine to its north; the recent armed conflict in Georgia and in Nagorno-Karabakh to its east; ongoing turmoil and bloodshed along its border with Iraq and Syria; and its strained relationship with Greece to its west—Turkey is truly in an unenviable position. Moreover, internal security threats in form of the large Kurdish minority, with its armed resistance movement known as Kurdistan Worker

Party or PKK, as well as recent terrorist attacks by ISIS-aligned terrorists demand close attention.

Despite this myriad of challenges at home and along its periphery, Turkey is now progressively expanding its ability to shape events farther from home. Turkey's reported efforts to establish military bases in Qatar, Djibouti, and Somalia, as well as the latest strategy paper identifying power projection and strike operations as important naval tasks, illustrate the current government's strategic vision.[22] Operating across great distances, of course, is not new to the Turkish navy and the sea service has contributed to a number of multinational maritime efforts over the past decades. These have included Operation Sharp Guard in the Mediterranean and Adriatic Seas, numerous deployments with NATO's naval standing forces, as well as Turkey's leading role in creating the Black Sea Naval Force in 2001, aimed at promoting closer cooperation among the states surrounding the Black Sea. Given the growing chasms between the various stakeholders in the region, joint exercises, such as those regularly conducted by the NATO allies, can mitigate the risk of unwanted incidents at sea. Pursuing common goals and utilizing shared operational procedures during these missions promotes mutual trust and respect among the sea services. As such, the Hellenic and Turkish navies as well as NATO's and Russia's naval forces have conducted joint training exercises on numerous occasions in the past.

Based on the decision by Turkey's political and military leadership to continuously modernize its existing force and replace its aging surface combatants with new warships on a one-to-one basis,[23] the Turkish navy has set itself the goal of "transforming from a force structure required for coastal operations, to a structure that could have a say in the open seas," over the next fifteen to twenty years.[24] Waters comes to the conclusion that as a result of this process, Turkey is the "operator of what is numerically the strongest of Europe's mid-sized naval forces." He continues, "Turkey has managed to combine the creation of a modern and well-balanced fleet with a progressive increase in the involvement of domestic industry in warships construction."[25] With the development of the *Ada*-class corvette and F-100 (MILGEM) frigate, Turkey has not only demonstrably shown its industrial capacity, but also "join[ed] the small group of countries able to both design and construct their own warships."[26] Yet numerous hurdles remain.

The announced development of the TF-2000 air-defense frigate in 1996 can be seen as an important step in the fleet's evolution into a blue-water navy, despite claims that "Turkey's naval defense concept is almost exclusively littoral-based."[27] However, not a single ship of this class has been laid down as of 2017. This unfortunate circumstance has caused a strategic "window of vulnerability" as Israeli defense analyst Micha'el Tanchum notes.[28] So far Turkey has been able to balance its naval forces against both the Hellenic navy as well as Russia's Black Sea Fleet. However, with Russia's naval buildup under way, Turkey can no longer rely on its naval parity. "Prior to the Crimean conflict, Russia's Black Sea fleet consisted of twenty-four major surface combatants and one diesel submarine while Turkey's major naval assets consist of approximately twenty-four surface combatants and fourteen submarines," Tanchum elaborates. The deployment of Russia's new *Admiral Grigorovich*–class frigates and Kilo-class submarines to the Black Sea (the first units have now entered service), "will quickly tilt the balance of naval forces in Russia's favor, giving Russia a significant strategic advantage for a window of four to eight years depending on the pace of Turkey's resumed production schedule." [29]

The problem of insufficient fleet air-defense capabilities will only be exacerbated by the introduction of the new assault ship in the near future. Although this ship and the addition of two new tank landing ships will, for the first time in recent history, give the Turkish navy robust amphibious capabilities, this iteration of the Spanish *Juan Carlos* is not intended to carry a SAM system, thus making it dependent on its escort for air defense. This circumstance goes to show how difficult it is to build a balanced fleet capable of conducting sea control as well as expeditionary and amphibious operations. Even if there are significant funds available, building numerous different types of ships, as well as training its crews, is a significant challenge. Without previously gained experience in constructing and operating these new platforms, the learning curve tends to be very steep for both the shipbuilders as well as for the Turkish navy itself. It will be interesting to see how the government deals with the financial burden such grand visions of Turkey's naval forces entails. One point many advocates of a large Turkish navy stress, however, is that "Turkey, unlike many European countries, always has money for defense."[30]

Greece

The Hellenic navy has also profited from decades of sustained defense spending of roughly 3 percent of the country's GDP. According to sources, Greece allocates the highest percentage of all European countries to national defense.[31] However, the percentage of GDP does not properly illustrate the ramifications of the economic crisis the country has found itself in for nearly ten years. Despite allocating more than 3 percent of its GDP to national defense in the period between 2009 and 2013, the budget shrunk by almost 50 percent in real terms due to the ailing economy—from 10.9 billion USD to only 5.5 billion.[32] Therefore, it is difficult to predict how the Greek armed forces are going to fare under these financial circumstances. Some evidence suggests that the Hellenic navy might be forced to forfeit some of its capabilities down the road. In short, it is unlikely that Greece will be able to modernize its fleet at the same pace it has pursued over the last twenty-five years. And maybe more importantly (from a Greek point of view), the strategic pendulum is therefore likely to swing even more toward its neighbor and principle antagonist—Turkey.

As noted, the two countries share common interests in a geopolitically highly volatile region. "Greece is located at the crossroads of three continents (Europe, Asia, and Africa). It is an integral part of the Balkans . . . and is also in close proximity to the Black Sea and oil-rich regions of the Middle East and Caucasus."[33] Throughout

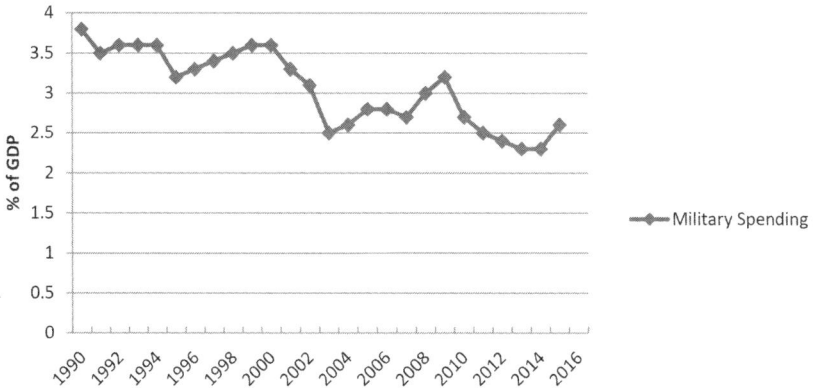

Figure 9-2. Greece: Defense Spending in % of GDP, 1990–2015
Source: SIPRI Military Expenditure Database.

history Greece has been considered a seafaring nation. It is no surprise that even now its navy cherishes the country's naval heritage that predates that of most modern sea powers. However, "[Greece's] strategic importance was eclipsed twice in history, once by naval technology, shifting the traffic of sea commerce to the Atlantic and the other, during the Cold War, when the central front of the continent attracted most allied attention."[34]

Throughout the Cold War, the United States and its allies considered the Mediterranean theater to be of somewhat less strategic importance, particularly when compared to the central front and the North Atlantic.[35] For Greece, the surrounding waters were of vital necessity; naval forces capable of controlling and protecting these waters were considered essential to the country's prosperity. Unfortunately, Greece and Turkey have not been able to put aside their differences over the islands and waters of the Aegean Sea and as a consequence Turkey's military power continues to dictate Greek defense policies. Nowhere can this be observed better than in the country's national defense strategy.

Although Turkey and Greece were essential NATO members during the Cold War (both joined NATO in 1952) and both were assigned with challenging Soviet expansion into the

Mediterranean and Middle East, conflicting interests between the two "allies" led to a number of precarious incidents throughout the second half of the twentieth century. Even the conclusion of the Cold War had little positive effect on their mutual belligerence. In fact, many Greeks—policymakers and citizens alike—perceived Turkey as an even greater threat than the Soviet Union.[36] "In trying to understand how Turkey is seen from the other shore of the Aegean Sea, we can compare it with . . . the Turks' perception of the USSR."[37] Two senior Turkish analysts elaborate: "As a neighbor and a historically conflicting partner of Tsarist Russia Turkey has perceived (and continues to perceive) [its] northern neighbor as a source of threat regardless of its regime. With sizeable territory, large population, enormous natural resources and the perennial aim of reaching the 'Warm Waters' *via* controlling the Turkish STRAITS . . . , this 'big neighbor of the North' has put potential threat and sometime actual pressure on Anatolia."[38] The analysts conclude, "Despite some differences, we can apply a similar scenario to the Turkish-Greek relationship. With a big territory, a large population, and a dynamic economy . . . , Turkey seems to be perceived as a considerable source of pressure [and threat] by Greece."[39]

Proof of this claim can be found in the Greek defense white paper from 1996. In this document the Ministry of National Defense laid out "the national military strategy which provides the directives for the use of the country's military power, . . . defense planning, . . . structure of the forces, [and] decision-making in defense matters."[40] The Hellenic armed forces were to be designed around a defensive doctrine; they were to be capable of protecting the so-called Greece-Cyprus Joint Defense Area against their most vexing opponent. Deterring the threat that emanated from the Turkish military represented the "central axis of Greece's military strategy."[41] The navy was to perform four principal tasks: 1) deterrence, 2) naval presence, 3) sea control, and 4) power projection ashore.[42] Effective power projection would have been difficult for Greece to achieve, given its limited amphibious capabilities.

In the early 1990s, this defense strategy was clearly highlighted in the Hellenic naval forces. Mostly designed for territorial defense among the many archipelagos of the Aegean Sea against a possible Turkish incursion, the navy exhibited effective ASW and ASuW capabilities. Its submarine force consisted of eight Type 209 vessels and two old U.S. submarines for training. Eleven destroyers and frigates, mostly relics from World War II, were in service and newer ships of Dutch and German design were either being procured abroad or built in Greek shipyards. The Dutch *Kortenaer* class, for example, represented "an excellent general-purpose frigate type optimized for the anti-ship and anti-submarine roles."[43] Ultimately, ten of these warships would sail under the Hellenic flag. The second type of surface combatant to enter service during the 1990s was the MEKO 200 class; they were similar to those built for the Turkish navy, except for a different propulsion system and CIWS. Four of these ships were built and remain in service today. Small surface combatants, especially patrol vessels and fast guided-missile attack craft, had always played an important part in Greece's naval doctrine and "there has been continued investment in this warship category in spite of the fact that it has increasingly fallen out of favour elsewhere."[44]

As tension decreased between the two neighbors at the beginning of the new millennium, so did Greek defense spending. While older vessels were decommissioned, the Hellenic navy made an effort to restructure and modernize its fleet. It had become apparent that an arms race with Turkey was neither useful nor could it be sustained. The navy's main role therefore remained hinged on the strategy of territorial defense and protection of the SLOCs. Investments were made to maintain the current fleet and replace older ships with more sophisticated vessels. As a result, it can be argued that this decision was the only reasonable approach to the fiscal realities of the time. Major Stergio Tsilikas offers the following assessment of Greece's strategy:

> Greek-Turkish relations have entered a period [in which] the prospects for resolution are better now than they have been

in years. A new rapprochement effort has unfolded between the two countries since the 1999 destructive earthquakes in Turkey, and the two sides have made gestures of reconciliation. Unfortunately, experience has shown us that similar efforts in the past [were of only a temporary nature and] in certain cases were followed by major crisis. Greece's deterrence doctrine includes those elements needed to restore the balance in the Greek-Turkish interaction and tries to ensure that a low or medium level crisis will not get out of hand.[45]

The modernization of the Hellenic navy proved to be a significant challenge as payment difficulties postponed a number of naval procurement projects. The navy's troubled quest to acquire a replacement of its aging Type 209 submarine flotilla being the most prominent example of recent mismanagement. With Germany leading the field in AIP submarine technology, the Greek government awarded ThyssenKrupp Marine Systems, who also owned Hellenic shipyards, a contract to build four new Type 214-class boats. Despite these being launched as long ago as 2004, financial constraints enticed the Greek government to reject the first vessel on the grounds of alleged technical shortcomings.[46] The legal feud, which lasted for years, "has become something of a cause célèbre in Greek political circles" an observer noted. "A former Greek defense minister has been jailed over the alleged handling of bribes from another company . . . and other Greek officials are under investigation."[47] The controversy might also affect from whom Greece chooses to buy its future air-defense frigate. While the German shipbuilder was previously considered a primary contender for the bid, Greece has been showing increased interest in the French version of the FREMM frigate, which has already been sold to Morocco and Egypt. However, any such procurement is far from certain as declining funds make large-scale investments in the future seem increasingly unlikely. Greece's obscure and sometimes dubious acquisition processes largely contribute to the difficulty of predicting the future of the Hellenic navy:

There have been no comprehensive analyses or systematic studies of arms procurement decision making in Greece, despite the high level of resources allocated to defence. The lack of previous research is a major obstacle to examining this process. The Greek defence planning process and in particular the arms procurement decision-making process are also fairly closed in terms of public accountability, transparency, parliamentary scrutiny, monitoring and oversight.[48]

What seems to be clear is that the Greek navy will want to retain a large number of warships in order to protect its interests in the Aegean and the Mediterranean. The defense white paper, published in 2014, acknowledges the fact that the United States is in the process of pivoting to the Asia-Pacific region, which will "create new conditions for the security and defence demands in the European area."[49] Greece intends to address these demands by participating in international peacekeeping operations, supporting the transformation of NATO, facilitating the creation of a joint European defense and security policy, and supporting the HADR effort in the Mediterranean Sea.[50] Like Spain, France, and Italy, Greece will have to shoulder the growing burden of mass migration from the African and Asian continents to Europe's shores. At the time of writing, Greek naval vessels (as part of NATO's SNMG2) were deployed to the Aegean Sea, in an effort to combat human trafficking and illegal migration.

Though the white paper does not provide any specific requirements in terms of military capabilities, it reiterates the basic tenets of Greece's defense strategy, which has largely remained unaltered since the end of the Cold War (and in fact since the creation of the deterrent strategy after the Turkish invasion of Cyprus in 1973).[51] Further, it stipulates that the main goals are the "enhancement of Hellenic Navy capabilities, area air defense capabilities, maritime cooperation aircraft and modern submarines."[52] To what extent the Greek government will be able to provide the necessary funding to achieve these goals remains unclear. It is quite possible that the size of the fleet will decrease after 2020 should no replacement for the *Kortenaer*-class frigates be found. Meanwhile the situation regarding the subsurface force appears somewhat more promising as both the long overdue upgrades for some on of the existing Type 209 and the delivery of the Type 214 have been completed. After years in which the "existing domestic construction [appeared] to be paralyzed whilst longstanding plans of new orders had been stalled,"[53] the Elefsis Shipyards have recommenced construction of the *Roussen*-class fast-attack craft. And, finally, four of the navy's former six P-3B Orion patrol planes are scheduled to be reactivated after a comprehensive modernization and upgrade program.

Both Greece and Turkey currently entertain robust naval capabilities and both countries continue to allocate significant amounts of treasure toward their national defense. Turkey has incrementally expanded its naval capabilities since the dissolution of the Soviet Union. It has also been able to revive a defense industry, capable of designing and building warships up to the size of frigates and to outfit them with domestically developed electronics and weapon systems—a great achievement by any standard. But there are some caveats to Turkey's ascendance toward being a greater naval power. Irrespective of the various domestic security considerations that need to be taken into account, the political decision makers in Ankara are running the risk of losing sight of which means justify which ends. With national pride soaring high, not least among the country's elites, advocates of sea power have already demanded the construction of an aircraft carrier in order to buttress Turkey's status as a regional power. Maintaining a large naval force is both costly and manpower-intense. There are already financial restrictions standing in the way of properly balancing all the navy's mission requirements. This will only grow more difficult as new assault ships, or even a carrier, are put to sea—not to mention the envisioned naval air wing of F-35s. In the long term, Turkey will also need to reconsider its increasingly authoritarian form of rule, or else it is likely to further alienate allies and partners, possibly

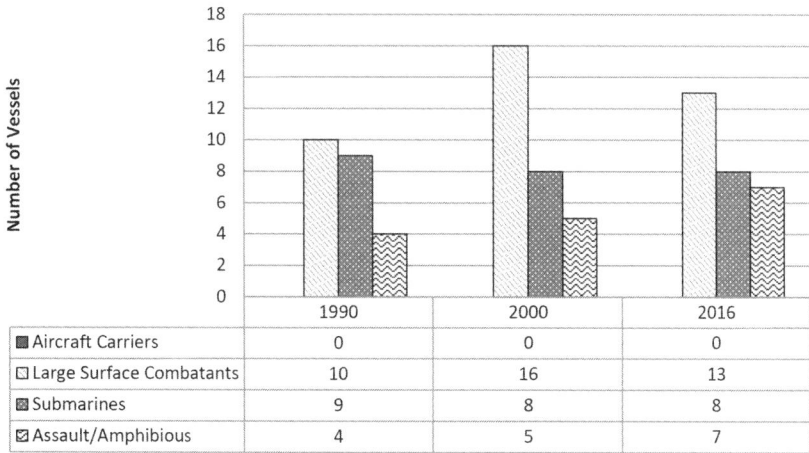

Figure 9-3. Greece: Number of Major Vessels

Sources: *The Naval Institute Guide to Combat Fleets of the World, Military Technology Almanac, World Naval Review*.

	1990	2000	2016
■ Aircraft Carriers	0	0	0
☐ Large Surface Combatants	10	16	13
▦ Submarines	9	8	8
☑ Assault/Amphibious	4	5	7

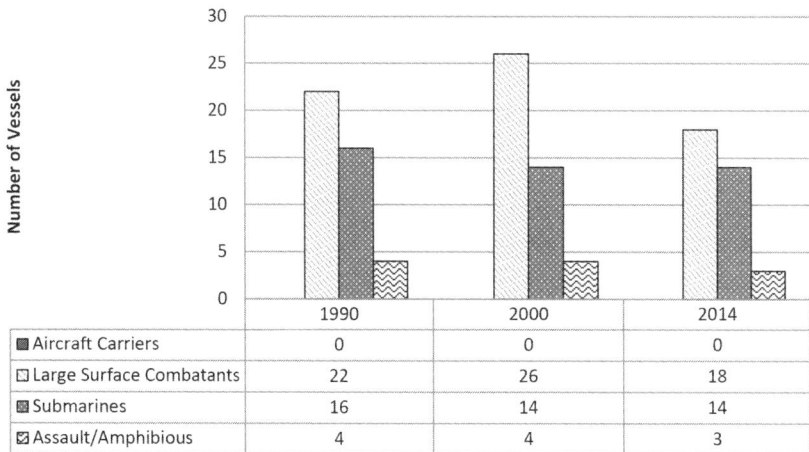

Figure 9-4. Turkey: Number of Major Vessels

Sources: *The Naval Institute Guide to Combat Fleets of the World, Military Technology Almanac, World Naval Review*.

	1990	2000	2014
■ Aircraft Carriers	0	0	0
☐ Large Surface Combatants	22	26	18
▦ Submarines	16	14	14
☑ Assault/Amphibious	4	4	3

leading to strong opposition from the EU and United States and even greater hostilities in the region.

The future of the Hellenic navy, on the other hand, looks somewhat bleaker. The ongoing struggle between the European Union and the Greek government regarding the latter's national debt, as well as an economy that is recovering at a very slow rate, make large-scale military investments more difficult. Greece will need to be far more prudent in its future procurement decisions and take vigorous action to prevent falling victim of corruption and dubious political schemes. In the near to midterm, Greece will likely have to streamline its forces to bring down the costs of training and personnel, reducing its naval capabilities.

What is most important, however, is that the two countries continue their political dialogue. Turkey and Greece will undoubtedly play an important role in Europe's future. They will also determine to what degree Europe has a say in world affairs and their respective maritime forces will be a significant factor in deciding the outcome.

Germany

Reluctance and Reductions—Not Stepping Up to the Plate

ince the end of the Cold War, the German armed forces have undergone one of the most drastic changes of all European states. Since its inception in 1949, and until the dissolution of the Soviet Union, the Federal Republic of Germany invested heavily in its military. At the same time numerous other NATO members deployed large forces on German soil in order to deter a possible attack by the Warsaw Pact. Similarly, East Germany, officially the German Democratic Republic, had a huge number of men and matériel deployed on its territory. At the height of the Cold War, the Soviets alone had more than 300,000 soldiers in East Germany, including 20 tank and motorized rifle divisions. These troops were considered "Category I": the best trained and equipped in the Soviet army.[1]

During this period of time, the common assumption was that if deterrence were to fail and war broke out, the decisive battle would be fought on the central European front: in Germany, western France, Italy, and possibly also in Austria.[2] American and NATO contingency planning called on the West German armed forces to

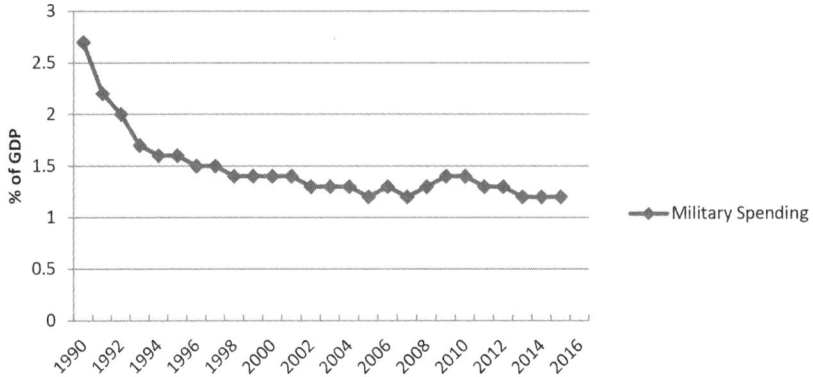

Figure 10-1. Germany: Defense Spending in % of GDP, 1990–2014
Source: SIPRI Military Expenditure Database.

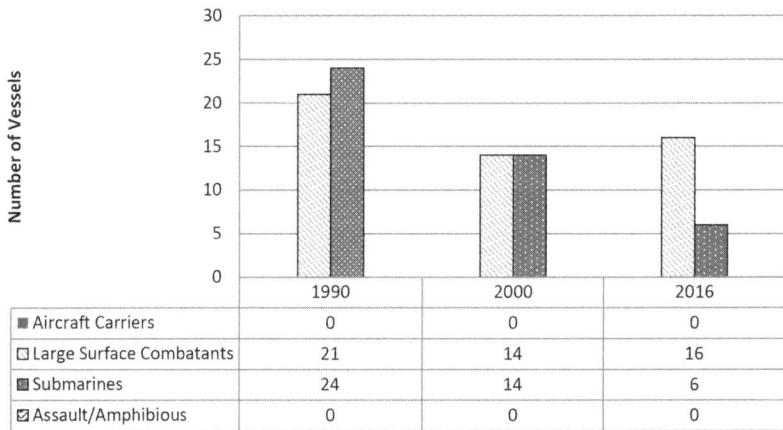

	1990	2000	2016
■ Aircraft Carriers	0	0	0
▢ Large Surface Combatants	21	14	16
▥ Submarines	24	14	6
▨ Assault/Amphibious	0	0	0

Figure 10-2. Germany: Number of Major Vessels
Sources: *The Naval Institute Guide to Combat Fleets of the World, Military Technology Almanac, World Naval Review.*

share the burden of confronting the bulk of Soviet heavy mechanized forces. For that reason, the German army and air force
received the lion's share of military funding.

The role of the German navy, the Bundesmarine, on the other
hand, was for the most part directed toward operations in the
littoral waters of the North Sea and the Baltic Sea. The navy was

designed to play a key role within NATO's contingency planning, and in case of conflict, was to conduct anti-submarine warfare (ASW), anti-surface warfare (ASuW), and mine warfare (MW) against Soviet naval forces.[3] In particular, the mining operations of the approaches to the Danish Straits, the most critical choke point in NATO planning, required the Germans to sustain a large fleet of mine warfare vessels and substantial mine inventory.[4]

Once the Iron Curtain had finally fallen, and East Germany and West Germany had celebrated their reunification, the joint German navy consisted of over a hundred vessels, including nearly a dozen destroyers and frigates, 42 guided-missile patrol boats and nearly 50 mine warfare vessels. In addition, the Howaldtswerke in Kiel had designed and produced what were considered among the best diesel-electric submarines in the world. The German navy operated 18 Type 206, and 6 older Type 205 submarines in 1991, while various other versions were sold to other states, including Venezuela, Chile, Norway, Greece, and Indonesia.[5] East Germany had operated a much smaller force throughout the Cold War. Unlike some advanced Soviet technology, most notably the Mikojan-Gurewitsch MiG-29 combat aircraft, which was of interest to Western defense analysts for its advanced capabilities, the handful of Soviet-built frigates, corvettes, and missile patrol boats were of no relevance in the post–Cold War era and were quickly taken from service or sold.[6]

Compared to other European powers, such as Great Britain, Italy, and France, Germany has for most of its history been considered a continental power. Its naval ambitions (and its maritime ambitions more generally) were squandered in both World Wars and, as a consequence, Germany lacks the naval history and culture of a blue-water navy that is capable of conducting the full range of naval warfare.[7] German sea power in both World Wars "was never imbued with that determination to close with, and destroy, the enemy which was the tradition in Britain's Royal Navy." As a large land power, "the Germans either lacked superiority in force or they had ulterior objectives in mind, in support of which the hazards of battle would be an arguably needless complication."[8]

Considering this relative strategic inaptitude throughout Germany's history, the evolution of the German navy since the end of the Cold War seems quite remarkable. Conceived as a littoral maritime force, limited both by its role and required capabilities within NATO, the navy has developed into a multimission fleet that can be deployed over great distances. The ability of this "expeditionary navy" to conduct so-called out-of-area operations[9] reflects the change in how the role of the Deutsche Marine of the twenty-first century is perceived by the German policymakers. The defense white paper published by the German Defense Ministry in 2006 called upon the navy to deploy, on short notice, in far-off regions of the world. Moreover, it should provide effective support to land operations and thereby project power onto enemy shores, even under threat.[10]

Based on these criteria and building on a series of reform efforts—including the suspension of compulsory military service as a major goal of the so-called Bundeswehr reform—the force structure has been under constant flux. In terms of ship hulls, the number of warships has plummeted over the last twenty years as older ships have gradually been replaced by fewer, ostensibly more capable, vessels. Moreover, the entire naval structure has undergone major reorganization. The current fleet is now divided into two flotillas, one in Kiel (Einsatzflotille 1: submarines, guided-missile craft, mine warfare vessels, K-130 corvettes, and tenders) and the second in Wilhelmshaven (Einsatzflotille 2: frigates and larger support vessels); naval command (Marinekommando) has been consolidated at Rostock while the only remaining naval aviation base is located at Nordholz.[11]

It comes as no surprise that these austerity measures have led to widespread skepticism among defense analysts and the broader public regarding the state of Germany's armed forces.[12] Given the string of shortcomings in capability and readiness of its forces, there is legitimate cause for concern. In the case of the navy, the reduced force levels are exerting considerable strain on the relatively few platforms and their crews. Existing (and numerous) standing commitments, from the Baltic to the Indian Ocean, have tied down all available naval assets. Moreover, there are numerous indicators suggesting that Germany will remain unwilling to conduct any form of high-intensity warfighting in the foreseeable future. Considering Germany's experiences in Afghanistan, its reluctance to take part in other large-scale military operations in recent years (Iraq 2003, Libya 2011, Syria 2014), and its self-perception of a "Zivilmacht" (Civilian Power), "the key question is whether Germany will be willing [and able] to deploy forces in contingencies beyond its borders."[13] Lacking the ability to project significant military power at the upper end of the intensity spectrum, and with apparent intention to only make modest investments in order to increase such capabilities in the near future, it is likely that we will continue to see Germany only taking part in low-threat arenas, HADR efforts, and peacekeeping operations, delegating responsibilities in high-risk operations to others. How the German Ministry of Defense intends to plan for and conceptualize the return of high-end challenges remains unclear; despite best efforts by the German naval community.[14]

In the mid-1990s the German Ministry of Defense and Armed Forces published several strategic white papers in an attempt to define the role of its military within the new security environment. One of the documents, the *Weißbuch 1994,* put forward a defense policy framework in which the German naval forces where to be transformed from the aforementioned littoral force to a modern blue-water navy (expeditionary navy).[15] It stated that the navy's principal task was to maintain the freedom of the seas and to provide maritime capabilities to international conflict resolution efforts, both as part of an alliance as well as on its own, and undertake crisis-management operations farther away from home.[16] This reorientation also led to changes in the navy's structure and fleet composition. In a far more austere financial environment, both the current size of the force as well as the future naval procurement plans had to be reconsidered.

Many of the navy's vessels were nearing the end of their service life, or were not considered capable of effectively conducting the new missions envisioned by the defense planners. For these reasons, further goals of the navy were outlined in the already ongoing "Marine 2005" naval modernization plan through its basic tenet: to gradually reduce the number of warships, but ultimately operate a well-balanced, yet somewhat smaller force than the four major European naval powers.[17]

The initial—and as is so often the case, overly optimistic—procurement plan—envisioned a fleet comprised of sixteen to twenty frigates, twenty to thirty patrols boats, twenty to thirty MW vessels, ten to fourteen submarines, fifteen to seventeen support ships, sixty to sixty-five naval fighter-bombers, thirty-five to forty search and rescue (SAR) helicopters and twelve to fourteen ASW and marine patrol craft.[18] In an article from 1992, the German naval historian Jürgen Rhades, rightfully stressed that these numbers were merely provisional as "it will be impossible to predict precisely what will be required after 2005."[19] And, in fact, the target figure of platforms for the Marine 2005 goals was quickly dropped in light of the peace dividend. By the time 2005 had come to pass, the austerity measures had reduced the navy not by one-third, as Rhades had predicted, but had effectively cut it in half.[20] Retired Admiral Sigurd Hess pointed to the fact that the German navy had to realize that it could neither replace its aging vessels at a satisfactory rate, nor build and deploy the platforms necessary to conduct the envisioned operations.[21]

Despite these drastic changes, Germany has been able to develop and deploy highly capable warships and weapon systems, manned and operated by skilled crews. Compared to the aging fleet of the 1980s, Germany has succeeded in gradually putting newer (yet fewer) ships to sea. These newly built surface and subsurface combatants were designed to conduct a larger variety of missions more effectively and over greater distances than before. Based on Germany's industrial prowess, its shipbuilding facilities have gained substantial experience in producing state-of-the-art vessels. In particular, shipbuilders such as Blohm & Voss, Howaldtswerke-Deutsche Werft (now ThyssenKrupp Marine Systems), and the Nordseewerke have developed innovative designs and delivered cutting-edge technology.

Besides the previously mentioned Type 206 submarine, the MEKO (Mehrzweck-Kombination), which has been built since the 1980s, serves as an example of German technical ingenuity. Although the MEKO was never procured by the German navy, the design has enjoyed considerable commercial success on the foreign market, and numerous units continue to operate under the flags of Australia, Argentina, and Turkey. In the process, the German engineers placed heavy emphasis on modular design, which offers shipbuilders and customers numerous benefits. For many navies, the need to "reconfigure or adapt ships in the face of changing operational requirements . . . has often proved prohibitively expensive."[22] Therefore, concepts like the German MEKO, the Royal Danish Navy's Standard Flexible (StanFlex) system, or the (badly managed) U.S. Navy's littoral combat ship mission packages can save costs and provide added flexibility.

As part of a more capable and globally deployable naval force, Germany was also at the forefront of submarine development. Relying on their technical know-how and rich operational history, the German shipbuilders pioneered the development of the air-independent propulsion (AIP) diesel-electric submarine. In general, diesel-electric powered submarines need to surface regularly to recharge their batteries and cannot stay submerged for extended periods of time.[23] Until the successful application of AIP technology, this capability was reserved for nuclear-powered submarines. First tests of a fuel cell-based air-independent propulsion system were conducted as early as 1988, but due to technical challenges and fiscal restrictions, it took another fifteen years until the first AIP Type 212A submarine was delivered to the German navy. The new submarine now gives its commander the unique ability to remain submerged for much longer periods of time than previously possible, owing to the vessel's fuel cells. What is so extraordinary about this technology is that the boats are very quiet, thus making them difficult for others to locate. Diesel-electric submarines are known, and feared, for their ability to operate at a very low noise level, loitering in shallow waters where their comparatively louder and larger nuclear counterparts are less willing to venture. With one of the inherent limitations of diesel-electric propulsion having been overcome (the other being the low speeds at which they can run while using fuel cells), the new German submarines are even more difficult to detect. With the Type 212A, the German navy now "has a submerged endurance bettered only by those few navies that are able to afford nuclear-propelled boats, as well as an overall level of stealth that is perhaps second-to-none."[24]

On the downside, Germany's intention to build and deploy ten to fourteen such submarines, as envisioned during the 1990s, "is little more than a distant memory,"[25] an analyst notes. All Type 206 subs have been decommissioned, leaving the navy with no more than six submarines.[26] And despite the Type 212A's increased endurance—necessary in out-of-area operations—the German navy is "still some distance away from furnishing the true offensive oceanic proficiency of high-speed attack submarines powered by high-capacity nuclear reactors,"[27] such as those operated by the United Kingdom or France.

Among all the navy's assets, the shift toward a more globally oriented force is most visible in its fleet of surface combatants. Not only have many of the former MW and ASuW vessels—such as the *Frankenthal* minehunters and *Tiger*-class guided-missile craft—been decommissioned, but far more capable surface platforms, such as the F-123, F-124, F-125, and K-130, have been or are in the process of being put to sea. Starting with the F-123 *Brandenburg*-class, a ship with a total length of 139 meters and a displacement of over 4,700 tons, the German navy commissioned the first in a line of very large and capable frigates. Despite being designed during the 1980s as a ASW platform to replace the increasingly obsolescent *Lütjens*-class destroyers (commissioned in 1969), the F-123 carried a wide variety of ASW, ASuW, and AAW weapons and at the time of construction also incorporated novel signature-reduction design elements. Additionally, the number of crew members was reduced owing to increased automation and prolonged maintenance cycles.[28]

Its successor, the F-124 *Sachsen* class, is in many ways a refined version of the F-123; it was based on a trilateral cooperation for a future frigate between Germany, the Netherlands and Spain. After the initial plan (the NRF-90 project) to build a common frigate for the eight most important NATO members failed in the late 1980s, a memorandum of understanding among the three nations was signed in 1990.[29] Its provisions required the future frigate to be deployable in operations across the intensity spectrum. Basically, the ship had to be a multipurpose platform. At the time, a German commentator pointed out that the focus had shifted away from anti-submarine warfare, toward anti-surface and antiair capabilities. Therefore, "this new emphasis [demanded] improved equipment in the areas of surveillance, communications, air defence and C2 [command and control]."[30] This, he concluded, could have "hardly been [achieved] by German, Dutch, or Spanish industry alone."[31] Although the final versions of each country's ships (the *Álvaro de Bazán* class, *De Zeven Provinciën* class, and *Sachsen* class) are different in design and combat systems, all of them exhibit substantial capabilities hitherto unprecedented in vessels of this class.

While the Spanish *Bazán* frigate (also known as F-100) relies on the American Aegis combat system to deal with aerial threats, the Dutch and German ships feature the long-range 3-D volume search radar (SMART-L) and APAR multifunction radar (an active electronically scanned array, or AESA). [32] "The APAR represented a very significant design, development and industrial challenge," while "the sophisticated technology used for [the SMART-L radar] allows its use even in littoral scenarios, [as] it was especially designed to deal with small low-flying targets."[33] Therefore, both radars on board the *Sachsen* class are excellent examples of Europe's defense industry holding its own in this specific sector.[34] Another common feature is that all three classes deploy the American SM-2 air-defense missile, fired from the ships' Mk 41 vertical launch system. Accordingly, the three units of the *Sachsen* class are considered among the most capable and well-balanced AAW frigates in the world, and, interestingly, are currently the only frigates to deploy antiair missile systems for all tiers of air defense.[35] Moreover, the ships could theoretically deploy the SM-3 missiles as part of the

United States' and NATO's plan to establish a sea based theater ballistic missile system. However, so far there are few indications that the German government will go forward with such plans.[36]

Within NATO, these vessels offer air and missile defense to other, less capable units and have also been deployed together with U.S. and French carrier strike groups over the past years. In 2013, and for the first time in history, a German frigate (F220, *Hamburg*) was assigned to coordinate the air space of Carrier Strike Group VIII (*Dwight D. Eisenhower*), thus being solely responsible for its air defense.[37] The growing interaction with other fleets is only part of Germany's effort to increase its international presence. By and large, the country's involvement in international operations has increased considerably over the past two decades. In the context of its strategic reorientation and growing engagement abroad, the German navy has been deployed in various theaters: from clearing mines in the Persian Gulf to fighting piracy off the coast of Somalia.

It did not take long until the Germany navy gained its first experiences in the post–Cold War era. In 1994, it conducted its first larger operation—Southern Cross—in an effort to evacuate German UNISOM II troops from Mogadishu, Somalia. Between July 1994 and July 1996, the navy also took part in enforcing the embargo against former Yugoslavia in the Adriatic. As a continuous part of NATO's Standing Naval Force Mediterranean (STANAV-FORMED, now SNMG 2), German destroyers and frigates participated in nearly 6,000 boarding operations and inspections at sea.[38] The navy's longest-standing naval deployment thus far has been its antiterrorism mission as part of Operation Active Endeavour. In an act of unprecedented solidarity, following the attacks of 9/11, the German Bundestag decided to deploy its naval forces to the waters around the Horn of Africa and consequently took command of joint task force CTF-150 on a number of occasions.[39] Though publicly criticized, the German government remained adamant that the mission was necessary to counter the threat that terrorist activities posed to the good order at sea.[40] Germany's commitment to peacekeeping operations was buttressed by its leading naval role in the United Nation's UNIFIL mission off the coast of Lebanon. Based on Resolution 1701, the German navy has been assisting and training the Lebanese navy since 2006.[41]

The latest additions to Germany's naval forces, the K-130 *Braunschweig*-class Corvette, the F-125 *Baden-Württemberg*–class frigate, and the *Berlin*-class combat support ship represent an ongoing effort to adapt to the new maritime security environment. As mentioned, the navy's guided-missile *Tiger*-class, *Gepard*-class, and *Albatros*-class patrol boats had limited ability to perform out-of-area operations. As naval commentator Guy Toremans points out, "the one-watch boats had a very limited endurance by nature of their limited seaworthiness and the fatigue factor impacting their crews."[42] Keeping these shortcomings in mind, in 2001 a consortium of three German shipbuilders was awarded a 880 million euro contract to build a first batch of five new corvettes. Incorporating signature-reduction features, modern combat systems and potent AAW and ASuW capabilities, the *Braunschweig* class undoubtedly can meet numerous requirements over the coming decades. However, despite being "dispatched worldwide to undertake surveillance missions, embargo and counter-drug operations, as well as, potentially, to participate in combat missions,"[43] the vessels are faced with limitations due to their small size. "One of the lessons already learned from the K-130 programme was that, although significantly larger than the fast patrol boats, the new corvettes have still proved to be a bit too small to operate comfortably and effectively in support of some of the German navy's growing mission requirements around the globe."[44] This will put more strain on the relatively small number of large surface combatants, such as the F-124s and new F-125 Stabilization Frigate and also calls into question Berlin's most recent decision to procure an additional batch of five ships to fill the gaps the delayed future frigate program (MKS-180) has created.

If there is one thing the navy's most recent addition, the F-125 *Baden-Württemberg* class, does not lack, it is size. Its builders proudly claim that with a length of 149 meters and a displacement in excess of 7,300 tons, it will be the largest frigate ever built. The four ships of the class will replace the 8 units of the Type 122 (*Bremen* class), starting in 2017. Unlike its predecessors (designed primarily for ASW), "the design of the new frigate class reflects everything that is important for littoral warfare."[45] Still based on the provisions of Germany's defense white paper from 2006, the ships will be able to conduct littoral operations that take place hundreds and thousands of miles away from home.[46] However, in light of the growing tension between East and West, defense planners will need to consider these ships operating in highly contested and confined waters of the Baltic and North Sea. In this scenario, the F-125 will not provide the same high-end combat capabilities the *Sachsen* class can bring to the table. Its air-defense and anti-submarine capabilities will be especially limited when compared to other ships of similar size, notwithstanding that the ships have considerable room for upgrades.

On the other hand, owing to increased automation, the crew will be considerably smaller than on previous ships (120 crew, compared to 200 on the *Sachsen*)—an important factor in times of shortages in military personnel. Moreover, the German navy intends to employ a dual crewing concept much like used on board U.S. submarines (rotating the crews while on deployment instead of long tours of a single crew), thereby allowing the frigate to conduct operations for up to two years and five thousand hours at sea per year.[47] Also, apart from the number of hulls, other important factors, such as "technical quality, professional skill, and maintenance efficiency," have to be considered in order to judge a navy's capabilities.[48] The German navy would, by any estimate, score high in the second and third category. However, under closer examination, Germany's commitment to the maritime realm does not pass the test. While "changes to the navy structure are expected to be less drastic than those to the army" and the navy overall was not hit as hard by past cuts as its sister services, there is not much reason to celebrate.[49]

The German navy is being stretched increasingly thin in support of its many security obligations. Currently, its vessels are engaged in the UNIFIL mission, the EU antipiracy operation *Atalanta*, the counterterrorism effort, and EU NAVFOR Operation Sophia in the Mediterranean. The Deutsche Marine regularly trains and exercises with other navies and various elements of foreign armed forces, contributes warships to the Standing NATO Maritime Groups as well as the Standing NATO MCM Groups (mine countermeasure) on a constant basis and, finally, integrates its air-defense frigates in U.S. carrier strike groups. At the same time, the force level has dropped to 11 frigates, 5 K-130 corvettes, and a small number of mine warfare vessels; the total mine inventory is rumored to be somewhere between 5 and 50 mines. While the third and final *Berlin*-class combat group supply replenishment ship represents an important addition to Germany's "expeditionary fleet," the decommissioning of the last *Gepard*-class fast patrol boats leave the navy with alarmingly few hulls at least until the middle of the next decade, possible even longer (27 submarines and surface combatants in total).[50] The aforementioned maintenance efficiency and ability to deploy forces will become increasingly challenging in the future, due to the wear and tear on the existing fleet.

Given Germany's economic health—and the political as well as military influence it could thus conceivably wield—the government has to accept criticism for its general reluctance to use hard power, even in cases where it would be generally considered justifiable. The NATO-led military intervention in Libya, for example, not only created deep rifts between the NATO members and emphasized the absence of a common European strategy, but it also illustrated the most likely form of the future Western response to conflict and humanitarian crisis. As part of the ad hoc Coalition of the Willing and Able, neutral Sweden took part in enforcing the no-fly zone over Libya, while Germany—which for over forty years has owed its safety and security to its NATO allies—watched from the sidelines. At the time, "the German decision not to participate in the Libyan operation caught many officials by surprise and raises questions whether the Alliance can rely on Germany's support for future power-projection missions—even ones, like Libya, that are carried out under a UN mandate."[51] Later events, such as the threat of force against Bashar Al-Assad's regime in Syria in the summer of 2013 or the current effort against the so-called Islamic State underscore Germany's aversion to committing its military forces to operations that pose a measurable degree of risk.

To sum up, since the end of the Cold War, the German navy has undergone drastic reform. Today it bears little resemblance to the Cold War fleet patrolling the waters of the Baltic and the North Sea. Apart from a small number of increasingly obsolete ships (F-122 scheduled for replacement), the navy has commissioned and operates state-of-the-art submarines, corvettes, and frigates. Germany continues to be a leader in key naval technologies and has had substantial commercial success on the naval market over the past two decades, securing contracts from states all around the world. In addition, the Germans have successfully deployed naval forces in a number of contingencies, though most of them were on the lowest end of the intensity scale.

However, the drastic budget cuts that ensued as a consequence of the Soviet collapse have taken a detrimental toll on the naval services. Vice Admiral Hans-Rudolf Boehmer's predictions from 1996 on the navy's future 15 years out would almost seem humorous, would they not have such far-reaching ramifications for Europe's security in an increasingly competitive maritime environment. By the year 2010, Boehmer predicted, "the navy will not be much different in size than it is today, however, it will be significantly more capable. There will be 15 frigates, 10–12 submarines and it will include a strong mine countermeasure capability. Further, there will be a mixture of modern corvettes and not-so-modern patrol boats [and the] naval air arm will still be flying the Tornados."[52] In reality, the German navy can call upon none of these capabilities. The surface and subsurface fleet remain considerably smaller than envisioned, while the naval air arm has lost its Tornado strike assets; its remaining helicopters and maritime patrol aircraft regularly have been left grounded due to mechanical issues and shortfalls in maintenance. The recent effort to integrate a German sea battalion into the Dutch amphibious assault ship cannot obscure the fact that the German navy does not have any noteworthy amphibious capability of its own.

Compared to other states of its size and wealth (the other European G-7 members, for example), Germany's naval commitment can be considered haphazard, lacking a clear-cut strategic aim and the corresponding provisions that spell out what force levels are required.[53] In his critical assessment of Europe's navies, McGrath summarizes Germany's naval abilities as "[falling] mainly within the lower end of the operational spectrum."[54] Although he, along with others, recognize Germany's contribution to peacekeeping and stabilization efforts (which follow from its strategic reorientation throughout the post–Cold War era), he makes it clear that its "cruising navy provides little in the way of power projection."[55] Given the considerable financial burden countries such as France, Italy, the U.K., and, to a lesser degree, Spain have to carry to maintain their well-balanced fleets (which also includes costly nuclear-deterrent forces in the case of France and the U.K.), Germany's naval investments seem disproportionally small. With tensions rising on Europe's northern and southern flanks and Russia's reemergence as a naval power, it remains to be seen if Germany's policymakers will take these changes within the geopolitical security environment to heart. While there are some indicators suggesting both an increased awareness and willingness to make investments toward defense on Germany's part, it is still too early to present a reasonable estimate if this can, or will, become a long-term trend. Ultimately, "the interesting question is not whether the Navy supports Germany's worldview and view of itself, . . . [but] it is whether a nation as powerful, rich, and networked as Germany, is underinvesting in naval power while free riding on the backs of U.S., U.K., and French naval capabilities to a greater extent than other European nations."[56]

CHAPTER 10

Denmark and the Netherlands
Commercial Might and Military Inaptitude

Both the Netherlands and Denmark offer interesting examples to illustrate how maritime powers have evolved over the
course of history. Centuries ago, both countries ranked among the
most prominent sea powers in the world, fashioning large merchant
fleets as well as powerful armadas of warships.[1] This union between
military and commerce—conducted by many, but refined by the
Dutch and ultimately mastered by the British—resulted in "control of
the sea by maritime commerce and naval supremacy [and meant]
predominant influence in the world."[2]

However, in this day and age it appears as if many European
governments no longer consider highly capable naval forces to be
an essential element for the prosperity of their respective states.
Apparently, it is a widely held view that despite being largely dependent on the on-time delivery of goods transported by sea, countries
fare quite well without maintaining large and expensive naval fleets.
Even more remarkable is the fact that this myopia has also befallen
traditional seafaring nations, such as those under discussion in this
chapter. Frankly, the political leadership across Europe seems to

worry little about being able to buttress their economic power with credible hard power.

There are a number of reasons for this development given the extent of geopolitical transformation over the past few centuries. First, one cannot disregard the fact that the Western world has evolved into a community of (mostly) shared values and comparatively little rivalry. Second, in a world of global commerce in which 90 percent of materials and goods are shipped by sea, the United States has taken it upon itself to protect the quintessential freedom of the sea and thereby has guaranteed access to the global commons (global resource domains). That this has only been possible by making substantial investment in its naval forces is self-evident. For countries such as the Netherlands and Denmark, this of course represents a welcome convenience. Unlike in previous centuries, neither state has to fear that its commercial ships will fall prey to commerce raiders or will be sunk by maritime marauders, which in the past were often of European origin. In turn, they can expand their commercial activities and gain large revenue by transporting goods to and fro between Europe, the United States, the oil-rich Middle East, and Asia. Indeed, throughout the twentieth century, both countries have expanded their commercial shipping, while their military capabilities have been truncated.

To briefly outline this growing disparity between commercial and military sea power, it is worth noting the level of investment in each area. For instance, the Netherlands is not only dependent on the unimpeded flow of commerce at sea, it has also invested huge sums to develop its shipping capabilities. Its seaport complex at Rotterdam is now the fourth-largest port in the world and the largest in Europe (based on the amount of containers—twenty foot equivalent unit or TEU—handled per day). At a size of over 12,500 hectares it can accommodate even the largest ship and has a throughput of 450 million tons of freight per year.[3] Denmark's commercial shipping industry is of even greater magnitude. As Parry highlights, "The Danes are the understated, high achieving denizens of the maritime industry."[4] The Danish Møller-Maersk shipping company is the largest and arguably most renowned of its kind in the world. Its huge Triple E container ships have been specifically designed for the route between Asia and Europe and can carry over 18,000 TEU.[5] A single ship of this class displaces over 249,000 tons fully loaded, which is 5 times the displacement of the entire Danish navy combined (around 54,000 tons including its auxiliaries). Although many of these commercial efforts are usually part of international consortium enterprises as well as private investors and are not necessarily state matters, it is nonetheless striking how successfully commercial shipping can be pursued in these countries without the national military power one would expect necessary to underpin and protect it in times of crisis.

With the end of the Cold War and the subsequent defense retrenchment across Europe, the naval forces of both the Netherlands and Denmark have been fighting an uphill battle against continuously declining government spending. While initially, new and highly innovative warships were able to absorb the gradual decommissioning of older vessels, years of defense cuts have either forced the navies to drastically reduce the size of their fleet (as in the case of the Netherlands), or to give up certain capabilities altogether (as in the case of Denmark). No matter how much more capable the new warships, OPVs, and replenishment vessels are from a technical standpoint, current defense spending will not allow them to be used to their full potential, nor will it permit the navies to keep pace with naval developments elsewhere. This circumstance might in fact lead to a similar detriment both countries already had to painfully experience when their prosperous seaborne trade fell victim to extrinsic events and hostile actors who chose to pursue their interest by military means rather than benign cooperation, ultimately ending in years of hardship for many Danish and Dutch citizens.[6]

Denmark

Unlike some of its neighbors who have remained important actors in world affairs to this day, Danish maritime might had already been eclipsed by the early nineteenth century. Since then the Danish military has only been able to maintain comparatively small naval forces, despite the country's strategically important position at the entrance to the Baltic.[7] During the Cold War it was understood that the brunt of a Soviet naval attack from the Baltic Sea had to be absorbed by West German, Dutch, and Norwegian forces, whereas Denmark's small flotilla could provide modest support to ASW and ASuW operations against the Soviets around the Danish peninsula and the outlet to the North Sea. Heavy mining of the critical choke-point was essentially the primary task of the Kongelige Danske Marine or Søværnet within NATO planning.[8] By 1990, the Danish navy maintained a fleet of five relatively old diesel-electric subma-rines of Norwegian and German design, three small *Niels Juel*–class frigates, a number of patrol vessels with limited war fighting capabilities (mainly used for protecting national fishing rights), as well as a number of guided-missile craft and torpedo boats from the 1960s and 1970s.[9] As one of the stakeholders in the High North and Artic Circle (Greenland is part of the Danish Crown lands), vessels capable of operating in icy waters as well as icebreakers have been an important element of the Danish maritime capabilities. It is safe to say, however, that in the event of war between NATO and the Warsaw Pact, the small Danish fleet would have likely not been able to reach Greenland.[10]

By the time the Cold War had drawn to a close, the Søværnet could hardly be considered even a second-rate naval force and pending defense cuts made the future of the navy seem hardly encouraging. Faced with these challenges, Danish shipbuilders came up with one of the most innovative ship designs to date: the "Standard Flex." One commentator observed, "It seems somehow appropriate that the country that produced Lego should have been a pioneer of naval warship modularization."[11] In the 1980s, Danish shipbuilders had proposed a similar concept as the German MEKO design—namely that a ship should be able to quickly adapt and transform to the needs of the navy. To make such a flexible design possible, the Standard Flex 300 multi-role vessels (*Flyvefisken* class) were built, each with four StanFlex container positions onboard. In each position, "among others, medium caliber guns, anti-ship missile launching systems, air defense missile launching systems, MCM control systems, Variable Depth (VD) sonars, equipment for pollution control and hydrographic equipment"[12] could be fitted and, if needed, swapped within a few hours.[13] These containers "are precisely engineered to allow connections with power, cooling, communications, water and data supplies [and the] weapon system or sensor is mounted on, or in the module, with the electronics, power machinery, magazine and supporting equipment inside."[14] As part of the necessary restructuring of the Danish navy after the Cold War, the Committee Concerning the Danish Armed Forces' Equipment laid down a long-term procurement policy that stipulated or, better said, "recommended" that a large part of the fleet (seventeen ships) should be replaced by a total of six large vessels, all of which were to incorporate the StanFlex modules.[15] Two units would evolve into the *Absalon*-class command and support vessel, upon which the three highly innovative, multipurpose *Iver Huitfeldt*–class frigates are based. These five ships constitute the mainstay of today's Danish navy and will be described in further detail.

In many ways, parallels can be drawn between the development of both the Dutch and Danish naval forces and those of other European NATO members over the past twenty-five years. Many navies—such as the British, French, Italian, Spanish and German—have shifted their focus from operations against the Soviet navy in the Atlantic, North Sea, and approaches to the European continent to expeditionary, out-of-area operations, most notably around the African continent. In essence, crisis management and peace enforcement over great distances and, more importantly, from the sea onto land took precedence over the concept of defense of territory and SLOCs. Therefore, European fleets acquired larger vessels with notably better sea-keeping characteristics, which are also capable of conducting a wider range of missions and can remain at sea over longer periods of time. This common strategic reorientation during the 1990s and 2000s can be summarized as follows:

"Traditional blue water navies [were] taking an increasing interest in littoral warfare and navies, which so far [had] focused upon operations in their national brown waters, [and were] seeking to improve their blue water capability in order to offer their littoral warfare experience in other parts of the world."[16]

Denmark's effort to transform the Søværnet into a blue-water capable navy strained the small Danish defense budget to such a degree that vital capabilities had to be relinquished outright. Although Danish defense planners had made tentative provisions for a replacement of the nation's aging submarine flotilla (three to four AIP submarines, as part of the failed trilateral *Viking* program between Norway, Denmark, and Sweden[17]), the underwater force was disbanded in 2004 and it remains to be seen if growing security challenges in the Baltic will mandate the renewed procurement of these very expensive systems.[18] Considering Denmark's dependence on commercial shipping and its exposed geographical position at the entrance to the Baltic Sea, more cautious observers may be tempted to question the judgment of the former leadership responsible for the disbandment of the submarine program.

Shifting the focus to Denmark's surface fleet, the situation appears to be somewhat less dire. In 2003, the keel of the first 4,500-ton *Absalon*-class flexible support ship was laid down in the Maersk Odense Staalskibsværft. At a length of 137 meters and a width of 19.5 meters it was much larger than the *Niels Juel*–class corvettes, which throughout their service life had suffered under their "inherent size handicap which basically is reflected in a limited endurance."[19] Not only was the *Absalon* much larger, it was an entirely different kind of ship, and in many ways unique. The relatively large superstructure was designed to reduce the ship's radar cross section and houses a multipurpose "flex deck" that can carry various modules. Main battle tanks can be transported, as well as containerized hospital modules for HADR operations. Two landing craft can embark and up to 46 vehicles can be taken on board via the stern ramp. Even more flexibility is provided by the weapon modules installed amidships. Four quad Harpoon SSM launchers

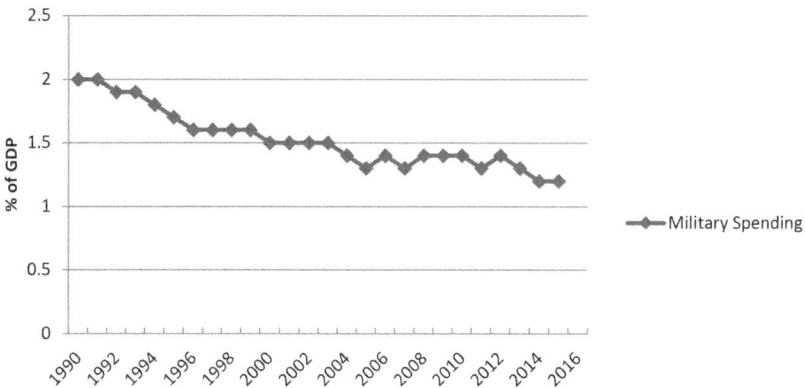

Figure 11-1. Denmark: Defense Spending in % of GDP, 1990–2015
Source: SIPRI Military Expenditure Database.

and 3 12-cell Mk 56 VLS find space between the main mast and funnels; they are able deploy a total of 36 ESSMs, in addition to the 16 Harpoon SSMs. A single 127-mm/62 caliber Mk 45 gun is mounted in the A position on the bow, which is overlooked by an Oerlikon 35-mm CIWS (B position). A second CIWS is mounted above the hangar. Finally, the *Absalon* class is designed to engage enemy surface and subsurface threats with its ship and helicopter-launched torpedoes.[20] Due to their impressive capabilities, these ships can rightfully be compared to other modern frigates, despite being appointed mainly to support duties.[21]

The reorganization of Denmark's defense sector continued throughout the first decade of the new millennium. The *Danish Defense Agreement 2005–2009* highlighted that "changes in the international security environment require[d] the Danish Defence to strengthen its capacities in two central areas: 1) Internationally deployable military capacities and 2) the ability to counter terror acts and their consequences."[22] As previously mentioned, the short-range submarine force was disbanded and a number of StanFlex 300 vessels and minelayers were phased out to gain sufficient funding for the rest of the fleet to "intervene in conflicts far beyond the immediate neighborhood that was the focus of operations during the Cold War,"[23] as part of NATO's Standing Naval Forces and Response Force.[24] At the same time, the country committed itself to the war on terrorism. In January 2002 the Danish Parliament decided to deploy its troops to Afghanistan as part of Operation Enduring Freedom. Its main battle tanks, infantry units, and special forces were heavily engaged over the course of the mission to Helmand Province and among all contributors, the country suffered the highest percentage of casualties.[25]

Although the Danish navy has been spared such painful experiences, it has been no less active in conducting joint maneuvers, providing its warships to NATO's standing maritime forces and participating in multinational naval operations. The list of Danish deployments is long: from Operation Desert Shield, the aforementioned Operation Sharp Guard in the Adriatic, and Operation Iraqi Freedom to the current deployments as part of the multinational Combined Task Force 150 and 151, where the *Absalon* has served as the task force's flagship. She and her sister ship have also been part of the NATO antipiracy operation around the Horn of Africa, known as Ocean Shield. (The Combined Task Force 151 is a multinational operation that cooperates closely with the European Union's Operation Atalanta and NATO's Operation Ocean Shield.)[26]

Over the years, Denmark has shown estimable willingness to participate in military and peacekeeping operations beyond its shores. Apart from its various naval activities and ongoing assistance to the Afghan government,[27] the Danish air force also took aggressive action in Libya in 2011. Surprisingly, the small number of Danish F-16 combat aircraft accounted for roughly 11 percent of all sorties flown against the Gaddafi regime. Considering that Denmark flew more sorties than Italy, which had the carrier *Giuseppe Garibaldi* deployed off the coast of Libya, this is quite a remarkable achievement.[28] Recent defense documents published by the Danish government indicate that the nation is willing to continue this effort, notwithstanding the significant shortage in personnel:[29] "The demand for Danish military contributions will not be diminished," one such document underscores.[30] The Danish armed forces, therefore, need to be able to conduct operations ranging from "armed conflict [to] stabilization tasks and international policing."[31] The production of the newest class of frigates, the *Iver Huitfeldt*, constituted a vital step toward enhancing "the ability of the Navy to participate in international operations, to support ground operations and to perform tasks in the North Atlantic and the Arctic."[32]

In naval circles, Denmark's principle surface combatant, the *Iver Huitfeldt* multipurpose frigate, has been one of the most discussed warships. It owes this flattering attention to the heated debate over the U.S. Navy's new frigate, also known as the littoral combat ship (LCS). Lightly armed and suffering with numerous teething problems, the current production variants of the LCS (the monohull LCS-1 *Freedom* class and the trimaran LCS-2 *Independence* class) have fallen out of favor in U.S. naval quarters. Despite their innovative design, which includes mission modules that were planned to be prepositioned in order for the ships to quickly adapt to new tasks in combat theaters, the rebalancing to a higher threat environment (Southeast Asia and the approaches to China) led two former secretaries of defense, Chuck Hagel and Ash Carter, to curtail production of the LCS. In a DOD press briefing, Hagel underscored these doubts by stating that "regarding the Navy's littoral combat ship, I am concerned that the Navy is relying too heavily on the LCS to achieve its long-term goals for ship numbers."[33] Quickly, many defense analysts were making the case for the U.S. Navy to drop the LCS altogether and preferably buy the Danish *Iver Huitfeldt* instead. I do not intend to add to the debate and would rather refer the reader to various articles on the subject.[34] The latest addition to the Danish navy does deserve closer attention. Naval journalist Guy Toremans provides an excellent overview of the *Iver Huitfeldt* class[35] and summarizes the development of the Danish navy over the past two decades: "With the introduction of the *Iver Huitfeldt*–class frigates, as well as the two *Absalon*-class flexible support ships, the RDN has been transformed from a 'small-ship' navy—focused on its adjacent waters—to a small 'big ship' force geared towards expeditionary operations at range from its home bases."[36]

The second version of the Flexible Støtteskibe (Flexible Support Ship) project capitalized on the experiences gained with the successful *Absalon* class. Given the tight defense budget, only three units (instead of four) were commissioned. Like its predecessors, the ships were also designed to utilize the advantages of the StanFlex system to the fullest. The hull is somewhat shorter than comparable surface combatants of other European navies, such as the German *Sachsen* or Dutch *Zeven Provinciën* class, but also noticeably wider. Even though a copious amount of off-the-shelf components were used in order to keep costs low, the frigates exhibit all the aspects of a state-of-the art warship. This includes "a comprehensive approach to signature reduction" with the missile launchers and other weapons installed behind a flushed superstructure that reduces the ship's radar cross section.[37] One of the main missions of the frigate is air defense. The modularity of the StanFlex weapons containers has proved expedient and the *Iver Huitfeldt* class can conceivably deploy 2 Mk 56 VLS for ESSMs in the E and F positions flanking the Mk 41 VLS centrally located between the main mast and the ships' funnels. The latter is able to fire a total of 32 Raytheon Standard SM-2 Block IIIA missiles and could also be updated to fire the SM-3 (capable of ABM defense), as well as Tomahawk cruise missiles. In combination with its APAR, active phased-array search and track radar and SMART-L long-range volume search radar, the ships' air-defense capabilities can rightfully be considered among the best in the world. Further, the radar system can be upgraded to track ballistic missile targets. In August 2014, the Danish government decided to go forward with its plans to join the NATO ABM missile shield and will invest around $70 million into modifying their SMART-L radar. However, there are currently no plans to procure the SM-3 missile, "the intention being that missile targets will be passed to other sea or land-based interceptors for engagement."[38] The decision was met with stark criticism from Moscow, causing the

Russian ambassador to Denmark to threaten the use of nuclear weapons against these ships.[39]

Confronted with Russia's supercharged rhetoric and growing military footprint in the Baltic and the North Atlantic, adequate funding remains a key concern within the Danish navy. This is not much of surprise given the country's sustained defense spending of around 1.4 percent of GDP over the last ten years. Despite making the smart decision to modernize the Søværnet, the Danish government discovered that the three *Iver Huitfeldt* frigates have proven to be quite expensive to operate, in spite of their relatively modest production costs. As the Danish chief of naval staff, Admiral Frank Trojahn, elaborates, "the high-end frigates/littoral combat ships are focused on international missions. [They] have been heavily engaged [and the] operational tempo is likely to remain high."[40] This puts great strain on both men and material. Given the declared "manpower problems,"[41] shared at least in some part by most other Western navies, the ships have all been designed to operate with a much smaller crew than their foreign counterparts. While the German, Dutch, and Italian frigates all require between 150 and 200 able-bodied sailors, the *Iver Huitfeldt* was envisioned to make due with a crew of 100. Yet Commander Fjord-Larsen has pointed to the impracticability of lean manning concepts. "The high level of specialization has potential problems because there is less slack available in the complement if someone goes sick or on leave. Personally, I think that we are at the lower end of the manning limit."[42] Lieutenant Commander Kenneth Jensen, deployed on the third unit of the class, the *Niels Juel,* acknowledges that the number was somewhat overoptimistic. As a consequence, seventeen more crew members are being hired in order to effectively operate the vessels.[43] Given the armed forces' manpower shortages, "the RDN may . . . face [increasing] manpower issue because the current Danish defense agreement does not currently provide the resources needed for three full crews," Toremans concludes.[44]

More problems related to the austere financial environment the Danish navy currently finds itself in become apparent when one

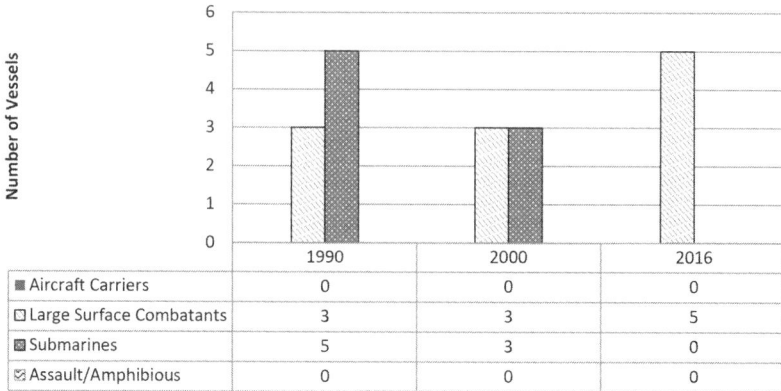

Figure 11-2. Denmark: Number of Major Vessels

Sources: *The Naval Institute Guide to Combat Fleets of the World, Military Technology Almanac, World Naval Review.*

takes a closer look at the latest fitting of the ships. The two 76-mm guns in the A and B positions are an interim solution until funds for the intended 127-mm/62 caliber Mk 45 gun and Oerlikon CIWS are approved. At the time of writing, the Mk 41 VLS was not yet armed, as the navy was waiting for the delivery of the Standard SM-2 missiles from the United States, while the two Mk 56 VLS have neither been bought nor installed; and finally, the CIWS on top of the helicopter hangar is in fact a dummy.[45] The ship's potential is unquestioned. However, both the incremental fitting of new combat systems and continuous deployment will heavily burden the crews as well as the defense budget.

The Danish navy has made great strides since the days of the Cold War. Over the past twenty-five years, the Odense Steel Shipyard has perfected the art of constructing multipurpose warships that can quickly and easily be reconfigured to conduct different tasks. From the navy's four small *Thetis* patrol boats to its large frigates, the StanFlex module fittings can accommodate anything from hydraulic cranes and towed sonar systems to rapid-fire guns and ESSM launchers. Despite its small size, the Danish navy has been very active; it has taken part in numerous multinational operations for more than two decades, playing a key role in antipiracy and antiterrorism operations in the Indian Ocean and Arabian Sea. The fleet's capable surface combatants also contribute to NATO's standing maritime groups.

Unfortunately, the fiscal realities of the post–Cold War era have ruled out the possibility of maintaining a more balanced fleet. With the defense budget steadily decreasing throughout the 1990s, leveling out at the 1.4 percent mark ($4.5 billion per year), the Danish armed forces did what they could to modernize their fleet. A deliberate decision was made to phase out the fleet's numerous smaller combatants as well as its submarines and instead, to build large multipurpose warships. As a result, the Danish fleet has been able to increase its power projection, as well as its amphibious warfare and air-defense capabilities. However, "today the fleet has no submarines, no fast attack craft and no dedicated minelayers."[46] This leaves questions as to what extent Denmark will be able to effectively deploy the remaining platforms in an increasingly contentious maritime environment abroad and, more importantly, closer to home. In addition, the melting of the polar caps will have profound geostrategic consequences, which is both exciting and vexing news for Copenhagen. Denmark's industry is heavily invested in commercial shipping—just barely maintaining its lead in this very competitive market—as well as in the exploration of natural resources, from the Baltic to the arctic waters around Greenland and the Faroe Islands. It is fair to say that Denmark's small navy will likely find it challenging to protect the country's national interests and effectively deal with the growing range of commitments in the future.

The Netherlands

By the end of the Cold War, the Royal Netherlands Navy (Koninklijke Marine) had rightfully earned its place among the world's most powerful navies. Its large fleet had been a force to reckon with, providing the Western allies with important sea-control capabilities for a large part of the Cold War. It is no wonder that in his authoritative almanac, *The Naval Institute Guide to the Combat Fleets of the World,* Bernard Prézelin mentions the Dutch navy in the same breath as the U.S., Soviet, Japanese, Italian, and Chinese navies.[47]

Designed to defend the critical strategic lines of communication in the North Sea and through the English Channel, the Dutch navy fashioned a large fleet of capable warships. In 1990, five domestically designed diesel-electric submarines were in service with the production of a follow-on class of four state-of-the-art boats under way. Two large guided-missile destroyers (the *Tromp* and *De Ruyter*)—easily recognizable by their large dome-construction housing the SPS-01 3D radar and armed with both Seasparrow and SM-1 MR missiles—had served in the air-defense role and as the fleet's flagship since the mid-1970s. Two of the 10 *Kortenaer*-class frigates had been sold to Greece in the early 1980s and were replaced by a modified version designed for the air-defense role.[48] A large class of minehunters was introduced throughout the 1980s and added significant capabilities to the already respectable MCM flotilla. Two large replenishment ships provided necessary fuel and supplies for the fleet conducting operations on the high seas and in protection of the Netherlands' overseas territories. Amphibious and littoral warfare capabilities, on the other hand, were quite limited, due to the geographical and strategic realities of the Cold War security environment. To keep a close eye on Soviet surface vessels and submarines, the Royal Netherlands Navy operated a total of 13 P-3C Orion anti-submarine and maritime surveillance aircraft as well as 22 WG-13 LYNX helicopters—all in all, a highly capable aviation element.

Like most NATO allies during this period, the Dutch navy relied heavily on American weapon systems, especially for AAW and ASW. Nonetheless, by the 1980s the country's defense industry had established itself as one of Europe's leaders in the field of electronics and sensor technology. Over time the Hollandse Signaalapparaten (or simply Signaal) became a powerhouse in the design and manufacturing of combat systems and radars. Among others, the APAR and SMART-L radars are highly successful systems developed by what is now known as Thales Naval Nederland.[49] The Netherlands were also able to maintain the proficiency to construct very large vessels in its shipyards at Vlissingen, Rotterdam, and Amsterdam and have cooperated closely with other European states to build powerful surface vessels. The trilateral frigate project between Holland, Germany, and Spain is but one example.

Though one runs the risk of confusing the procurement process of the Danish and Dutch naval forces since the end of the Cold War given the similar figures, there are some marked differences that should be considered. In 1999–2000, the Danish long-term procurement plan recommended the decommissioning of seventeen vessels, gradually being replaced by six (ultimately trimmed to five) new multipurpose frigates by 2011.[50] Interestingly, in the same period of time, the Dutch navy also decommissioned seventeen ships, adding only four new escort vessels to the fleet.[51] The main difference in the outcome of these processes is that while the Danish navy has been able to expand its naval capabilities in some important areas relative to other naval forces (also owing to the inherent limitations and obsolescence of its older warships), no such testimony can be made for the Dutch fleet. As Conrad Waters laments, "Once one of the more significant European maritime forces, the Royal Netherlands Navy has been progressively reduced in size and stature since the end of the Cold War until it barely ranks amongst Europe's second-tier fleet."[52]

This remarkable decline can largely be ascribed to two factors: first, the austerity measures during the decade following the Soviet breakup, when the defense budget plummeted from 2.5 percent to 1.5 percent of GDP; and second, the fact that the Dutch navy was faced with a number of large-scale procurement projects, such as the replacement of its submarines and large elements of its surface fleet. Four new *Walrus*-class submarines and eight *Karel Doorman* (or M-class) frigates entered service between 1990 and 1998.[53] In addition, the *Rotterdam* amphibious transport ship (a joint project between Spain's E. N. Bazán and Netherlands' Royal Schelde) was commissioned in 1998 and provided the navy with the ability to deploy a battalion of marines from a single ship.[54] This set of

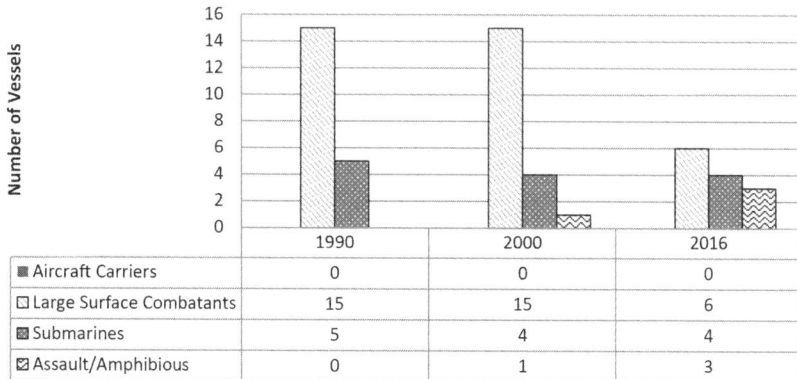

	1990	2000	2016
■ Aircraft Carriers	0	0	0
▢ Large Surface Combatants	15	15	6
▦ Submarines	5	4	4
☑ Assault/Amphibious	0	1	3

Figure 11-3. The Netherlands: Number of Major Vessels

Sources: *The Naval Institute Guide to Combat Fleets of the World, Military Technology Almanac, World Naval Review*.

capabilities was deemed necessary to allow the Dutch naval forces to expand their participation in multinational peacekeeping operations and to project military power over great distances. Accordingly, the commander in chief of the Royal Netherlands Navy, Vice Admiral Luuk Kroon, at the time reiterated these tasks as the key function of the armed forces:

> In order to fulfill these primary tasks [of crisis management as well as national and allied territorial defense] the Dutch armed forces will be capable of: Maintaining a capacity for simultaneous participation in a maximum of four peacekeeping operations under the aegis of the United Nations or the OSCE. In either case the contribution will have the size of a battalion, or equivalent; [as well as maintaining] rapidly deployable assets in peacetime for the protection of the NATO treaty area and for adequate contribution to peace-enforcing operations.[55]

Kroon also stressed that although the new security environment the navy found itself in "has its impact on the RNLN, the structure of the Navy [would] be unaffected."[56] And in fact only relatively modest reductions in the fleet's composition were initially made (as the graph illustrates). Rather, the organizational structure was streamlined, shedding some unnecessary ballast in the process. The somewhat more upbeat financial environment at the end of the 1990s gave the armed forces a short period of reprieve.[57] Maintenance costs and the overhead expenses were also reduced by the withdrawal of two *Tromp*-class destroyers and four *Kortenaer* frigates. Meanwhile, the four new *De Zeven Provinciën* air-defense frigates were laid down and a comprehensive modernization to the fleet's aging ships and aircraft seemed to be secured. The acquisition of a second LPD as well as the procurement of the new NH90 helicopter by 2007 was stipulated in the Dutch defense white paper of 2000.[58] However, in hindsight, the principle goals of the white paper, namely to increase the armed forces' combat readiness and ability to sustain power-projection operations over longer periods of time, were probably overly optimistic and could not be met under the growing fiscal restriction.[59]

Marcial Hernandez of the American Enterprise Institute provides some insight into the momentous decline of the Netherlands' armed forces throughout the previous decade: "With the exception of the bump in the Dutch base defense budget in 2001, [any] increase in defense expenditures has largely gone to Dutch operations needs connected with the Netherlands' deployment to Afghanistan. With the base defense budget . . . remaining essentially flat until [2015] and with the government's [past decision] to cut planned defense spending substantially, the result is a Dutch military that falls well short of the 2000 white paper's goals."[60]

A brief glance at the military force structure is telling: in 1990, the Dutch army had more than 900 main battle tanks. Today it has nil—having sold its last units to Finland in 2014.[61] Current efforts, such as to integrate Dutch mechanized forces into Germany's 1st Panzer Division, exemplify Europe's growing defense cooperation but highlight its apparent lack of heavy forces. The Dutch air force, for example, has lost more than half of its F-16 fighters and the navy has been stripped of all its P-3C maritime patrol aircraft. Last but not least, the navy's escort fleet has shrunk from 15 frigates and destroyers in 1990, to merely 6 ships.[62] This process has been accompanied by a reduction of the active-duty force (including civilian employees) from 103,000 to 53,300 by 2016. Since 2011 alone over 12,000 jobs have been cut. That such measures will likely have long-term effects on the Netherlands' military capabilities is self-evident.

In terms of numbers, the decommissioning of all but two *Karel Doorman*–class frigates (two were sold to Belgium, with which the Netherlands has an exemplary joint defense agreement[63]) left a large gap in the navy's escort fleet. The defense cooperation with Belgium and the introduction of the *De Zeven Provinciën*–class air-defense frigates, formally known as the LCF (Luchtverdedigings en Commandofregat) have partially filled this gap. The trilateral cooperation between Spain (F-100), Germany (F-124), and the Netherlands (LCF) has been discussed at length. The ships' capabilities are largely on par with the two foreign designs and can be considered highly capable platforms. In contrast to the Spanish Álvaro de Bazán class, which uses the Aegis combat system, the Dutch ships rely on the SEWACO IX combat system as well as the APAR and SMART-L radars, all designed by Thales. The above-mentioned upgrades to the long-range radar, to track (and engage) ballistic missiles, are under way and scheduled to be completed in 2017.[64] Akin to the decisions of Germany, Spain, and Denmark, the Dutch government has not shown any intention to buy the Standard SM-3 missile, rather relying on U.S. ABM-capable ships based in the naval port at Rota (Spain) and land-based facilities in Poland and Romania.

Based on NATO force levels requirements and the general approach of the Netherlands' closest allies (U.S., U.K., and Belgium), the Dutch navy continued to strengthen its amphibious capabilities with the goal to deploy brigade-sized elements in high-intensity operations.[65] The 28,000-ton joint support ship *Karel Doorman* is arguably the most significant result of this effort. Fighting an uphill battle against unabated defense cuts during the height of the European economic crisis, the completion of the *Karel Doorman* was under question several times: "Additional reductions in defense spending revealed in September 2013 [threatened] to see the new joint support ship . . . sold before she had even entered into service."[66] Fortunately, this decision was revoked and she formally entered service in 2014, adding considerable power projection and capabilities to the Dutch navy. Moreover, the Netherlands and Germany have signed a far-reaching agreement that includes the joint use of the *Karel Doorman* and deploying the German navy's Seebatallion from the ship.

The third high profile acquisition was that of the four *Holland*-class patrol vessels, commissioned between 2011 and 2013. At a total displacement of 3,750 tons, these ships exhibit characteristic features of the current trend toward larger and more sophisticated off-shore patrol vessels. Though being lightly armed, these new OPVs are well suited to their intended mission environment; designed for low-intensity operations, they constitute the "workhorse of the maritime security mission."[67] With no need for expensive long-range weapon systems and powerful propulsion for sustained high speeds, they are more affordable to build and to operate than first-rate warships. Moreover, the systems onboard the latest OPV's, such as the *Holland* class, are specifically designed to conduct antiterrorism, antipiracy, and other constabulary tasks on the high seas.[68] Deploying an exorbitantly expensive air-defense destroyer to stop and search a rogue dinghy in the Gulf of Aden, despite being common practice, does not represent the most efficient way of dealing with such maritime security challenges. Therefore, the new patrol boats offer the Dutch navy much-needed capabilities in low-threat environments (such as policing of their overseas territories). Conversely, they do not qualify as first-rate warships because they cannot provide the necessary deterrent and operational advantages of a ship of similar size but heavier armament, such as the older frigates (i.e., *Karel Doorman*).[69] Considering the Netherlands' self-imposed liabilities and the country's continued effort to play an active role in multi-national operations across the intensity spectrum, the decision to reduce the escort fleet to only six frigates can rightfully be viewed with reservations.

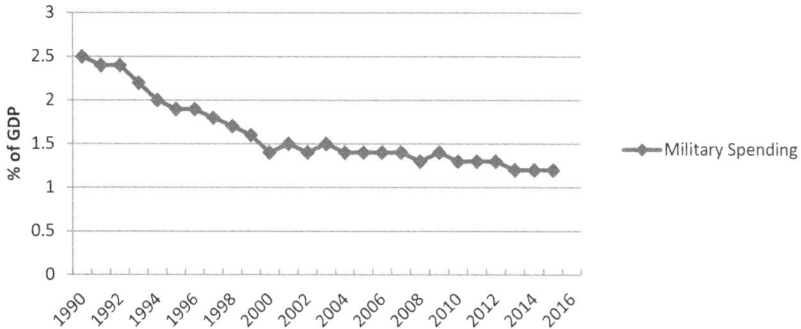

Figure 11-4. The Netherlands: Defense Spending in % of GDP, 1990–2013
Source: SIPRI Military Expenditure Database.

Since 1990, "ongoing cuts to the Dutch defence budget have had a dramatic effect on the size and effectiveness of the RNLN," a Dutch naval analyst noted.[70] While a similar development can be observed in nearly all other Western navies, over the last two decades, successive Dutch governments have failed to make necessary provision for the navy to successfully adapt to the post–Cold War security environment but have largely stood by while traditional naval capabilities have withered away. Relative to others, as of 2017 the Dutch military and its naval branch are both smaller and less well-balanced than their equivalent of twenty-five years ago. Despite efforts to cooperate more closely with other NATO allies and a substantial reorganization of its force composition and command structure, these measures were not sufficient to outweigh the negative impact the fiscal restraints have had on the military. This is not to say that the Netherlands should return to their former war footing, given the general security the country enjoys. "Obviously, no one expects the Netherlands to sustain a military the size and character of the one it had during the height of the Cold War,"[71] Marcial Hernandez underscores. However, a country with the fifth-highest GDP per capita in Europe[72] that spends more than 50 percent of its budget on health care and social services,[73] it can be argued, should be expected to allocate a little more toward its national defense than it has in the recent past.

The Netherlands is inevitably dependent on the security of the global SLOCs, the good order at sea, as well as NATO's deterrent posture and its promise of collective defense to maintain their wealth and prosperity. However, this fact seems neither to have struck a chord with the Dutch population nor with their elected representatives. As a result, the navy's effort to enhance its capabilities has largely remained unsuccessful. Ultimately, after a quarter-century of reductions, it is time that the Netherlands rethinks its defense priorities and recalibrates its budget appropriation accordingly.

CHAPTER 11

Sweden and Norway

Scandinavian Navies Sticking to Their Guns?

The two Scandinavian countries described in this chapter provide a good example of how smaller European navies have been rather successful in adapting to the changes in the global security environment since the end of the Cold War. Although the graphs below indicate a steady decrease in defense appropriation, the navies of Norway and Sweden are able to deal with a broader range of maritime tasks than they were twenty-five years ago. More importantly, unlike many other navies in Europe, they still remain capable of conducting sea-control, sea-denial, and territorial-defense operations. Notwithstanding cost-saving measures, neither country is committed to the general fallacy that the end of the Cold War heralded an era of smaller threats, hence, reduced needs. On the contrary, the political and military leadership have for the most part made wise choices in how to best modernize their fleets under difficult fiscal conditions. Defense cooperation has been considered crucial as has the development of leap-ahead technologies. Consequently, the navies of Norway and Sweden arguably rank among the most innovative small navies in the world.

A major reason not to include Denmark in this chapter, but rather to draw comparisons between the Dutch and Danish navies, is founded in these respective states' underlying political and military strategies. As we have seen, many European navies underwent a far-reaching strategic reorientation after the end of the Cold War. The principle of sea control, so it seemed, had to give way to the idea of crisis management in the littorals far from Europe. Both Denmark and the Netherlands made what they believed were necessary adjustments to their defense policies and built large and expensive warships capable of conducting amphibious operations, but consequently had to cede other, more traditional, naval capabilities in return. None of the other Scandinavian states (including Finland) were willing to take such a risk. Geographic and political realities (lack of NATO membership, the continued perceived threat posed by Russia) arguably trumped the idea of creating expeditionary-focused fleets for peace enforcement in distant regions of the world.

Sweden

In October 2014, several eyewitnesses reported suspicious underwater activity near the Stockholm archipelago. In the days that followed, the Swedish military conducted one of the largest submarine hunts since the end of the Cold War. To date, the identity of what was believed to be a small submarine remains shrouded in mystery. This incident came at a time of increased tensions between Europe and Russia due to the forced annexation of Crimea and Russian support to the separatists in eastern Ukraine. Western media was quick to point to Russia's aggressive naval buildup as the only possible source of the incursion. Regardless of the origin and nature of the sighting, the incident provided the Swedish armed forces with an opportunity to display the credibility of its naval capabilities.

For over three decades, the Royal Swedish Navy has gone to great lengths to build and maintain a small, yet highly capable fleet. This effort originates in Sweden's status as a nonaligned state and the requirement to defend its territory and people on its own.[1] Located on the Baltic Sea—one of the world's most critical junctions of energy, commerce, data, as well as converging political interests—the country's national defense strategy has relied on similar strategic principles as its neighbors Finland and Norway, namely territorial defense. Over the larger part of the Cold War, the navy's main duty was to defend the country from aggression from the sea. For that purpose, the fleet was conceived as a sea-denial force. To date, the navy is still designed to protect Sweden from hostile incursion or even invasion. While other European nations were quickly lulled to sleep by the ostensible absence of great power rivalry, Sweden remained vigilant, albeit with quickly shrinking financial means. The military's outlook is reflected in the remarks of Vice Admiral Peter Nordbeck in an interview from 1996. Although the chief of the Swedish navy pointed out that at the time there was no direct threat to Swedish sovereignty, caution was well advised:

> The fact remains . . . that Europe is still resolving many areas of conflict and that all nations do indeed value military strength to support their international security politics. Therefore we cannot, within the foreseeable future, neglect the risks of war and that Sweden could be subject to an armed aggression. [The] main task for the Swedish Armed Forces is to demonstrate such a wartime operations capability that it deters an aggressor from planning or executing any armed attack against our country.[2]

With these directives in mind, the Swedish navy was designed to "deny the aggressor secure sea lines of communication to Sweden; establish full control over [Swedish] territorial waters; and defend [Swedish] ports and naval bases."[3]

To better understand the evolution of the Swedish naval forces we have to go further back in time, to another fateful naval incident that occurred in 1981. In October of that year, the Soviet S-363, *Whiskey*-class submarine, ran aground only ten kilometers from a Swedish naval base, supposedly having lost its ability to navigate. For many observers, the "Whiskey on the Rocks" incident provided evidence that the Soviet Union was regularly conducting illegal intrusions into Swedish territorial waters. As a result, a vigorous effort was undertaken to modernize the Swedish fleet. The navy's anti-submarine warfare capabilities in particular were enhanced, while a more balanced approach toward ASuW and MCM capabilities was conceived. New submarines and larger corvettes were to complement a sophisticated sea-denial network composed of underwater acoustic sensors, minefield, and coastal artillery.[4] "Seldom has a single peacetime event had such profound an impact on the development of a navy," senior naval analyst Hans Harboe-Hansen notes.[5]

By 1990, the Swedish navy had evolved into an effective fighting force, operating within the confined waters of the Baltic Sea and adjacent North Sea. Its domestically produced submarine flotilla consisted of four new *Västergötland*-class, three *Näcken*-class, and five older, but still capable, *Sjöormen*-class submarines. Pioneering the Swedish iteration of air-independent propulsion, the Kockums shipbuilder in Malmö installed an additional Stirling closed-cycle diesel engine into a six-meter hull extension onboard the *Näcken*. This not only enabled the boat to carry out operations at much lower acoustic levels but increased the time it could stay submerged to almost two weeks.[6] Based on the experiences gained with the Sterling propulsion in the *Näcken*, all three AIP *Gotland*-class submarines were delivered to the Royal Swedish Navy in 1996, underpinning the already renowned underwater capabilities. At the time, Admiral Nordbeck expanded on the capabilities of this new vessel: "The greatest threat against conventional submarines occur when they are forced to snort when charging their batteries. With the Gotland class we are receiving the first non-experimental AIP conventional submarine in the world. In combination with the diesel-electric machinery we are doubling the operational time at sea. [However this] is no reason to reduce the total … number of submarines."[7]

The Swedish surface fleet consisted of nearly three dozen fast-attack craft, armed with torpedoes, Saab RBS-15 SSMs, the

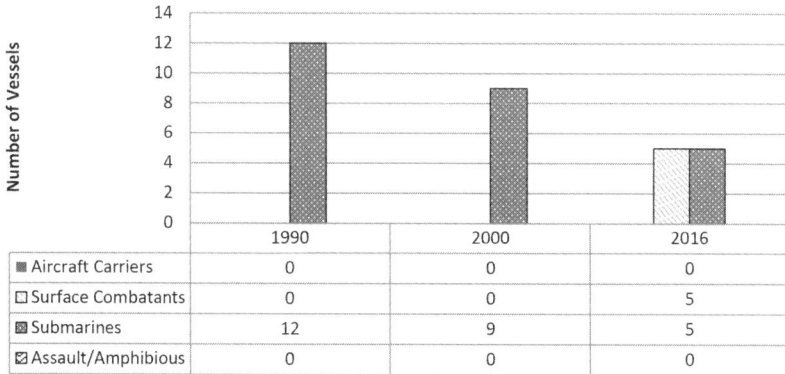

	1990	2000	2016
■ Aircraft Carriers	0	0	0
☐ Surface Combatants	0	0	5
▩ Submarines	12	9	5
☑ Assault/Amphibious	0	0	0

Figure 12-1. Sweden: Number of Major Vessels

Sources: *The Naval Institute Guide to Combat Fleets of the World, Military Technology Almanac, World Naval Review.*

Norwegian Penguin Mk 2 SSM, as well as 57-mm Bofors guns. The RBS-15 was a fire-and-forget weapon so no large shipborne target illuminators had to be installed. Moreover, the navy was designed to operate under the umbrella of the Swedish air force; hence, antiaircraft weapon systems (apart from the Bofors gun, which could also be used against aerial threats)[8] were also considered superfluous. As they were largely focused on operating in relative proximity to the Swedish coast (in the Baltic Sea and the Gulf of Finland), none of the ships needed a powerful propulsion system for high-speed transitions over long distances, allowing the warships to be of rather small size.

Sweden's maritime intelligence-gathering efforts are particularly noteworthy. Few navies, especially not small ones, are willing to invest their scarce resources in ships specifically designed to conduct intelligence operations (collecting signals intelligence, for example). For the most part, regular naval vessels are assigned such duties. Historically, submarines have lent themselves to such operations, utilizing their inherent stealth characteristics to operate almost unimpeded and gain vital information regarding the enemy's strength, movement, and intent. In some cases, submarines were also used to tap or cut underwater communication cables.[9] However, for obvious reasons, specialized vessels are even more effective in conducting these tasks. Sweden's *Orion* intelligence-gathering ship is one of few such vessels in service among European navies.[10]

Besides the *Gotland*-class submarine, the YS2000 corvette represented Sweden's second major procurement project in the post–Cold War era. Radically different in its appearance, this surface combatant broke new ground in naval ship design. Preliminary drawings of the ship hinted at the uncompromising application of state-of-the-art technology; signature reduction across the entire spectrum lies at the heart of the corvette's clean, sharp lines. Water jets, powered by a combined diesel or gas (CODOG) propulsion system, enables the ship to reach sprint speeds of up to 35 knots while long-duration missions are also possible at lower speeds. Substantial automation has reduced the number of hands necessary to operate the ship at sea. This is an important factor on a ship that displaced no more than 650 tons fully loaded. "[Despite the relative scarcity of space, the] living conditions and accommodation provided for the complement of six officers, twenty petty officers and seventeen ratings is excellent. This is partly a reflection of the specialist nature of the crew, who have to maintain high standards of efficiency and flexibility to operate and understand multi-task software and to handle extremely complicated instruments and sensors."[11]

The sensor and weapon suite of each vessel is equally impressive for a ship of such small size. Most systems on board are of Swedish origin. For example, the ship's Sea Giraffe radar is built by Saab Systems as is the CEROS 200 fire-control director, which is necessary to direct the Bofors 57-mm/70 Mk 3 cannon. The gun itself is mounted in a stealth turret to minimize the ship's radar cross section. Additional AAW capabilities have been tentatively planned. For the moment, the reported price tag of $150 million for 5 South African Umkhonto SAM systems appears to be too expensive for Sweden's MOD.[12] In light of the deployment of advanced sea-skimming anti-ship missiles (K-300P Bastion-P) in Kaliningrad and increased tensions with Russia, more robust air-defense capabilities might become necessary.[13] Moreover, "such a capability is an essential requirement for the Royal Swedish Navy if it is to participate in international naval activities."[14]

The main reason to include the *Visby* class in Figure 12-1 (although it cannot be classified as a "large surface combatant") is based on the ship's ability to effectively operate in littoral waters, as well as on the open seas. Commander Erik Uhren commented on the latest improvements, which include a sonar system and landing system for Lynx helicopter, noting that they "are intended to allow the corvettes to participate in EU and NATO task groups on 'out-of-area' operations and exercises."[15] The modular design enables the *Visby*-class ships to adapt to new threats that might arise and will give these (somewhat) multipurpose surface combatants sufficient room to grow in the future.

Cooperation between Sweden and its neighbors has expanded significantly over the past two decades. The Nordic Defense Cooperation between the Scandinavian states (which includes Iceland), despite being based on "a cooperation structure, not a command structure,"[16] has resulted in a very high degree of political and military collaboration. Moreover, the Swedish defense policy has highlighted the need to increase the armed forces' participation in international operations and to provide significant capabilities to the European Rapid Reaction Force.[17] In this context, Sweden's defense cooperation with Finland is particularly interesting. Originally outlined in a defense white paper more than ten years ago,[18] this fruitful effort was reiterated by Sweden's defense minister, Karin Enström, in a recent interview: "As regards defense cooperation between Sweden and Finland, both countries signed an action plan for deepened cooperation in May [2014]. This plan aims at increasing capabilities and efficiency through combined use of resources, increased interoperability and a closer dialogue on common challenges."[19]

Sweden is strengthening its partnership with the Baltic States and consequently with NATO as a whole. Although public support for joining the alliance remains well below the 50 percent margin, this step remains a matter of open discussion, not least because of

Russia's recent behavior and belligerent military posture.[20] Currently, Swedish forces are contributing to NATO operations as part of the Partnership for Peace initiative and can be rightfully considered "NATO's most active and most capable partner."[21] Jan Joel Andersson also points to the fact that "many in the political and military establishments in Sweden and Finland have grown increasingly positive about [joining NATO]."[22] Ultimately, however, any such decision will have to be made by the general public of both countries, the majority of which still remain skeptical.

Despite some analysts' remarks that Sweden's admission into NATO is a "no-brainer,"[23] it remains unlikely that the country will join the alliance in the near future. Consequently, the Swedish government will be hard-pressed to continue its investment in naval capabilities in order to protect the country's territorial integrity and strengthen its political and military ties with its Western partners. In contrast to many other countries, Sweden has shown no interest in building an amphibious capability worth noting. Should the Swedes become more engaged internationally, the need to create an even more balanced fleet is likely to arise sometime in the future. Costly provisions would have to be made to effectively project power over greater distances as well to operate a fleet capable of dealing a broader range of security challenges farther away from home.

For the time being, the focus remains clearly set on security matters close to home and important steps are being made to steadily modernize the existing force. The introduction of two new A-26–class submarines is scheduled for the end of the decade while the latest fitting of mine-clearance equipment onboard the *Visby*-class vessels will contribute to the navy's mine warfare capabilities. In addition, $40 million is being allocated toward the procurement of a new SIGINT ship to replace the aging *Orion*.[24] With defense spending reaching an all-time low in 2014, the Swedish government has announced that it is willing to invest in excess of $2 billion over next 5 years in order to strengthen its armed forces.[25] With an increase in spending, Sweden's defense industry will be better positioned to maintain its technical prowess and innovative naval

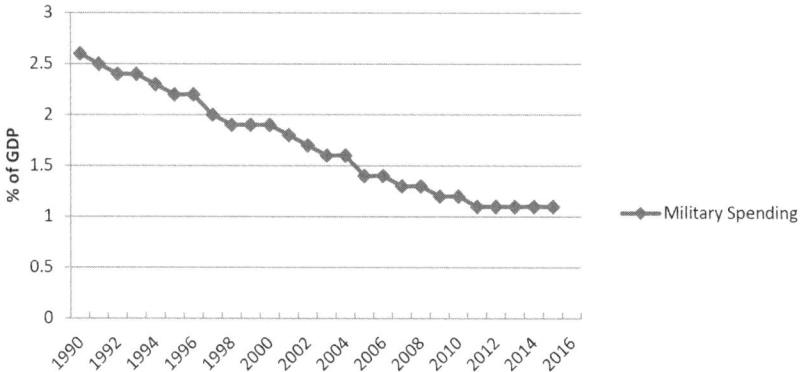

Figure 12-2. Sweden: Defense Spending in % of GDP, 1990–2015
Source: SIPRI Military Expenditure Database.

craftsmanship, while the Royal Swedish Navy in turn will be provided with greater means to live up to the high standards it has set for itself.

Norway

Given its unique geographical position in northern Europe, Norway has played an important role throughout the twentieth and early twenty-first century. While Norway remained a neutral ally to the Entente during the First World War, German forces invaded Norway in 1940 and occupied its territory until the end of the war, utilizing its geographical position to threaten Allied naval units in the North Atlantic. During the era of the Cold War, Norway's proximity to the mainstay of the Soviet Union's naval forces around the Kola Peninsula was of particular significance. From a naval perspective, the defense of Norway would have been a true litmus test for the U.S. efforts to repel a Soviet attack on the West. Even if the initial thrust of the Red Army through central Europe could have been brought to a halt, or at least slowed down, the European allies were dependent on reinforcements from America via the strategic lines of communication across the Atlantic to win a possible war of attrition against a numerically superior enemy. The Soviet navy, so it was feared, could utilize its large submarine fleet to rush out from its sea bastion in the High North and raise havoc among the convoys crossing the Atlantic. Faced with the continuous growth of the Soviet naval capabilities during the 1970s, U.S. maritime strategy focused primarily on protecting its convoys; the doctrine envisioned small carriers (such as the *Principe de Asturias* later built by Spain) and their assigned escort fleet engaging the Soviet "hunter-killer" submarines.

John Lehman, secretary of the navy during the Reagan administration, strenuously objected to any such defensive plans. Under his auspices, a new American "Maritime Strategy" doctrine statement was commissioned, which planned to put full-forward pressure on the Soviet Union's flanks, such as the Mediterranean and North Sea, as well as in other theaters of war (Pacific, Middle East). Moreover, areas of Soviet sea control, for example, the sea bastions in the High North, would be challenged by the deployment of large elements of U.S. naval forces, directly threatening the Soviet ballistic-missile submarines and thereby relieving pressure on the central front.[26] However, the entire plan hinged on confining Soviet naval forces to the waters north of the GIN gap (Greenland-Iceland-Norway gap, also called the GIUK gap[27]) in order for NATO to reinforce the northern and central front.[28] Defending Norway, and thus being able to use it as a base of operations, was considered pivotal. In fact, provisions were made for American, Canadian, British, and Danish ground forces to support the Norwegian army against the likely attempt by the Soviet Union to occupy Norwegian territory. To this end, territorial defense lay at the heart of Norwegian defense planning.

The concept of territorial defense was also reflected in the composition of the Royal Norwegian Navy (RNoN) at the end of the Cold War. Ten modernized German Type 207 submarines were operational with a class of six *Ula* (Type 210) boats entering service between 1990 and 1992. The five *Oslo*-class missile frigates were based on an older U.S. design and exhibited robust ASW, AAW, and ASuW capabilities. The two *Sleipner*-class corvettes were over thirty-five years old. Although they were "attractively modelled corvettes, [they were] obsolescent even in the coastal protection role."[29] The opposite can be said about many of the navy's guided missile patrol craft. Their primary task was to defend the shores from an enemy invasion fleet. In this role, their highly potent Penguin SSM qualified them as a significant deterrent force. The Norwegian naval shipbuilding industry also invested heavily in mine warfare vessels. A class of air-cushion minesweepers under construction in the early 1990s represented a first step in Norway's revolutionary utilization of this technology.[30]

Even after the seismic shift in world politics at the end of the Cold War, the aforementioned defensive strategy mindset remained prevalent among Norway's leadership. In their view, the country would have to become more self-reliant when it came to national defense, as Admiral Torolf Rein, chief of defense of Norway, elaborated in the mid-1990s:

> From being situated at a pivotal point of opposed superpower interests, in the eyes of our allies, Norway is in the process of being reduced to an ally of marginal interest, located at the outskirts of the current events. . . . With this background I, therefore, do not see any development that entails a fundamental change in the assessment of the challenges our defense forces could be faced with.[31]

The threat of invasion and the necessary provisions to "prevent an enemy from quickly gaining a foothold on Norwegian soil"[32] continued to dictate the shape of the Royal Norwegian Navy.

Although the defense budget had shrunk considerably by the mid-1990s, the size of the fleet remained largely intact. More important, as Admiral Rein stressed at the time, was the quality of the fighting force. "For the Navy the maintenance of a high quality submarine [and surface] force was essential for [Norway's] ability to counter an amphibious assault and to prevent enemy naval

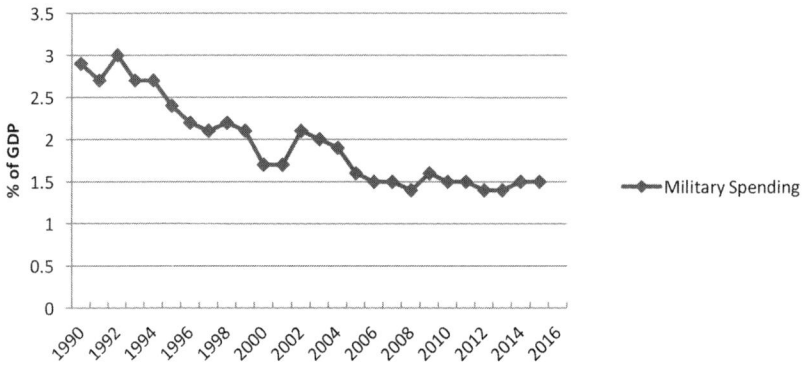

Figure 12-3. Norway: Defense Spending in % of GDP, 1990–2015

Source: SIPRI Military Expenditure Database.

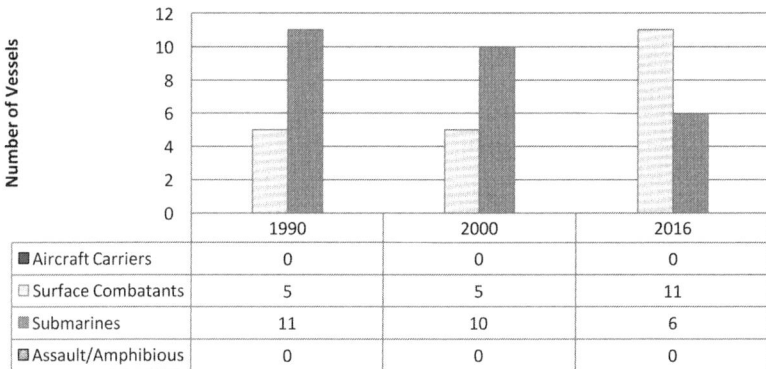

	1990	2000	2016
■ Aircraft Carriers	0	0	0
▢ Surface Combatants	5	5	11
▨ Submarines	11	10	6
▨ Assault/Amphibious	0	0	0

Figure 12-4. Norway: Number of Major Vessels

Sources: *The Naval Institute Guide to Combat Fleets of the World, Military Technology Almanac, World Naval Review.*

domination of Norway's territorial waters."[33] Consequently, weapon systems were continuously upgraded and naval personnel kept at a high level of readiness.[34]

In regard to its territory, a brief glimpse at a map of Norway makes it easy to identify the country's inherent strategic vulnerabilities. While the southern tip is 1,750 kilometers from the northern shores, most of its territory only expands a few hundred kilometers from the coast inland. The Norwegian hinterland is largely dominated by rough mountainous terrain, thus forcing the population to live close to the sea. Moreover, the few land lines of communication, running from north to south, could be easily enfiladed in the case of war. This means that the "coastal Sea Lines of Communication are of the utmost importance . . . and protecting [them] is therefore one of the major missions of the RNoN," Admiral Rein stressed.[35]

To protect the SLOCs a new class of frigates was to be delivered to the navy between 2004 and 2010. After the *Oslo* (F-300) ran aground and sunk in 1994, only four ships of the class remained in service and by the year 2000—and all were reaching the end of their respective service lives. Their successors were planned to be far larger (4,900 tons compared to 1,670 tons) and considerably more capable in all areas of warfare. Initially, proposals from three different manufacturers were considered but in the end Spain's Empresa Nacional Bazán (now Navantia) was awarded the $1.6 billion contract to build a class of five ships.[36] From the start it was clear that the project would prove to be immensely expensive for a relatively small country such as Norway, whose entire yearly defense budget amounted to approximately $5.5 billion. Although the construction process was spread out over a long period of time to save costs, the new frigates amounted to roughly a fifth of a Norway's entire annual defense budget. In comparison, the most expensive procurement project in the history of the U.S. Navy is the latest order of ten *Virginia*-class submarines worth $17.5 billion. However, the U.S. defense budget amounts to roughly $600 billion.[37]

While many foreign frigates were either too expensive or did not provide the desired capabilities, the Navy Material Command Norway decided "not to procure an off-the-shelf design from abroad,"[38] but instead to buy a ship that satisfied the navy's needs. The result of this effort was the *Fridtjof Nansen*–class frigate, which entered service with only a year's delay (very little in comparison to other projects). Compared to other European frigates, such as the Dutch *Zeven Provinciën,* the German F-124, or the FREMM class, the

Norwegian vessels are somewhat smaller and less heavily armed. However, their sophisticated sensors and combat systems nonetheless make them very capable warships.

The *Nansen's* design is similar to that of the Spanish Àlvaro de Bazán, which is not surprising given that both types were designed and built by Navantia. While the Spanish frigates are the smallest vessels to carry the American SPY-1D radar, the Norwegian surface combatants, at two-thirds the displacement of their Spanish counterparts, also use the Lockheed Martin Aegis system. However, they have to rely on a scaled-down version of the radar—the SPY-1F. It could conceivably be used to fire the Standard SM-2 missile, yet only the Evolved Seasparrow Missile is currently deployed in a single 8-cell Mk 41 VLS. The ship relies on the Italian Oto Melara 76-mm/62 caliber gun to engage air, surface, and land targets. (Note that many foreign frigates already have larger 127-mm guns.) Its hull-mounted sonar is provided by Thales and the new NH90 helicopter can be deployed for ASW operations in addition to the ship's Stingray torpedoes. Further space has been reserved for two quad SSM launchers, firing the Kongsberg's stealthy Naval Strike Missile. Despite having undergone successful testing at the RIMPAC exercise,[39] the missile has, as of 2017, only been integrated into one of the five vessels. Further, no CIWS system has yet been fitted either. Notwithstanding these shortcomings, the *Fridtjof Nansen* class has enabled the Royal Norwegian Navy to punch well above its weight.

Needless to say, these improvements come at a substantial price: the entire project cost more than $2 billion, putting the navy under substantial financial pressure. In fact, in 2013 rumors surfaced that the third ship of the class, the *Otto Sverdrup,* was no longer operational because it was being stripped for spare parts in order to keep the rest of the class in frontline service.[40] Arguably, stagnant defense spending over the past few years has been one reason for this development.

On a more positive note, after a long-pending decision, all six *Skjold* air-cushion attack-missile craft have been ordered. Initially planned as a class of twenty-four to replace the aging fleet of small surface combatants, the highly complex stealth craft underwent "comprehensive testing with focus on speed, sea-keeping, [electromagnetic compatibility], signature and functionality, as well as the operational reliability tests—mainly in northern Norway [where the sea-conditions are particularly demanding]."[41] These tests were necessary as the design of the *Skjold* probed unknown territory in ship design. In fact, it took ten years for the second unit of the class to be commissioned.

At first glance it is obvious that these warships differ in most respects from what we have seen in naval shipbuilding thus far. Most parts of the hull and bridge structure are made of carbon fiber to increase its stealth features. The propulsion system is based on the experiences gained with the navy's air-cushion minesweepers and is designed around four gas turbines driving two water jets (similar to those in the Swedish *Visby* class). In order to maintain speeds of over 40 knots (75 km/h), two lift fans located in the bow blow air into the pocket between and under the catamaran's hull. The bow and keel of the ship are sealed by rubber flaps, thus enabling it to ride on a cushion of air (also known as surface effect). Speeds of up to 60 knots (>110 km/h) have been reached, making it the fastest naval vessel in the world.[42]

At the same time these ships pack a powerful punch. A single 76-mm/62 caliber gun is installed on the ship's deck, while two retractable quad launchers for the Naval Strike Missile are located aft of the bridge. Portable Mistral SAM launchers can also be installed for point air defense. Despite being quite small in size, they are not only among the most innovative warships designed to date, but can rightfully be considered an essential element of Norway's fleet of surface combatants, "capable of contributing substantially to a wide range of operations in both the littoral and in blue water. Although designed to patrol Norway's littoral waters, the units have already proved to be amongst the most flexible [naval] assets."[43] A lengthy deployment as part of the U.S. Navy in 2002 and 2003 proved that long-distance, out-of-area operations were not only possible but that "[the ship's] top speed of 60 knots could prove quite useful to the EU or NATO counter-piracy operations."[44]

As Norway slowly freed itself from its somewhat parochial concept of territorial defense and shifted toward a more multinational-
oriented defense policy at the turn of the millennium, so did the
Royal Norwegian Navy. Consecutive defense white papers in the
mid-2000s stated that, apart from securing Norwegian sovereignty, the contribution to multinational crisis management, which
included multilateral peace operations, were to be furthered:[45] "Our
security cannot be maintained through a one-sided focus on the
conventional defence of Norwegian territory,"[46] one such capstone
document stated. A further publication in 2008 emphasized the
latter point by postulating that "Norway's most important contribution to the strengthening of international, and therefore Norwegian
security, is active and constructive participation in the UN and
NATO."[47] As a result of these decisions, Norway's shore-defense
artillery was disbanded[48] and its naval forces became more actively
engaged in cooperative endeavors (such as joint exercises with its
Scandinavian and Baltic neighbors and the EU antipiracy operations off the coast of Somalia), while its sister services have been
deployed to Afghanistan, Mali, South Sudan, and the Middle East.

In the long term, however, the focus of Norway's attention
will remain directed toward the High North and the Arctic. Even
before Russia's intervention in eastern Ukraine, the Armed Forces
Joint Headquarters was moved from Stavanger to Bod, inside the
Arctic Circle; all military operations have been directed from this
location since 2010.[49] More importantly, Norway has expanded its
conscription to both sexes. (Sweden reintroduced conscription in
2017.)[50] Norway is also actively seeking to foster even closer military cooperation with the United States and the United Kingdom to
enhance situational awareness and collective defense in the Artic,
North Atlantic, and the North Sea. (The three nations will likely
operate F-35 Lightning II combat aircraft and P-8 maritime patrol
aircraft by the mid-2020.)[51] All of these efforts have been spurred by
growing security concerns in the region. Future conflicts over commercial interests—for example, fishing rights and the exploration of
natural resources on and under the seabed—might lead to disputes

between the different parties in the region. More dramatically, the possibilities of increased instability and even hostility between the Russia and the West persist. In the future, the fundamental question regarding the freedom of access to the commons of this region will become more pressing, particularly in light of Russia's recent behavior and the expansion of its military footprint along Europe's northern flank. In the long term, the Royal Norwegian Navy is likely to be confronted with threats that are "multi-domain, multiregional, and multifunctional"[52] in nature and range across the intensity spectrum. So far, it has been able to adapt to the diverse security environment of the post–Cold War era. It is fair to say that under a more favorable financial environment, the Norwegian navy will remain a relatively small yet credible naval force in the region.[53]

PART

Analysis and Observations
Quo Vadis Europe?

Having profiled major components of European naval capabilities, it is time to place the development of European sea power within the larger context. Purely by numbers, Europe could lay claim to being a military superpower in its own right: the European continent is more populous than the United States and also has a higher gross domestic product, thus making it the greatest combined economic power in the world. In terms of per capita GDP, Europe's wealth becomes even more tangible: thirteen of the twenty richest countries in the world are located on the Continent. Furthermore, two of the five permanent UN Security Council members are European (France and Britain)—both of which have nuclear forces—and together with Germany and Italy they constitute more than half of the G-7 members. All European armies combined have more men and women under arms than the United States and they are among the most professional and best trained in the world. And even its collective naval forces would at first glance seem more than sufficient in size to protect Europe's interests and satisfy its security needs: European navies can deploy a nuclear-powered aircraft carrier with an air wing of highly sophisticated aircraft alongside 2 smaller carriers (Spain and Italy) operating the venerable Harrier jump jet; 15 amphibious warships are able to project aerial and naval assets over great distances and onto distant shores; 8 strategic ballistic missile submarines provide a constant nuclear deterrent while the European navies operate a mix of 12 nuclear-attack submarines and 50 diesel-electric boats (some of which are the most capable in the world); more than a hundred mine countermeasure vessels are in service, compared to the U.S. Navy's 13, and an escort fleet of more than 130 destroyers and frigates is complemented by numerous highly sophisticated missile-attack craft and stealthy corvettes. How can one speak of neglect and decline in light of such impressive numbers?

As mentioned at the outset of this book, Europe's heterogeneity and its inability to utilize its vast military resources in pursuit of common security goals was probably best summarized by Henry Kissinger's tongue-in-cheek query: "Who do I call if I want to call Europe?" Although decades of close cooperation among European states have resulted in tight military ties being forged, more recent events have shown how little the political and military leadership in Europe can agree upon common goals and actions when they involve inherent risks. Over the last decade, U.S.- and NATO-led campaigns have therefore often consisted of ad hoc coalitions of more or less willing European states, while other members watched from the sidelines. This disunity has led some defense analysts to call the credibility of NATO's Article 5 mutual-defense agreement into question.[1] Moreover, under President Donald Trump, it remains unclear if the United States will remain fully committed to its NATO allies. His "America First" policy is eliciting widespread uncertainty among the Europeans regarding the organization's future.

The truth of the matter is that, despite being a powerful force on paper, the European naval forces suffer from considerable limitations in fulfilling traditional naval missions, especially at the upper end of the force spectrum. With vital deterrence and warfighting capabilities atrophied, the most basic element of European sea power has significantly deteriorated since the days of the Cold War. As the case studies have revealed, many navies have ceded important capabilities as a direct result of the post–Cold War peace dividend and after years of continued austerity measures and shifting priorities. Notwithstanding innovations in shipbuilding, far-reaching automatization, and advancements in sensor technology, considerably fewer naval platforms are available to deal with the current abundance of maritime tasks.

The British fleet, for example, has been truncated by nearly 60 percent while the French Marine Nationale currently has to rely on a fleet half the size of what it was in 1990. Italy's forces are stretched thin by the nation's interests in the greater Mediterranean theater and the growing burden of mass migration, and Spain is barely able to maintain its current multipurpose fleet due to a decade of economic woes and halfhearted defense appropriations. Likewise, Greece continues to be caught in a quagmire of financial crises and it is therefore questionable if the country will be able to sustain its comparatively high defense expenditure in the future. As a result, the Hellenic navy is unlikely to retain its current capabilities. Turkey has been able to establish itself as a major naval power in the Black Sea and the Aegean Sea and perhaps more importantly, has developed a domestic defense industry able to indigenously design and manufacture warships. However, reservations regarding the effectiveness and morale of the Turkish navy persist in the light of the recent coup d'état.

On Europe's northern flank, the Netherlands, one of the richest countries in the world, has cut its surface fleet by more than half, while its next-door neighbor Germany has up until very recently been hesitant to step up to the plate. As the world's fourth-largest economy and Europe's industrial powerhouse, Germany operates some of the most capable surface combatants in the world. However, compared to other medium-sized powers such as the U.K. or France, it has remained unwilling to create a well-balanced, multipurpose fleet and lacks comparable power-projection assets.

On a somewhat more positive note, the Scandinavian navies have shown some encouraging signs of effectively adapting to the evolving security environment. They have not only modernized their armed forces but strengthened cooperation and interoperability in the High North and the Baltic Region. Because of Russia's growing military involvement in numerous regions of the world—most notably illustrated by the forced annexation of Crimea and the military intervention in Syria—Norway, Sweden, and Finland, as well as Poland and the Baltic states, will seek to revitalize territorial defense.

The latter countries have not been included in this study as they operate comparatively small naval forces. While Latvia, Lithuania, and Estonia have very modest defense budgets and only a handful of small warships, Romania and Bulgaria likewise have little ability to hedge against Russia's growing naval presence in the Black Sea. Poland, despite efforts to expand its capabilities in the waters of the Baltic Sea, will also find it difficult to secure funding for new surface combatants and submarines. Poland's border with Russia's ally, Belarus, and with the Russian exclave Kaliningrad provide ample reason to strengthen the country's land forces rather than diverting funds to naval matters: "The overall future of the Polish Navy continues to look relatively bleak . . . given the increasing obsolescence of the two FFG-7 type [*Oliver Hazard Perry*–class] frigates and four *Sokól*-class [Kobben] submarines that form the core of the fleet and the priority given to financing army and air force,"[2] an analyst notes. Entertaining the possibility of further Russian aggression in the theater, the aforementioned countries will likely not be able to make substantial investments toward their naval posture in the short term. Rather, they will want to rely on strengthening cooperation with better-equipped partners while gradually adding to their defense expenditure.[3] This in turn will put additional stress on those European navies that already have difficulties in sustaining their current operational tempo (as in the case of Norway, Britain, and Germany).

In many instances the navies find themselves unable to provide sufficient means to conduct their daily tasks, as "demonstrated by the 'gapping' of certain standing commitments to allow warships to be released for increasingly important NATO taskings."[4] Consequently, OPVs and auxiliaries fulfill missions traditionally conducted by potent frigates and destroyers.[5] In the case of a major crisis (imagine a revolution and civil war in Egypt that threatens free transit of the Suez Canal, for example), little or no surge capabilities are extant and no large-scale military operation can be maintained without the indispensable assets of the United States. The austere financial environment after the Cold War has forced many navies to continuously adapt to new and more varied challenges with less and less money—or as Rear Admiral Parry puts it, "The peace dividend was spent a long time ago and, in some cases, many times over."[6]

The past twenty-five years have been a period of constant strategic naval reorientation for European navies. First, the principle notion of sea control in the waters of the North Atlantic, Baltic, and Mediterranean against the Soviets was by and large replaced by the understanding that a "post-modern navy" needed to be able to conduct expeditionary warfare, contribute to stability operations, and maintain the good order at sea. Only since Russia has reemerged as a serious competitor to NATO are traditional tasks such as ASW and ASuW—and thus exercising sea control—again considered a critical naval skillset.

During the 1990s, the numerous stability operations and humanitarian interventions in relative proximity to the European continent required naval forces to assume an expeditionary posture for prolonged out-of-area operations. Large investments were made to build warships capable of projecting power over great distances. Both the U.K. and France had already maintained such forces at the end of the Cold War and continued to expand these capabilities. By the year 2000, the Netherlands, Spain, Italy, and others had followed suit and today even small fleets, such as the Royal Danish Navy, operated large warships designed with such missions in mind. However, procuring these highly expensive capital ships accounted for significant portions of each navy's budget. Further, the cost of maintaining and operating such platforms over their entire service lives has quickly become a major concern for defense planners.

Against the backdrop of new operational requirements and an increasingly austere financial environment, large naval exercises and wargaming for high-threat scenarios were curtailed, adding to the degradation of traditional naval skills.

The shortage of manpower is at least as pressing as the issue of the inadequate number of warships and the lack of routine naval exercises. Today, most European militaries have shifted from mandatory service to a volunteer force and almost all armed forces are finding it increasingly difficult to attract young citizens to join their ranks; indeed, in 2017 Sweden became the first country in Europe to reintroduce conscription. Even if a navy receives additional platforms, they are of little use if they cannot be properly crewed and kept in readiness. Retention remains an equally challenging proposition, as the military must compete with the often better-paying private sector.

At the same time, views of the future are not encouraging. "This is my prediction for the future," opined J. B. Haldane. "Whatever hasn't happened will happen and no-one will be safe from it." Sam J. Tangredi concluded, "In the dynamic security environment, any assessment of the future is truly only as valuable as its facility for being upgraded."[7] Naval forces are now routinely called upon to effectively tackle all possible contingencies, from drug interdiction to deploying special forces into hostile areas far from home. Naval sea power is also very likely to become an even more important factor in an increasingly competitive world—one in which the access to the ocean's vital resources of fish, oil, gas, and raw materials may become more heavily contested.

Both the European Union and NATO represent the politico-military pillars on which European sea power rests. With the United States shifting its attention toward the Asia-Pacific region, the North Atlantic alliance is likely to remain the defining element in Europe's security architecture. "NATO will remain critical in maintaining an equilibrium in the Western hemisphere, just as suitable arrangements for the USA and its allies to provide assurance and to support their friends (and interests) will be critical in the Eastern hemisphere."[8] With significant elements of U.S. naval forces shifting their priorities to the APR, the European NATO allies must again provide their naval forces with the necessary means to assume the roles the Americans have conceded as well as create synergies so that European sea power can be more than the sum of its parts.

One of the most promising developments over the last two decades has been the ability of many European states to successfully join forces in building state-of-the-art ships and weapon systems. Although the proficiencies in high-end defense technology could not be maintained in all areas, British, Italian, and Danish warships with their sophisticated array of sensors, radars, missiles, artillery, and electronic countermeasures can rightfully be considered among the best in the world. To this end, "NATO helps to reduce defense duplication and prevents the renationalization of defense. Without NATO, the individual alliance member would be forced to spend considerably more money on defense than they currently do."[9]

In this day and age, it is exorbitantly expensive to build warships, submarines, and aircraft from scratch and no European country's defense industry is able to provide all the necessary parts and manufacturing processes for such an undertaking. Therefore, joint ventures such as the Franco/Italian *Horizon* and FREMM projects, the trilateral cooperation between Spain, Germany, and the Netherlands for a new air-defense frigate, the multinational NH90 helicopter program, and the construction of the *Rotterdam/Galicia*–class LPDs are high-profile examples of the successful and necessary measures European governments have made so far.

In terms of interoperability, the European navies have made great strides in being able to conduct a wide range of maritime missions with naval detachments from other countries. NATO's Standing Maritime Groups are continuously at sea, constituting an immediate reaction force as well as a conventional deterrent. European warships regularly participate in a number of multinational naval exercises (i.e., Trident Juncture, Joint Warrior 17–2, Dynamic Mongoose 2017, etc.) and military operations, such as Operation Enduring Freedom, Operation Atalanta, and, since 2015, in Operation

Sophia in the Mediterranean. These joint ventures have provided an excellent basis for trust-building and interoperability among European and foreign navies and military services. Meanwhile, bi- and multilateral cooperation, such as the Belgian-Dutch naval cooperative (BeNeSam), the combined Dutch-British amphibious force, the SIAF (Spanish-Italian Amphibious Battlegroup) EU Battlegroup, and the German-Dutch amphibious battalion, have created synergies and offset some of the capability gaps among the individual navies. Such increased interoperability in theory would also allow each navy to specialize in specific areas. Lieutenant Chris Pagenkopf of the U.S. Navy offers this explanation:

> With enhanced coordination of the alliance's operational capabilities, member states could completely cede certain mission areas in which they struggle to maintain a competency because of a scarcity of resources. This would allow them to reallocate funding to focus on becoming a world-class capability leader in their assigned mission areas. As a result, the overall NATO force would be more integrated and effective, as it would be a confluence of capabilities leaders rather than a collection of independent militaries that are jacks of all trades but masters of none.[10]

Although such trends toward more specialized navies with niche capabilities has been noticeable (the Danish navy's air-defense capability is a good example), daunting political and operational considerations militate against pursuing such an approach any further.

A highly specialized navy would find it far more challenging to adapt to a rapidly evolving security environment and might be caught off guard, having invested large sums of money in the wrong areas. At the same time, these countries would have to realize that they are utterly dependent on other states to conduct basic tasks their own navies could no longer perform. Italy, for example, would have found it very challenging to operate near the shore of Libya in 2011, had it not commanded a well-balanced fleet, able to defend its aircraft carrier from air, surface, and subsurface threats. Were Italy to decide to abandon its subsurface flotilla and transfer this role to, say, the French navy in order to operate two aircraft carriers instead of one, it would have to hope that in the case of conflict France would deem it politically and military justifiable to commit its forces to such a task. In times of ad hoc coalitions and alliances, and with a range of domestic factors weighing heavily on the equation, such a plan is inherently risky.

A multipurpose navy, on the other hand, can adapt to changes in the strategic environment more easily and thus reduce the risk of having backed the wrong horse, while being left to its own devices by its supposed allies. In the Asia-Pacific region a number of states are actively engaged in building such naval forces. India, China, South Korea, Japan, Vietnam, Singapore, and Australia are all strengthening their blue-water capabilities and are in the process of creating more powerful multipurpose navies, despite the steep learning curve this effort involves.[11] The construction of aircraft carriers, amphibious assault ships, large surface combatants, and long-range submarines are the most obvious indicators of this trend. The graphs in the appendix provide a valuable comparison between the rise of naval power in the Asia-Pacific region and the apparent decline of European naval forces.[12]

Only four countries in Europe can claim to operate a modern, multipurpose navy. And although some states, such as Norway and Denmark, have shifted from purely littoral to blue-water operations, and again others, like Turkey, are seeking to operate more powerful fleets, their navies are still restricted by both smaller budgets and arguably more limited strategic interests than their Asian counterparts.

It is therefore pivotal for the European navies to retain the broadest possible range of capabilities. Even if short-term fiscal restrictions are limiting factors in putting each specific capability into full effect, in times of crisis they would constitute a crucial stepping stone from which to expand (although this process is likely to take considerably longer than imagined). From a platform-centric point of view, provisions need to be made so that surface combatants, submarines, and aircraft can be incrementally brought up to date over time. Luckily, modern European warships are designed with such provisions in mind. Many frigates and destroyers, such as the Norwegian *Nansen* class and British *Daring* class, are relatively lightly armed when compared to their Asian and American equivalents. However, they have room for additional weapon systems and their sensor suites can be upgraded if necessary.

The necessity to quickly shift priorities at sea has been illustrated by the renewed operational challenges NATO is faced with in the North Atlantic. After a hiatus of more than two decades, European anti-submarine warfare capabilities are again being put to the test by Russian submarine deployments.[13] Formally a forte of the northern European navies, especially of the United Kingdom, these proficiencies have to be regained. At the same time, constabulary duties on the southern flank as well as ongoing crisis throughout North Africa and the Middle East have effectively tied down large parts of European navies operating in this region.

It is safe to say that regardless of Europe's growing willingness to invest in its own defense, it will remain largely dependent on American military capabilities over the next decade. This includes the U.S. Navy's auxiliary forces. Without America's fleet of support vessels, large naval operations are not sustainable. Unfortunately, current trends indicate that the so-called teeth-to-tail ratio of U.S. combat ships to supply and replenishment vessels is becoming increasingly critical. This is even more critical with Europe's already limited sealift capabilities. While European powers were able to field, deploy, and sustain division-sized units in the war against Iraq in 1991, such deployment has largely become impossible.[14] Even the two most powerful amphibious forces in Europe—the French and the British—are "unlikely to be deployed in a high-threat environment without considerable U.S. force protection."[15] In essence, despite having tried to strengthen its amphibious forces, Europe's militaries lack the ability to get significant forces (mechanized forces have been drastically reduced across the board) to the scene of action and they do not have the necessary high-end capabilities to sufficiently protect themselves from harm once they get there. In the areas of air defense, close-air support, airborne-early warning, aerial-refueling, intelligence, surveillance and reconnaissance, and long-range precision strikes, Europe has to rely on U.S. assets.[16]

That U.S. military might—and especially its naval power—stems from a sustained defense expenditure of roughly 4 percent of the national GDP, more than twice that of the average European state,[17] seems to be more of a welcome convenience to the Europeans than a goal worth aspiring to. In the long term, the United States is likely to become increasingly frustrated by its allies' tendency to free-ride on the backs of U.S. taxpayers. With the Americans' attention already shifting toward China and the greater Asia-Pacific region, Europe will have to carry a larger share of the security burden in the Western Hemisphere as well as becoming more assertive in protecting its interests in other regions of the world. That it will have to do so with much smaller and often less capable naval forces than twenty-five years ago seems to be a foregone conclusion.

Conclusion
Whose Sea Power Will It Be?

By any reasonable estimate, sea power will be one of the defining elements in the future of world affairs. Like the centuries before, the twenty-first century will be governed by various powers at sea, interacting with each other in peaceful cooperation, tough competition, and possibly even in bloody conflict. In this book I have argued that the ability to influence decisions on land has in the past often depended upon holding military power at sea. However, I have thus far only alluded to the questions of which actors will be able to utilize the maritime realm to a greater extent than others and thereby shape the world in their vision in the future. *Whose sea power will it be?*

Three basic trends are likely to remain constant in the foreseeable future. First, the United States will maintain its global naval dominance by a considerable margin for at least another thirty years. However, the U.S. Navy's ability to maintain sea control will be challenged by the emergence of increasingly sophisticated anti-access/area-denial networks in proximity to the shores of Russia, China, and to a lesser degree Iran, North Korea, and elsewhere.

Moreover, the emergence of large blue-water navies in the Indian Ocean and the Pacific will force the United States to reevaluate its current maritime strategy. Ultimately, the U.S. Navy (including the Marine Corps) is likely to remain the only naval force able to project significant power into any region of the world and sustain a military confrontation over an extended period of time.

The second trend also coincides with one of the most profound geopolitical developments in modern history: the ascent of previously poor countries—such as India, South Korea, Indonesia, Vietnam, and, most importantly, China—which, for the first time in more than five hundred years, has caused the geopolitical center of gravity to shift from Europe and the Atlantic toward the Asia-Pacific region. In many countries in the APR, the maritime domain has assumed a prominent position. This is exemplified by Chinese naval scholars studying the writings of the most renowned naval strategists, Alfred T. Mahan and Julian S. Corbett, while other navies in the region are trying to emulate Western (U.S.) naval capabilities. Apparently, leaders from Tokyo to New Delhi have discerned the strategic gains to be made by developing a large commercial fleet as well as a powerful navy to protect the country's political and economic interests at home and abroad. These efforts have been highly profitable for these states, strengthening their domestic shipbuilding industry as well as their commercial markets. However, the possibility of conflict looms large as the current naval buildup among the conflicting actors in the region is joined by the United States.

The third trend allows us to infer which role Europe will play in this maritime century. Over the past twenty-five years, the European navies discussed in this book have all had to deal with paradigmatic changes to the global order. During the later years of the Cold War, all European states under discussion were either NATO members or aligned with the West and thus (at least in theory) part of the overarching maritime strategy against the Soviet Union. As such, each navy had specific tasks to fulfill—from mining critical choke points through which the Soviet forces had to pass in the case of war, to protecting the strategic lines of communication between the

United States and Europe upon which the vital reinforcement for the besieged European allies would be transported. The perceived threat that emanated from the enemy's naval forces had to be contained in order to maintain sea control. This principle of sea control was a strategic axiom for Europe's naval forces.

With the demise of the Soviet Union and the end of the Cold War, these plans were shelved. New forms of conflict necessitated novel approaches to naval operations. Expeditionary capabilities were expanded in order to conduct military interventions, stability operations, and peace-keeping missions in distant regions. Soon many European navies operated expeditionary forces in the form of amphibious assault ships and other large multipurpose surface combatants, capable of projecting power from sea onto land. Only a handful of smaller European states, such as Greece or Sweden, remained focused on territorial defense in the green waters closer to shore.

The fact that large sums of money, which would have formerly been allocated to national defense, could now be invested elsewhere was of even greater relevance to the transformation of European naval power. As part of the so-called peace dividend, the large military forces in Europe underwent drastic reductions. In an age when ships were becoming increasingly expensive to build and young men and women more difficult to recruit and train, far-reaching cuts to the military budgets made it difficult for many European navies to effectively modernize their fleets and maintain operational readiness. This process continued for more than two decades and was exacerbated by the global economic crisis that struck in 2008. Across the board, from Portugal to Finland, the armed forces had to find ways of doing more with less. By 2014, apart from the United States, only four of the twenty-eight NATO members were spending more than 2 percent of their GDP on defense and most budgets had reached an all-time low.

However, against the backdrop of Russia's intervention in the Ukraine and its annexation of the Crimean Peninsula in the spring of 2014, the European NATO members have pledged to shoulder greater responsibility and "to move towards the 2% guideline"[1] within a decade: "These decisions will further strengthen the Transatlantic Bond, enhance the security of all Allies and ensure a more fair and balanced sharing of costs and responsibilities," the official statement after the NATO summit in Wales 2014 read.[2] While it is quite difficult to envision a scenario in which all European states actually reach this ominous 2 percent benchmark, it is fair to say that the resulting defense appropriations would constitute the appropriate compromise in terms of feasibility and capability for the alliance. In fact, it appears as if we are witnessing a reversal in trends. Russia's military interventions in the Ukraine and Syria, the bloody terrorist attacks throughout Europe, and the ongoing refugee crisis have all given cause for greater security concerns among the European population than we have seen since the fall of the Berlin Wall. In 2015, for the first time in more than twenty-five years, defense spending on a whole has increased across Europe and numerous countries have committed themselves to strengthening their militaries over the coming years. However, it remains to be seen if the promised provisions toward collective European security and defense are part of a long-term development or just lip service, as governments return to their previous myopia once the political atmosphere becomes more favorable.

Although the safety and prosperity of all European states relies heavily on maritime security, on the unimpeded flow of commerce on the oceans' great highways, and access to the global commons, it will be difficult to convince the average citizen that more money has to be allocated to naval forces in order to protect Western values and to maintain Europe's material wealth. Therefore, it is the responsibility of the current political and military leadership to refrain from continuing down the road of mismanagement and negligence.[3] The increase in defense spending we are seeing as of late (albeit often uncoordinated and arbitrary), and the ongoing effort to buttress and revitalize collective defense by enhancing interoperability and by conducting large-scale, multinational naval exercises, needs to continue for the naval forces to regain and maintain their proficiency.

In numerous strategic defense papers, Europe's naval forces are not only called upon to fulfill their primary military function—to attack, defend, or deter—but far more often are used for diplomatic and policing duties. At any given point in time, navies are conducting humanitarian assistance and disaster-relief missions, such as those relating to the hurricanes that devastated large parts of the Caribbean in 2017 or rescuing refugees in the Mediterranean. British, Spanish, and German destroyers and frigates, designed to protect entire battlegroups from the onslaught of enemy aircraft and missiles, regularly conduct antipiracy operations against small motorboats and modern-day freebooters, armed with nothing but AK-47 rifles. Meanwhile, smaller, less sophisticated, and less expensive ships, which would be better suited to such tasks, are spread thin over the vast oceans, conducting other constabulary duties, such as drug interdiction and fishery protection in their country's territorial waters and exclusive economic zones.

I have made a point to stress the consequences the truncation of naval capabilities already have had on Europe writ large and what prospects this could have for Europe's future. Over the past five hundred years, most major powers in the world have understood the utility of sea power, both in economic as well as military terms. Naval historian Colin S. Gray goes so far as to argue that "great sea powers or maritime coalitions have either won or, occasionally, drawn every major war in modern history."[4] Ultimately, however, it was the successful marriage of commercial and military might during the larger part of the modern era that allowed successive European powers to accumulate vast territorial gains and secure wealth as well as political influence. After the end of the Second World War the United States succeeded the British as the preeminent sea power and has remained the "claviger and steward" of the international trade regime.[5] Meanwhile, Europe's economies continue to enjoy a free ride on the maritime security that the United States Navy has upheld for nearly seventy years. In the future it is unlikely that this practice will suffice. The oceans are becoming an increasingly contested area of interests. Chris Parry warns: "States will seek to extend their jurisdiction, control and regulation over offshore areas up to the limits of their exclusive economic zones (EEZs)." They will try to "exploit the resources that lie on and below the seabed and in the water column."[6]

Yet, most naval forces in Europe have suffered such grave reductions in size and funding since the end of the Cold War that they are barely able to fulfill the military, diplomatic, and policing roles they are called upon to perform. Although utterly dependent on trade by sea, it is questionable to what extent European states can contribute to the protection of the global SLOCs, and thereby, to the freedom of the sea outside their immediate sphere of influence. "On paper, NATO, with its Standing Maritime Groups, seems to be capable of deploying relevant naval forces across the globe. . . . In practice, however, any mission with a NATO logo needs approval of 28 member states [and] many members would object [to] any new NATO involvement outside the Euro-Atlantic Area," one German analyst stresses.[7] The European Union likewise has little leverage regarding security issues outside its rather limited area of influence, "showing Brussels' enduring strategic irrelevance in the Indo-Pacific."[8]

Closer to home, growing threats within Europe (ranging from terrorism to far-left/right political pressure) as well as the instability along Europe's borders remains a key security consideration. Further, Russia is making its presence felt from the High North to Europe's eastern border, and all the way to the southern Mediterranean flank. The country has reemerged as a major player at sea as well as in international affairs; skillfully applying hard power and coercion to expand its sphere of influence. Many in the West are taken aback by Moscow's strategy of hybrid warfare, fait accompli tactics, and plausible deniability operations, but are still in search of appropriate responses. Apart from Russia's growing presence along Europe's northern flank, the steady thawing of the polar caps might also have significant repercussions. The Scandinavian states, the Netherlands, Germany, and the United Kingdom all rely heavily on seaborne trade and could profit from the emergence of new trade routes along a navigable Northeast Passage. However, it would also place an additional burden on their naval forces, especially if Russia was to use its geographical and military advantage in the theater as political leverage.[9]

Meanwhile the eastern European states, which were formerly under Soviet rule, find themselves under pressure to strengthen their defenses, given their vulnerability to Russian incursions. Any such provision will have little effect on the overall state of European naval power. Because military forces for air and land warfare are considered the quintessential linchpin of deterrence in this theater of operation, "NATO's pivot to Russia will [likely] shift attention away from the maritime domain back to the continent. Armies and air forces will receive, once again, much more attention than navies."[10]

And finally, in the south, more effective responses and more money will be needed to deal with both high-end threats as well as with the influx of refugees from Africa and the Middle East. At the upper end of the intensity spectrum, Russia's naval capabilities as well as the proliferating asymmetrical threats need to be accounted for, while on the lower-end, continuous human assistance and border control operations will continue to keep Europe's navies occupied.

Sadly, notwithstanding the common defense agreements within NATO, the European Union, and the growing bilateral and multilateral military cooperation, the continent remains a conglomerate of highly diverse states, all of which have their individual domestic and foreign interests to satisfy. In short, "military capabilities remain in national hands," according to the Lisbon Treaty.[11] Nowhere does this become more apparent than when the lives of young men and women, as well as substantial amounts of treasure, are at stake.

The apparent rifts within Europe are not likely to disappear overnight, as the current effort to degrade and destroy the Islamic State in Syria and Iraq exemplifies. While American and French combat planes have flown strike missions from aircraft carriers stationed in the Persian Gulf and the Mediterranean, most other European countries have shown little interest in stepping up to the plate. Meanwhile, the Italian and Hellenic navies are heavily engaged in humanitarian assistance operations in the Mediterranean and

Aegean Sea. Yet to date, no comprehensive approach to dealing with this human catastrophe has been put forward by the European Union. Again, contradictory political views among the various states limit their ability to effectively put their naval forces to use.

So is this divided Europe going to be relegated to the fringes of a world centered on the Asia-Pacific region as I postulated at the outset of this book? Perhaps the somewhat encouraging answer is *not necessarily*. The developments we have been witnessing since 2014 give reason for hope. However, "countries need to be prepared for the long haul and the long view, in anticipation of risks and opportunities."[12] This means that sufficient investments must be made to provide the European populace with both security and access to the amenities of the global market. In the twenty-first century, naval forces will continue to represent one of the most effective tools for achieving both.

Much has been said in regard to burden-sharing and strengthening cooperation among the European partners. However, streamlining measures in force composition, as well as the effort to effectively engage with friends and allies to alleviate the burden that is placed upon each individual navy, pale against the drastic reductions of Europe's naval forces since the end of the Cold War. They have merely slowed the process of overall naval decline. Unless the previous propensity to reduce the size, readiness, and capabilities of the naval forces is revoked and the traditional elements of naval forces are again understood as multifaceted tools of first rather than last resort, European naval power will be unable to protect and promote the continent's broader economic interest and satisfy its security needs.

The twenty-first century will in all likelihood be one of American sea power, challenged by the rise of Asian sea power. Based on the past, current, and future global trends, it is still questionable if it will also be a century of European sea power.

APPENDIX

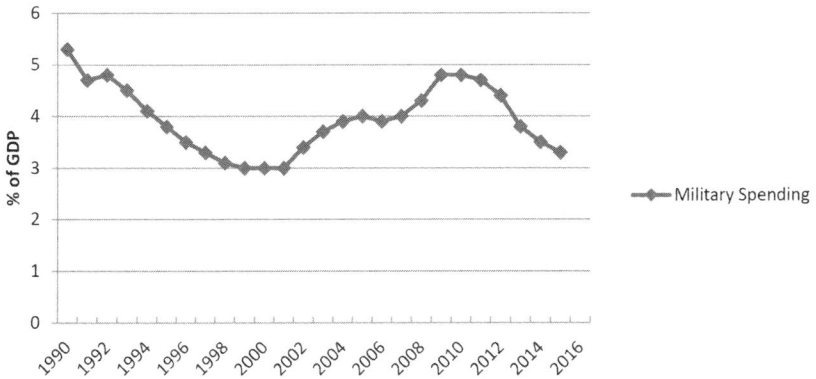

United States: Defense Spending in % of GDP, 1990–2015

Source: SIPRI Military Expenditure Database.

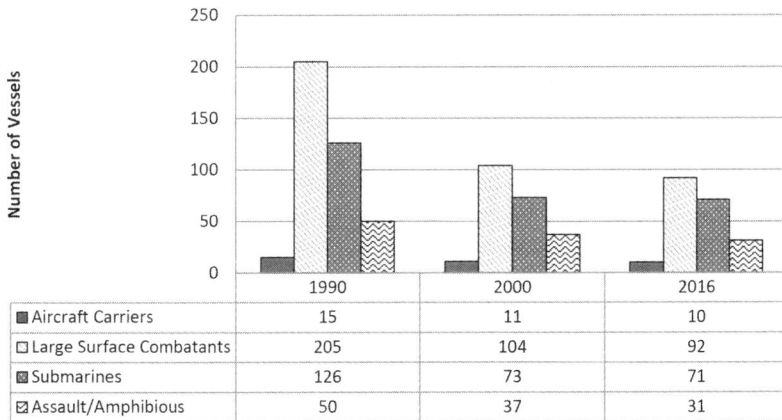

	1990	2000	2016
■ Aircraft Carriers	15	11	10
☐ Large Surface Combatants	205	104	92
▨ Submarines	126	73	71
▧ Assault/Amphibious	50	37	31

United States: Number of Major Vessels

Sources: *The Naval Institute Guide to Combat Fleets of the World, Military Technology Almanac, World Naval Review*.

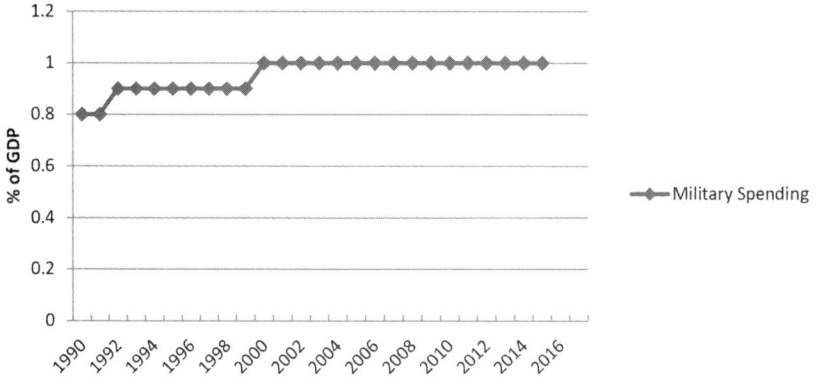

Japan: Defense Spending in % of GDP, 1990–2015

Source: SIPRI Military Expenditure Database.

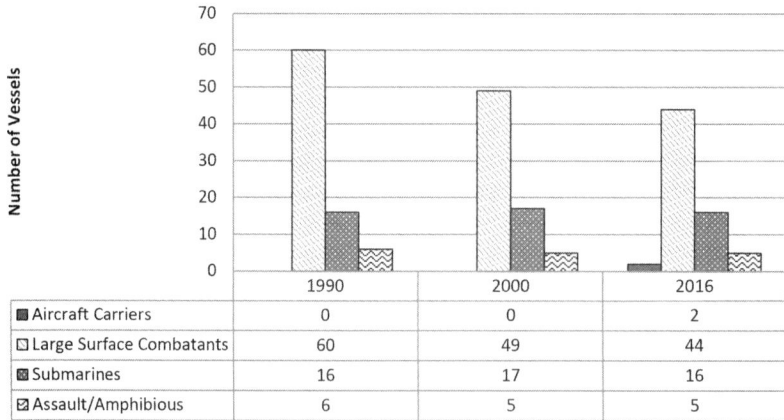

	1990	2000	2016
■ Aircraft Carriers	0	0	2
▢ Large Surface Combatants	60	49	44
▩ Submarines	16	17	16
▨ Assault/Amphibious	6	5	5

Japan: Number of Major Vessels

Sources: *The Naval Institute Guide to Combat Fleets of the World, Military Technology Almanac, World Naval Review*.

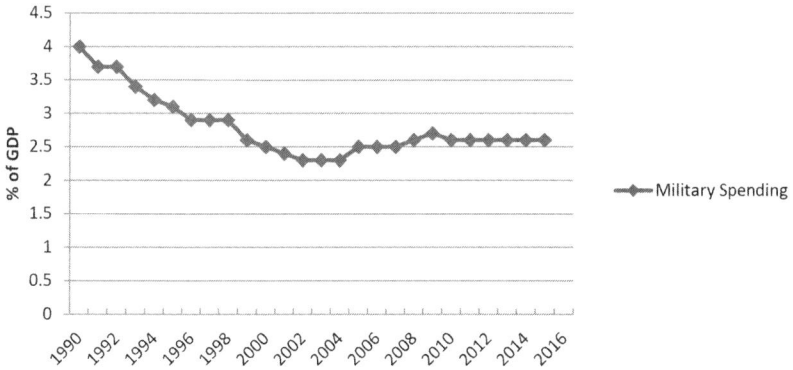

South Korea: Defense Spending in % of GDP, 1990–2015

Source: SIPRI Military Expenditure Database.

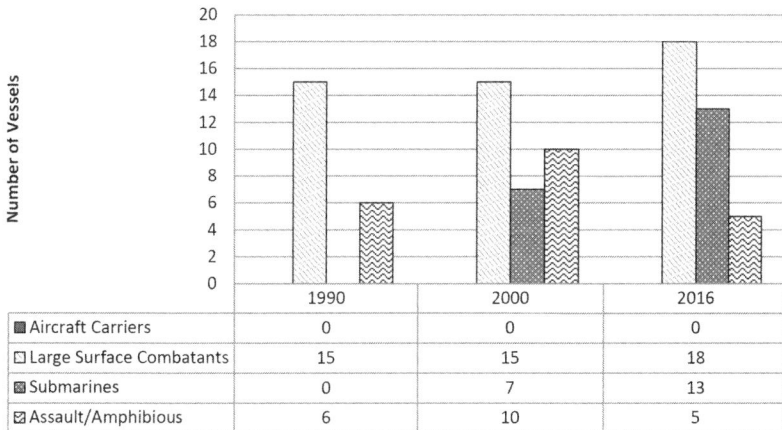

	1990	2000	2016
▣ Aircraft Carriers	0	0	0
☐ Large Surface Combatants	15	15	18
▩ Submarines	0	7	13
☒ Assault/Amphibious	6	10	5

South Korea: Number of Major Vessels

Sources: *The Naval Institute Guide to Combat Fleets of the World, Military Technology Almanac, World Naval Review.*

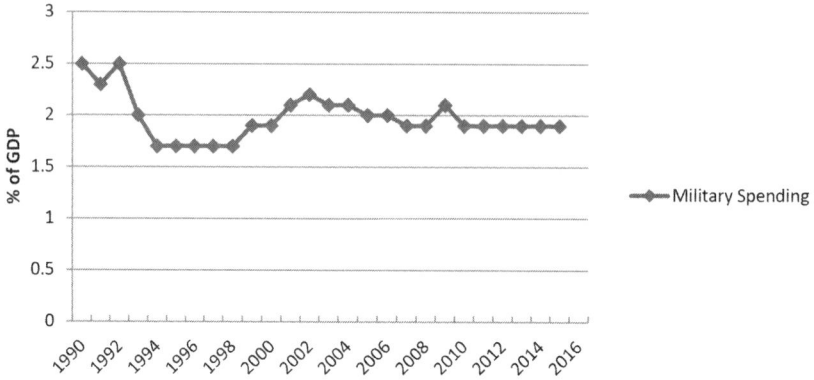

China: Defense Spending in % of GDP, 1990–2015

Source: SIPRI Military Expenditure Database.

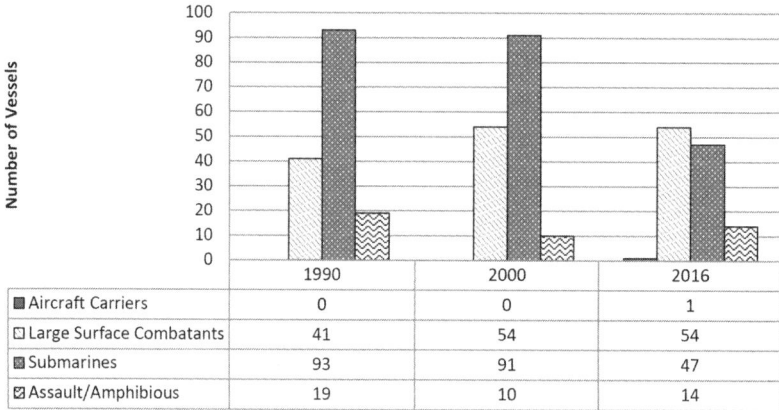

	1990	2000	2016
▣ Aircraft Carriers	0	0	1
☐ Large Surface Combatants	41	54	54
▦ Submarines	93	91	47
☑ Assault/Amphibious	19	10	14

China: Number of Major Vessels

Sources: *The Naval Institute Guide to Combat Fleets of the World, Military Technology Almanac, World Naval Review.*

Note that many vessels, in particular large parts of the submarine force, had already been rendered obsolete by 1990 and have since been put out of service.

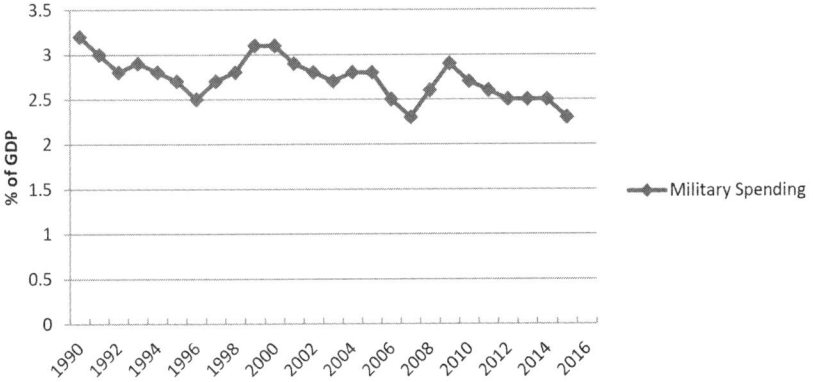

India: Defense Spending in % of GDP, 1990–2015

Source: SIPRI Military Expenditure Database.

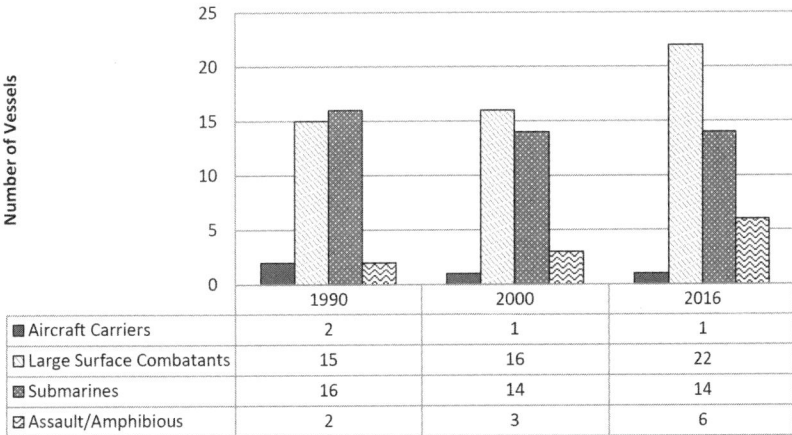

	1990	2000	2016
■ Aircraft Carriers	2	1	1
☐ Large Surface Combatants	15	16	22
▩ Submarines	16	14	14
☑ Assault/Amphibious	2	3	6

India: Number of Major Vessels

Sources: *The Naval Institute Guide to Combat Fleets of the World, Military Technology Almanac, World Naval Review.*

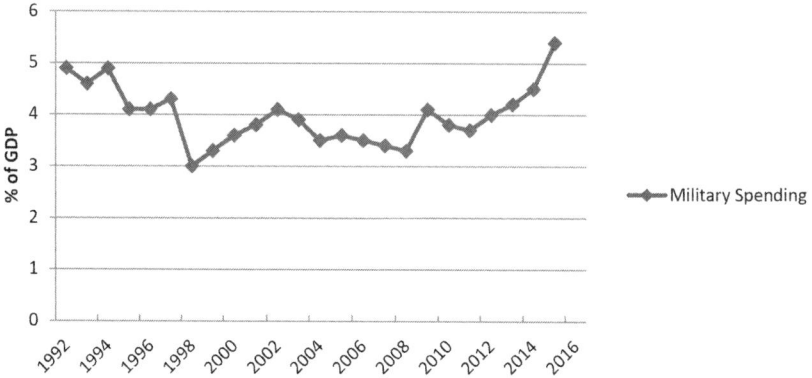

Russia: Defense Spending in % of GDP, 1990–2015
Source: SIPRI Military Expenditure Database.

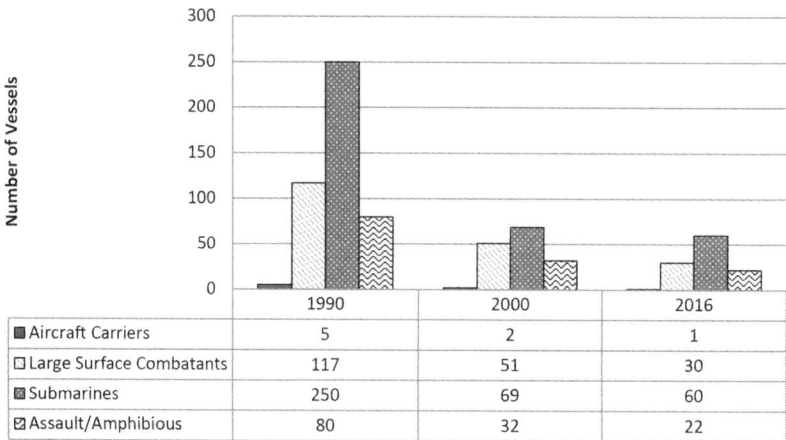

	1990	2000	2016
■ Aircraft Carriers	5	2	1
▢ Large Surface Combatants	117	51	30
▨ Submarines	250	69	60
▨ Assault/Amphibious	80	32	22

Russia: Number of Major Vessels
Sources: *The Naval Institute Guide to Combat Fleets of the World, Military Technology Almanac, World Naval Review.*

Note that these are highly tentative figures, especially those from 1990. The actual readiness of Russian warships is difficult to assess.

NOTES

Introduction

Epigraph. Colin S. Gray, *The Leverage of Sea Power: The Strategic Advantage of Navies in War* (New York: The Free Press, 1992), 289.

1. Chris Parry, *Super Highway: Sea Power in the 21st Century* (London: Elliot and Thompson Limited, 2014), 65. Economist and historian Niall Ferguson discussed Western ascendency more broadly in *Civilization: The West and the Rest* (New York: Penguin Books, 2011).

2. Parry, Super Highway, 10–23.

3. Gray, *Leverage,* 290.

4. Surprisingly, a number of Austrian scholars have produced some insightful research on naval matters. This includes Brig. Gen. Bruno Hofbauer's volume on modern sea power: *Moderne Seemacht. Grundlagen—Verfahren—Techniken;* Dr. Nikolaus Scholik published a comparative study of U.S. and Chinese sea power in 2015: *Seemacht im 21. Jahrhundert: Handbuch & Lexikon;* and Michael Haas, a nonresident fellow of the Institute for Security Policy Kiel, is in the process of finishing his dissertation on U.S. naval strategy during the Cold War.

5. Parry, *Super Highway,* 37.

6. The term "great highway" was coined by Admiral Alfred Thayer Mahan, one of the most prominent naval strategists. See Alfred Thayer Mahan, *Mahan on Naval Warfare: Selections from the Writing of Rear Admiral Alfred T. Mahan,* ed. Allan Westcott (1941; repr., Mineola, NY: Dover Publications, 1999), 17.

7. NATO, *Alliance Maritime Strategy* (18 March 2011), II:4.

8. The global commons are generally referred to as the global domains of shared resources. This includes the world's high oceans, the atmosphere, and outer space, as well as the World Wide Web.

9. See Peter D. Haynes, *Toward a New Maritime Strategy: American Naval Thinking in the Post–Cold War Era* (Annapolis, MD: Naval Institute Press, 2015).
10. Parry, *Super Highway,* 85.
11. Geoffrey Till, *Seapower: A Guide for the Twenty-First Century*, rev. 3rd ed. (New York: Routledge, 2013), xv.
12. F. Stephen Larrabee et al., *NATO and the Challenges of Austerity* (Santa Monica: RAND Corporation, 2012), 28.
13. Ezio Bonsignore et al., "Germany," *Military Technology: The World Defense Almanac 2014* (n.p.: Mönch Publishing Group, 2014), 1:130.
14. For an excellent account of the development of war, see Rupert Smith, *The Utility of Force: The Art of War in the Modern World* (London: Penguin, 2005).
15. See Robert M. Cassidy, *Counterinsurgency and the Global War on Terror: Military Culture and Irregular War* (Westport, CT: Praeger Security International, 2006).
16. Missions include "sea-control, expeditionary operations, stability operation/humanitarian assistance, inclusive good order at sea, and cooperative naval diplomacy." Till, *Seapower,* 35f.
17. For a detailed description of naval functions see ibid.
18. Smith, *Utility,* 3.
19. Julian S. Corbett, *Some Principles of Maritime Strategy* (1911; repr., Mineola, NY: Dover Publications, 2004), 89.
20. Sir Walter Raleigh quoted in Parry, *Super Highway,* 3.
21. The proliferation of advanced weapon systems and other forms of disruptive technologies, however, have the potential to greatly impact how sea power is employed in the future.

Chapter 1. Principles of Sea Power

1. NATO, *Maritime Strategy,* II:4.
2. Ibid.
3. Parry, *Super Highway,* 258.
4. The term was coined by Joseph Nye in his book, *Bound to Lead: The Changing Nature of American Power* and expanded in

2004 in *Soft Power: The Means to Success in World Politics.* In the preface of his latter publication the author briefly defines what he considers to be "soft power": "What is soft power? It is the ability to get what you want through attraction rather than coercion or payments. It arises from the attractiveness of a country's culture, political ideals, and policies." Joseph S. Nye Jr., *Soft Power: The Means to Success in World Politics* (New York: Public Affairs, 2004), preface.

5. Parry, *Super Highway,* 65.

6. Ibid., 4.

7. Ibid.

8. Mahan quoted in Till, *Seapower,* 57.

9. Till, *Seapower,* 349.

10. Alfred Thayer Mahan, *The Influence of Sea Power upon History* (1890; repr., Mineola, NY: Dover Publications, 2014), 88. A digital version is accessible at: https://archive.org/details/seanpowerinf00maha.

11. Mahan, *Naval Warfare,* 4.

12. Ibid.

13. Ken Booth, cited by Karl Rommetveit and Bjørn Terjesen in introduction to *The Rise of Naval Power in Asia and Europe's Decline,* ed. Bjørn Terjesen and Øystein Tunsjø (Oslo, 2012), 10.

14. James Eberle, "Maritime Strategy," *Naval Forces* 8, no. 2 (1987): 38.

15. Carlisle A. H. Trost, "Looking Beyond the Maritime Strategy," in *U.S. Naval Strategy in the 1980s, Selected Documents,* ed. John B. Hattendorf and Peter M. Swartz (Newport, RI: Naval War College Press, 2008), 263.

16. Parry, *Super Highway,* 64.

17. Corbett, *Principles,* 89.

18. Ibid., 87.

19. Mahan, *Naval Warfare,* 52.

20. Corbett, *Principles,* 90.

21. Ibid., 90.

22. Till, *Seapower,* 1–5.

23. Gray, *Leverage,* 281.

24. Ibid., 5.

25. See Department of the Navy, *A Cooperative Strategy for 21st Century Sea Power* (Washington, DC: GPO, 2007) and Department of the Navy, *A Cooperative Strategy for the 21st Century Sea Power: Forward, Engaged, Ready* (Washington, DC: GPO, 2015). For extensive debate on U.S. maritime strategy see U.S. Naval War College, *EMC Chair Symposium: Maritime Strategy.* Symposium took place 23–24 March 2016, Newport, RI.

26. Gray, *Leverage,* 284.

27. An excellent article on the development of naval sensors and weapons and their effect on naval warfare can be found in Norman Friedman, "Technological Reviews—Naval Sensors and Weapons," in *Seaforth World Naval Review 2010,* ed. Conrad Waters (South Yorkshire, U.K.: Seaforth, 2009), 167–76.

28. See John Richardson, "Chief of Naval Operations' White Paper: The Future Navy," *USNI News* (16 May 2017), 4.

29. Lord Nelson quoted in Mahan, *Naval Warfare,* 80.

30. Sam J. Tangredi, *Anti-Access Warfare, Countering A2/AD Strategies* (Annapolis, MD: Naval Institute Press, 2013), 238.

31. Ibid., 78.

32. Ibid., 77.

33. Rommetveit, introduction, 10.

34. Robert Gascoyne-Cecil, Marquis of Salisbury, "Letter to Robert Bulwer-Lytton, 1st Earl of Lytton (15 June 1877)," in Lady Gwendolen Cecil, *Life of Robert Marquis of Salisbury* (London: Hodder and Stoughton Limited, 1921), 2:153.

35. Till, *Seapower,* 121.

36. Ibid.

37. Parry, *Super Highway,* 262.

38. Ibid.

39. Till, "British Approach," 21.

40. Ibid., 21.

41. Department for Transport, *Statistical Release—Shipping Fleet Statistics 2014* (18 February 2015). For more information see Parry, *Super Highway,* 48–51.

42. Parry, *Super Highway,* 326.
43. "It is always difficult to sketch out the future that defence planners need to prepare for, but never more so than now, since in addition to the usual sets of challenges to do with the rise and fall of nations and the deadly quarrels so often associated with this (which may well be hugely exacerbated by the perfect storm of shortages in energy, food and water foreseen by some by the 2030s), we also have to grapple with a range of asymmetrical threats from a variety of non-state actors including terrorists and pirates. And then there are the faceless threats and challenges brought about by climate change—such as the increased propensity for catastrophic weather events or the rising importance of the increasingly ice-free water of the High North both of which could have both a direct and an indirect impact on Alliance security." Till, "British Approach," 17.

Chapter 2. The Pivot toward Asia and the Consequences for Europe

Epigraph. Barry Posen, "Panel Discussion: A Moment of Transition," min 33:00.

1. John G. Ikenberry, "The Illusion of Geopolitics. The Enduring Power of Liberal Order," *Foreign Affairs* (May/June 2014), 81.
2. Walter Russel Mead refers to these powers as "revisionist power." See Walter Russel Mead, "The Return of Geopolitics: The Revenge of Revisionist Power," *Foreign Affairs* (May/June 2014), 69–79.
3. John F. Lehmann, "The 600-Ship Navy," in *U.S. Naval Strategy in the 1980s, Selected Documents,* ed. John B. Hattendorf and Peter M. Swartz (Newport: Naval War College Press, 2008), 248.
4. Parry, *Highway,* 58.
5. Till, *Seapower,* xv.
6. While the term "Asia-Pacific region" was commonly used in the discussion pertaining to the shift in global power distribution,

the term "Indo-Pacific region" more aptly points to the importance of India and the Indian Ocean in global affairs.

7. "Europe and North-East Asia matter because that's where the great powers are, and they are potential threats to the United States; and the Middle East . . . matters because that's where the oil is, and oil is a critical resource like no other." See John Mearsheimer, "Imperial by Design," min. 13:00.

8. Mearsheimer, "Imperial," min. 15:00–17:00.

9. Only ten months after the last batch of M1 Abrams main battle tanks had left Europe in April 2013, twenty-nine tanks arrived in Germany. Ezio Bonsignore et al., "United States of America," *Military Technology: The World Defence Almanac 2014,* I (2014), 32.

10. Till, "British Approach," 23.

11. Although the percentage of defense spending has remained relatively constant, the dramatic increase in total GDP has enabled China to allocate significantly more money to its defense sector. Sam Perlo Freeman et al., "Trends in World Military Expenditure, 2013," SIPRI Fact Sheet, April (2014), 2.

12. Anti-access and area denial are strategic approaches to warfare. Their aim is to deny enemy forces the ability to operate in a contested area. Essential to this strategy, however, is the understanding that the enemy is strategically superior and a force-on-force engagement should be avoided by all means. Asymmetric technologies and tactics, as well as niche capabilities, are sought by states relying on anti-access strategies to offset the opponents' military advantage. For obvious reasons, superior intelligence, misinformation, and deception play a vital role in A2/AD efforts. See Tangredi, *Anti-Access,* 1–5.

13. Ibid., 1.

14. Department of Defense, *Defense Strategic Guidance: Sustaining U.S. Global Leadership, Priorities for 21st Century Defense* (Washington, DC: GPO, 2012), 2.

15. Defense Secretary Chuck Hagel quoted in Robert S. Dudney, "Verbatim," *Air Force Magazine,* July (2013), 45.

16. Øystein Tunsjø, "Maritime Developments in Asia: Implications for Norway," in *Oslo Files on Defense and Security: The Rise of*

Naval Powers in Asia and Europe's Decline, eds. Bjørn Terjesen and Øystein Tunsjø (Oslo: December 2012), 94.

17. Department of Defense, *Annual Report to Congress, Military and Security Developments Involving the People's Republic of China—2014* (Washington DC: GPO, 2014), 15.

18. Ibid., i.

19. Department of Defense, *Military Power of the People's Republic of China—2009* (Washington, DC: GPO, 2009), i.

20. The term *yuanhai fangwei* (远海防卫), which translates to "distant/far sea defense," began appearing with increasing frequency in Chinese publications. Authors associated with the Naval Research Institute (NRI) called the "shift from offshore to open ocean naval operations" an "inevitable historic choice" for China noting that naval power must "match the expansion of China's maritime interests." Department of Defense, *Military and Security Developments Involving the People's Republic of China—2011* (Washington, DC: GPO, 2011).

21. The United States' ability to close the Strait of Malacca is one of the biggest concerns to the PRC. See DOD, *China 2009*, 3f.

22. See Nikolaus Scholik, "Mahan oder Corbett: Das maritim-strategische Dilemma „Chinamerika" im indo-pazifischen Raum," *Österreichische Militärische Zeitschrift* 2 (2013): 140–51.

23. Robert C. Rubel, "Straight Talk on Forward Presence," *Naval Institute Proceedings* (March 2015): 25.

24. In the light of numerous crises around the globe, the U.S. Navy has shown that it remains capable of reacting to the ever-changing security environment, deploying a total of four carrier battle groups at the same time in June of 2016. See Christopher P. Cavas, "US NAVY Deploys Most Carrier Groups since 2012," *Defense News* (6 June 2016).

Chapter 3. Case Studies

1. The precise wording of the quote is not known. However, in an interview with *Der Spiegel*, Kissinger acknowledges having asked such a question. "SPIEGEL Interview with Henry

Kissinger: 'Europeans Hide Behind the Unpopularity of President Bush,'" *Spiegel Online International* (18 February 2008).

2. In principle, the most important capstone documents that promulgate joint European defense and security strategies are NATO's *Strategic Concept* document as well as the European Union's *Common Security and Defence Policy.* See NATO, *Strategic Concept for the Defence and Security of the Members of the North Atlantic Treaty Organization: Active Engagement, Modern Defense* (Brussels: NATO Public Diplomacy Division, 2015); and EU External Action, *A Global Strategy for the European Union's Foreign and Security Policy: Shared Vision, Common Action: A Stronger Europe* (Brussels, 2016).

3. "Austrian Jagdkommandos to Embark German Tender for EU Mission Sophia," Navaltoday.com (1 March 2017).

4. The Portuguese navy is not discussed in this study, despite its colorful history and current strength of more than three dozen warships, which include five frigates and two modern submarines.

5. Note that aircraft carriers are not referred to as surface combatants.

6. Till, *Seapower,* 117–24

7. Tangredi, *Anti-Access,* 149–60.

8. See contributions by John Andreas Olsen and Svein Efjestad in John Andreas Olsen (eds.), *RUSI Whitehall Paper 87: NATO and the North Atlantic, Revitalising Collective Defense* (Abingdon, U.K.: Taylor & Francis, 2017).

Chapter 4. United Kingdom

1. Despite not including the same geographical areas, the terms Great Britain and United Kingdom will be used synonymously.

2. Jorge Benitez, "Alliance at Risk," AtlanticCouncil.com (26 February 2016).

3. Nick Childs, *Britain's Future Navy,* rev. ed. (Barnsley, U.K.: Pen & Sword Maritime, 2014), 7.

4. The term "peace dividend" refers to the practice of allocating money that would have been invested in defense to other areas, such as health care or social services, as the result of dramatic changes in the global security environment.

5. See Bryan McGrath, "NATO at Sea: Trends in Allied Naval Fire-power," American Enterprise Institute (18 September 2013), n.p.; Benitez, "Alliance," n.p.; Francis Beaufort, "Today's RN Frigate & Destroyer Force Is 'Woefully' Inadequate," *Warships International Fleet Review* (January 2017): 5.

6. See Scholik, "Mahan oder Corbett," 140–51.

7. See Mikhail Tsypkin, "The Challenge of Understanding the Russian Navy," in *Oslo Files on Defence and Security: The Rise of Naval Powers in Asia and Europe's Decline,* eds. Bjørn Terjesen and Øystein Tunsjø (Oslo: December 2012), 90.

8. See DOD, *China 2014,* i.

9. Manohar K. Bangar, "Nobody Asked Me but . . . The Royal Navy: Whither Goes Thou?" *Naval Institute Proceedings,* March (2008): n.p. Brown-water and green-water navies generally are not able to sustain operations over great distances and longer periods of time on the open ocean. A brown/green-water fleet also tends to operate warships that are smaller than those of blue-water navies.

10. Yoji Koda, "Naval Developments in Japan," in *Oslo Files on Defense and Security: The Rise of Naval Powers in Asia and Europe's Decline,* eds. Bjørn Terjesen and Øystein Tunsjø (Oslo: December 2012), 57.

11. John Roberts, *Safeguarding the Nation: The Story of the Modern Royal Navy* (Barnsley, U.K.: Seaforth Publishing, 2009), 202.

12. The paradigmatic shift in armed conflict and the consequences it had on the U.S. armed forces is discussed in Jeremy Stöhs, "US Defense Policy since the End of the Cold War: The Difficulty of Establishing a Balanced Force Structure," *JIPSS,* 8, no. 1 (2014): 139–53.

13. Claire Taylor, *A Brief Guide to Previous Defence Reviews* (House of Commons Library, 2010), 9.

14. Ibid.
15. The number of warheads was later reduced to forty-eight. Ezio Bonsignore et al., "United Kingdom," *Military Technology. The World Defence Almanac 1995–96,* 1 (1996): 168.
16. Benjamin Bathurst, "The Royal Navy in the 1990s," *Naval Forces* 14, no. 4 (1993): 21.
17. Peter Hudson and Peter Roberts, "The UK and the North Atlantic: A British Military Perspective," in *RUSI Whitehall Paper 87: NATO and the North Atlantic. Revitalising Collective Defense,* ed. John Andreas Olsen (Abingdon, U.K.: Taylor & Francis, 2017), 81.
18. See Bathurst, "Navy 1990s," 21. Also in Bonsignore, "United Kingdom," 168.
19. It is possible that these upgrades saved the battleship USS *Missouri* when it was fired upon by Iraqi forces during the Gulf War. Fortunately for the Americans, the Type 42 air-defense destroyer *Gloucester* successfully tracked and destroyed the Silkworm missile racing toward the battleship. The *Missouri,* however, was also fitted with two Phalanx CIWS on each side of the ship. See Roberts, *Safeguarding,* 214.
20. A. D. Baker III, *The Naval Institute Guide to Combat Fleets of the World 2000–2001: Their Ships, Aircraft, and Systems* (Annapolis, MD: Naval Institute Press 2000), 860–62.
21. A comprehensive article on the ship can be found in Conrad Waters, "Significant Ships—HMS Daring: The Royal Navy's Type 45 Air-Defence Destroyer," in *Seaforth World Naval Review 2010,* ed. Conrad Waters (South Yorkshire, U.K.: Seaforth Publishing, 2009), 133.
22. NFR-90 is short for NATO Frigate Replacement for the 1990s. A more detailed description of this program is provided in the chapter on the Italian navy.
23. Alcibiades Thalassocrates, "A Fateful Name—Horizon," *Naval Forces,* 18, no. 2 (1997): 14.
24. Waters, "HMS Daring," 143.
25. Funds permitting, additional weapons could be fitted. This includes Harpoon or future anti-ship missiles, torpedo tubes, CIWS, and cruise missiles of European or American make.

26. HM Ministry of Defence, *British Maritime Doctrine* (BR 1806), 2nd ed. (London: The Stationery Office, 1999), foreword.

27. HM Ministry of Defence, *Strategic Defence Review* (London, 1998), n.p.

28. LPD stands for landing platform dock, LSD for landing ship dock. For more details on the differences between the types, see Department of the Navy, "The Amphibs," http://www.navy.mil/navydata/ships/amphibs/amphib.asp.

29. Ministry of Defense, *Strategic Defence Review*, n.p.

30. Ibid.

31. E. R. Hooton, "Britain's Strategic Defence Review: Smiles All Around," *Military Technology*, 22, no. 9 (1998): 34.

32. "UK: BAE Systems Secures $1.92 Bn. Submarine Deal," Navalto day.com (11 December 2012).

33. Taylor, *Guide*, 11–12.

34. Hooton, "Smiles," 36.

35. Childs, *Future Navy*, 7.

36. Ibid, 7.

37. For an excellent overview of the navy's operations during this period, see Roberts, *Safeguarding*, 202–34. Note that the book was published in 2009. For more recent information on deployments visit, http://www.royalnavy.mod.uk/.

38. See Royal Navy "Cougar 14," http://www.royalnavy.mod.uk/news-and-latest-activity/operations/mediterranean-and-black-sea/cougar.

39. Seidler, "Europe's Role," n.p.

40. Dave Sloggett, "Norway Leads Where Others Should Follow," *Warships*, 5 (2009): 23.

41. Stephan Maninger, "Der Schattenkrieg—Ergänzungen zur „Counterinsurgency—Debatte," *Österreichische Militärische Zeitschrift* 3 (2013): 305. An interesting article comparing the two forms of warfare is Michael J. Boyle, "Do Counterterrorism and Counterinsurgency Go Together?" *International Affairs*, 86, no. 2 (2010): 333–53.

42. Carlo Kopp, "COIN Reorientation—Too Far or Not Far Enough," *Defence Today,* 9, no. 2 (2011): 24–27.

43. HM Ministry of Defence, *Delivering Security in a Changing World, Defense White Paper* (London: 2003): 2–3. While in early 2001 the requirement stood at twelve vessels it was subsequently reduced, first to eight then six ships. Compare E. R. Hooton, "Britain's Type 45 Destroyers Advantage," *Military Technology,* 25, no. 6 (2001): 57–60 and E. R. Hooton, "'Delivering Security in a Changing World': UK Defence White Paper 2003," *Military Technology,* 28, no. 2 (2004): 76–78.

44. Hooton, "Security," 77.

45. HM Ministry of Defence, *Securing Britain in an Age of Uncertainty: The Strategic Defence and Security Review* (London: The Stationery Office, 2010).

46. Larrabee, *Austerity,* xii.

47. HM Ministry of Defence, *Securing Britain,* 22.

48. See Lee Willett in RUSI (eds.), "Accidental Heroes. Britain, France and the Libya Operation—An Interim RUSI Campaign Report," RUSI.org (11 September 2011), 8–9.

49. Dave Sloggett and Ian Ballantyne, "Charting a New Course for the 'Special Relationship' at Sea," *Warships,* March (2015): 18–19.

50. Jamie Merrill, "MoD Asks for American Help in Searching for Russian Submarine Near Scotland," *Independent* (1 April 2014).

51. Larrabee, *Austerity,* 6.

52. McGrath, "NATO Trends," n.p.

53. Ibid.

54. Larrabee, *Austerity,* xvii.

55. Lee Willett, "The Strategic Defence and Security Review, a Preliminary RUSI Assessment," min. 04:52.

56. Iain Ballantyne, "The Big Interview, First Sea Lord of the RN," *Warships* (Sept. 2009): 7.

57. Richard Beedall, "The Royal Navy: Mind the Gaps," in *Seaforth World Naval Review 2014,* ed. Conrad Waters (South Yorkshire, U.K.: Seaforth Publishing, 2013), 80.

58. Sir David Richards quoted in ibid.

59. Till, "British Approach," 25.
60. Andrew Chuter, "Cameron: UK Will Operate 2 Aircraft Carriers," *Defense News* (5 September 2014).
61. HM Ministry of Defence, *A Secure and Prosperous United Kingdom, National Strategy and Strategic Defence and Security Review 2015* (London: The Stationery Office, 2015).
62. In particular, if only three SSBNs would be built, this would severely change the strategic principle of an at-sea nuclear deterrent force, as Britain would no longer be able to have one ship at sea all the time. See RUSI, "Debating Continuous-at-Sea Deterrence: Britain's Nuclear Security."
63. McGrath, "NATO Trends," n.p.
64. Till, "British Approach," 18.
65. Ibid., 26.
66. Ibid., 28.

Chapter 5. France

1. Although the French armed forces were no longer incorporated into NATO's command structure, France had significant forces stationed in Germany. Throughout the Cold War NATO contingency planning was largely based on the assumption that France would join the other NATO forces in the event of war with the Soviet Union. See Norman Friedman, *The Fifty Year War: Conflict and Strategy in the Cold War* (London: Chatham Publishing, 2000), 295–98.
2. Seidler, "Europe's Role," n.p.
3. The "Law of the Sea" is largely "codified in the United Nations Convention on the Law of the Sea, signed Dec. 10, 1982. . . . Beyond its territorial waters [12 nm], every coastal country may establish an exclusive economic zone (EEZ) extending 200 nautical miles (370 km) from shore. Within the EEZ the coastal state has the right to exploit and regulate fisheries, construct artificial islands and installations, use the zone for other economic purposes (e.g., the generation of energy from

waves), and regulate scientific research by foreign vessels. Otherwise, foreign vessels (and aircraft) are entitled to move freely through (and over) the zone." Robin R. Churchill, "Law of the Sea," *Encyclopedia Britannica*, https://www.britannica.com/topic/Law-of-the-Sea#ref913546.

4. "The two [destroyers] are the most modern and doubtless the best equipped in all the navies of Western Europe, in particular with respect to electronic warfare equipment." Bernard Prézelin, *The Naval Institute Guide to Combat Fleets of the World, 1992–93: Their Ships, Aircraft, and Systems* (Annapolis, MD: Naval Institute Press, 1992), xiii.

5. "The system under which the French Navy procures its warships and naval equipment is unique. The main responsibility falls on the Direction des Constructions Navales [DCN], an official design bureau answerable to the General Armament Authority. This resembles the structure of other leading navies' procurement processes, but the bureau is also responsible for running the dockyards, markets its products for export, undertakes a surprisingly wide range of manufacturing, and collaborates with industry." Antony Preston, "Warship Design for the French Navy," *Naval Forces* 13, no. 1 (1992): 16.

6. Tons submerged: *Améthyste*-class SSN, 2,680 tons; *Oyashio*-class SSK, 3,600 tons; *Soryo*-class SSK, 4,200 tons; *Trafalgar*-class SSN, 5,200 tons; *Los Angeles*–class ca. 7,000 tons; *Akula*-class SSN, greater than 9,000 tons. See Eric Wertheim, *The Naval Institute Guide to Combat Fleets of the World, 16th Edition: Their Ships, Aircraft, and Systems* (Annapolis, MD: Naval Institute Press, 2013), 34. Ibid., 37, 200, 359, 581, 797, 847.

7. A number of *Agosta* boats were sold to Pakistan, Spain, and Malaysia, while the *Daphné* saw service with the Portuguese and Pakistani naval forces. See Chris Chant, *Ships of the World's Navies* (London: Brain Trodd Publishing House, 1990), 30–31.

8. Jean-Louis Promé, "'Optimar 95' For The French Navy," *Military Technology* 16, no. 9 (1992): 52.

9. See Prézelin, *Combat Fleets,* xii-xiv, 136–81.

10. Promé, "Optimar 95," 51.

11. Ibid. See Chapter 7 for description of Spanish developments.

12. See initial plan in "'Optimar 95,'" 51–54. Current forces in Jean Moulin, "France: The Marine Nationale: The Bare Minimum for the Job," in *Seaforth World Naval Review 2015*, ed. Conrad Waters (South Yorkshire, U.K.: Seaforth Publishing, 2014), 85.

13. Jean-Charles Lefebvre, "The French Navy in a Phase of Transition," *Naval Forces* 13, no. 5 (1992): 41.

14. The state-owned shipbuilder DCNS has secured a contract to design and build a total of twelve submarines for the Australian navy. In total the deal is worth more than $40 billion. Other contracts include submarines for the Malaysian navy, and frigates for the Moroccan navy and the Egyptian naval forces.

15. "It was originally planned to build four air defense destroyers to escort the *Charles de Gaulle,* but the *Cassard*-class was cut back to two ships. More air defense ships will be needed." See Anthony Preston, "France's Naval Industry in the 1990s," *Naval Forces* 13, no. 5 (1992): 16.

16. Jean-Louis Promé, "The French 1992–94 Military Programme Law: A Case of 'Let's Wait and See' While Adapting," *Military Technology* 16, no. 9 (1992): 42.

17. Promé, "Military Programme," 42.

18. "La Fayette Frigate Programme: A Major Success," *Naval Forces*, Special Issue: French Naval Technology (1994): 21–22. Alan Hinden, "La Fayette Ship Profile (I)," *Naval Forces* 19, no. 2 (1999): 45–47.

19. Hinden, "La Fayette Profile," 22.

20. Wertheim, *Combat Fleets,* 207.

21. Ibid.

22. A helicopter can land at up to sea state six. See Hinden, "La Fayette Profile," 22.

23. Hinden, "La Fayette Profile," 48.

24. Ibid.

25. Ministère de la Défense, *French White Paper, Defense and National Security 2013* (Paris 2013), 131.

26. Conrad Waters, "France's Aquitaine: First French FREMM Heralds a Renaissance for Its Surface Fleet," in *Seaforth World Naval Review 2013,* ed. Conrad Waters (South Yorkshire, U.K.: Seaforth Publishing, 2012), 90–107.

27. Waters, "French FREMM," 99.

28. Ibid., 95.

29. The thermal layer, or thermocline, is a general feature of large bodies of water, such as major lakes or oceans. This layer separates the upper more turbulent and mixed layer from the calm dark water below. The depth of the thermocline is not constant but, generally, is found at around 100 meters below the surface.

30. Ministère de la Défense, *Livre Blanc sur la Défense 1994* (Paris, 1994), 117–19.

31. Ministère de la Défense, *The French White Paper on Defence and National Security* (Paris, 2008), chapter 2, 9.

32. The new SM-3 is generally considered the currently best air-defense missile against high-altitude targets and has successfully been tested in the ballistic missile defense role. Moreover, Raytheon is now also building the Standard Extended Range Active Missile or SM-6 ERAM with an active seeker in order to engage targets beyond the horizon of the ships sensors.

33. For general data on carriers see Wertheim, *Combat Fleets,* 195–96.

34. Philippe Remon-Beauvais quoted in Jean-Paul Philippe, "The CHARLES DE GAULLE Takes Shape," *Military Technology,* 16, no. 10 (1992): 45. This is a very well-written article about the envisioned design features and requirements of the carrier in 1992.

35. Patrick Zimmermann quoted in Henri-Pierre Grolleau, "RAFALE Demonstrates Interoperability," *Military Technology* 32, no. 10 (2008): 92.

36. Ibid., 94.

37. Larrabee, *Austerity,* 26.

38. Ibid., chapter 2, 9.

39. Ministère de la Défense, *Defense, 2013,* 12.

40. Ibid., chapter 11.

41. An overview of American naval information warfare capabilities is provided in Jeremy Stöhs, "Intelligence and Deterrence at Sea: The Role of US Naval Information Technology During the 1980s and Today," *JIPSS* 8, no. 2 (2014): 73–91.

42. See Larrabee, *Austerity,* 19.

43. Ministère de la Défense, *Defense Key Figures, 2015 Edition,* (Paris, 2015), 20.

44. Keel of the lead vessel *Mistral* was laid down in 2003. The third and final unit, *Dixmude,* was commissioned in 2012. LHD stands for landing helicopter dock. These vessels can embark helicopters, as well as landing craft, small vessels, and in some cases hovercraft from its well deck. Examples would be the American *Tarawa* and *America* class, the French *Mistral* class, or the British *HMS Ocean.*

45. Compare McGrath, "Decline," n.p.

46. HM Ministry of Defence, FJS, *Combined Joint Expeditionary Force (CJEF) User Guide* (Swindon and Paris: The Development, Concepts and Doctrine Centre and Centre Interarmées de Concepts, de Doctrine et d'Expérimentations, 2012).

47. Dave Sloggett and Iain Ballantyne, "Franco Russian Carrier Saga," *Warships* 1 (2015): 13–14.

48. Mikhail Tsypkin, "The Challenge of Understanding the Russian Navy," in *Oslo Files on Defence and Security: The Rise of Naval Powers in Asia and Europe's Decline,* eds. Bjørn Terjesen and Øystein Tunsjø (Oslo: December 2012), 90.

49. Frédéric Lert, "Egypt to Acquire FREMM Frigate," IHS Jane's 360 (23 February 2015).

50. Ben Jones, "Franco-British Military Cooperation a New Engine for European Defence?" Occasional Paper 88 (February 2011): 5.

51. Ibid.

52. See Ministère de la Défense, *Defense, 2013,* 54.

53. Moulin, "Marine Nationale," 87.

54. Benitez, "Alliance," n.p.

Chapter 6. Italy

Epigraph. Angelo Mariani, "A Strategic View of the Italian Navy,"
  Naval Forces Special Issue 1 (1997): 6.

 1. Gray, *Leverage,* 135.
 2. Enrico Cernuschi and Vincent P. O'Hara, "Fleet Review—Italy:
    The Marina Militare: A Well-balanced Force in Time of Crisis,"
    in *Seaforth World Naval Review 2013,* ed. Conrad Waters (South
    Yorkshire, U.K.: Seaforth Publishing, 2012), 82.
 3. Original quote: "Il Libro Bianco del 1985 . . . conteneva alcune
    indicazioni importanti, mirando alla ristrutturazione della Dif-
    esa nella direzione di una migliore integrazione delle forze sia
    a livello operativo che di pianificazione e gestione delle risorse,
    a partire dalla definizione delle missioni, dall'unificazione della
    linea di comando, fino all'organizzazione del settore industriale
    e della politica degli approvvigionamenti." Giampaolo Di Paola,
    "L'evoluzione della Difesa italiana negli ultimi trent'anni,"
    Ministero della Difesa (28 September 2012).
 4. Fabrizio Coticchia, "Il Lungo Sentiero sul Lago di Ghiaccio:
    L'Evoluzione della Politica di Difesa Italiana dalla Fine della
    Guerra Fredda all'Operazione Leonte" (PhD diss., IMT Institute
    for Advanced Studies, Lucca, 2009), 185.
 5. Ibid. Original quote: "Il punto-chiave dell'intero documento
    appare l'identificazione tra la sicurezza e la salvaguardia degli
    interessi politici ed economici all'estero, attraverso una nuova
    capacità di *power projection* dello strumento militare, elemento
    cardine della politica estera del paese [italics in the original]."
 6. Umberto Guarnieri, "Roles, Missions and the Force Structure of
    the Italian Fleet," *Naval Forces,* Special Issue 1 (1997): 10.
 7. Guarnieri, "Italian Fleet," 10.
 8. Of the 42,000 refugees who registered in 2013 in Italy, 34,141
    had come by sea. Rivista Italiana Difesa, "Mare Nostrum: Com-
    mando e Controllo e Operazioni Aeronavali," *Foto X-tra'gli
    speciali di RID,* 10 (2014): n.p. See also Elisabeth Braw, "How
    Migrants Rescued the Italian Navy," *Foreign Policy* (31 May
    2016).

9. Parry, *Super Highway,* 245.

10. Cernuschi and O'Hara, "Marina Militare," 84.

11. Prézelin, *Combat Fleets,* xv.

12. In particular, during the 1970s and 1980s, Italian shipbuilders spearheaded the design of minehunters. Since then, the situation has become somewhat more difficult for Italy's naval industry. Antony Preston, "The Italian Navy Today," *Naval Forces* 14, no. 6 (1993): 32.

13. Ibid.

14. Cernuschi and O'Hara, "Marina Militare," 89.

15. Among the states capable of operating aircraft carriers including fixed-wing manned aircraft are Argentina, India, Spain, the United States, Britain, France, and Russia.

16. Cernuschi and O'Hara, "Marina Militare," 80–81.

17. Guarnieri, "Italian Fleet," 16.

18. Prézelin, *Combat Fleets,* xv.

19. Chant, *Ships,* 144, 158, 160, 166.

20. Guarnieri, "Italian Fleet," 10.

21. Mariani, "Strategic View," 7.

22. Ibid., 7.

23. Cernuschi and O'Hara, "Marina Militare," 82.

24. Alcibiades Thalassocrates, "Glimmer on the HORIZON," *Military Technology,* 19, no. 7 (1995): 17.

25. Thalassocrates, "Glimmer," 10.

26. The numerous reasons are explained in ibid., 27–34.

27. Guarnieri, "Italian Fleet," 15.

28. Alcibiades Thalassocrates, "A Fateful Name—Horizon," *Naval Forces,* 18, no. 2 (1997): 15. The allure of buying a tried and proven SAM system from the United States also caused Britain to consider installing the Mk41 VLS on its own destroyer design (the *Daring* class). Ultimately, however, they also decided to rely on the SYLVER VLS.

29. Thalassocrates, "Fateful Name," 15.

30. A very detailed chapter on the Italian version of the FREMM can be found in Conrad Waters, "Significant Ships—Italian

Fremms: Carlo Bergamini (General Purpose) and Virginio Fasan (Anti-Submarine) Frigates," in *Seaforth World Naval Review 2015,* ed. Conrad Waters (South Yorkshire, U.K.: Seaforth Publishing, 2014), 89. The Type 212 is discussed in more detail in chapter 9 on the German navy. For more information on the Type 212 see Conrad Waters, "Significant Ships—Germany's Type 212A Submarines: Cutting-Edge Technology Drives German Maritime Transformation," in *Seaforth World Naval Review 2014,* ed. Conrad Waters (South Yorkshire, U.K.: Seaforth Publishing, 2013), 137–52.

31. Waters, "Italian FREMMs," 89–107. An article describing the early stages of the program can be found in "France and Italy Launch Joint Frigate Programme," *Military Technology* 27, no. 2 (2003): 64–68.

32. The FREMM frigates incorporate impressive stealth features and the French *Aquitaine* supposedly has an even smaller radar cross-section (RCS) than the *La Fayette* class. For more information see Waters, "Aquitaine," 90–107.

33. Ibid., 94.

34. Waters, "Aquitaine," 107.

35. Italy also looked into cooperating with Britain's Future Surface Combatant (Type 24 frigate) and Germany's F-125 project. However, because of the aging fleet, it was decided that a joint venture with France would be more favorable and make the frigates available at an earlier point. See "Joint Frigate," 2003, 64–68.

36. Waters "Italian FREMMS," 90.

37. Ibid., 89.

38. "Fincantieri and Finmeccanica Will Renew the Italian Navy Fleet," defense-aerospace.com, 7 May (2015).

39. Ibid., 107. "The Italian defense budget is divided into three major areas: (1) investment (what the U.S. calls research and development, plus procurement), (2) personnel, and (3) training, maintenance, and operations. Since switching to an all-volunteer military in 2006, the Italian goal was to spend roughly

50 percent of their budget on personnel, 25 percent on investment, and 25 percent on training, maintenance, and operations. In reality, personnel costs have consumed roughly 70 percent of Italian military spending." Larrabee, *Austerity*, 36.

40. The 2005 defense white paper remains on point when it says that "the multilayered and unpredictable nature of future threats . . . demand development of a capability to prevent and, when necessary, to intervene quickly and efficiently even at a great distance from the homeland. In other words, unlike in the past, the military contribution to national security can no longer depend exclusively on the capability to guard and provide static defense of the metropolitan areas ("Homeland defense"); it must develop the capability to dynamically face threats whenever they occurs [*sic*]." Giampaolo di Paolo, "Il Concetto Stregico del Capoi die Stato Maggiore dell Difesa, 2005," 10–11.

41. Andy Nativi, "Mission Ready: Italy's New Carrier Has Multiple Roles," *Defense Technology International,* 2, no. 8 (2008): 19–20.

42. Enrico Cernuschi and Vincent P. O'Hara, "Significant Ships— The Aircraft Carrier Cavour: Doctrine and Sea Power in the Italian Navy," in *Seaforth World Naval Review 2010,* ed. Conrad Waters (South Yorkshire, U.K.: Seaforth Publishing, 2009), 127.

43. Cernuschi and O'Hara, "Marina Militare," 85.

44. McGrath, "Decline," n.p.

45. Agence France-Presse, "Italy Removes Aircraft Carrier from Libya Campaign," *Defense News* (7 July 2011), n.p.

46. See ibid.

47. Bruno Branciforte, "The Commanders Respond: Italian Navy," *Naval Institute Proceedings* (March 2012).

48. Ibid.

49. Gary J. Schmitt, "Italian Hard Power: Ambitions and Fiscal Realities," American Enterprise Institute (1 November 2012), n.p.

50. Italy has decided to build five new offshore multipurpose patrol vessels, with an option of four additional ships. "The Pattugliatore Polivalente D'Altura (PPA) vessel will replace Minerva-class corvettes, Cassiopea-class patrol vessels and two Duran de la

Penne–class destroyers." Needless to say, the new class will in any case number fewer than the ships being decommissioned. Tom Kingston, "Italy Closing in on Patrol Vessel Deal," *Defense News* (26 October 2014).

51. Lizzy Davies and Arthur Neslen, "Italy: End of Ongoing Sea Rescue Mission 'Puts Thousands at Risk,'" *Guardian* (31 October 2014).

52. Cernuschi and O'Hara, "Marina Militare," 86.

53. Giorgio Giorgerini, "The Italian Navy in the 1990s," *Military Technology*, 14, no. 5 (1990): 48.

Chapter 7. Spain

1. Elmar B. Potter, Chester W. Nimitz, and Jürgen Rohwer (eds.), *Seemacht. Eine Seekriegsgeschichte von der Antike bis zur Gegenwart* (München: Pawlak Verlag, 1986), 24–47.

2. R. G. Grant, *Battle at Sea: 3,000 Years of Naval Warfare* (London: Dorling Kindersley Limited, 2008), 120.

3. "Spain was the big loser of the war and the settlement. Although it signed a series of treaties with its military opponents, it never accepted their terms until forced to do so in 1719–20. As soon as the Succession War was over and the Utrecht Treaties signed, Spain set out to undo the entire settlement. It had been stripped of the Netherlands, all of its Italian holdings, and Gibraltar and Minorca. It was compelled to grant British participation in the Asiento trade, shipping African slaves to Latin America and to the Spanish West Indies. Philip V had been forced to renounce his claim to the French throne. The settlements were thus a major national and dynastic humiliation. . . . The assault on the settlement came quickly." Kalevi J. Holsti, *Peace and War: Armed Conflicts and International Order 1648–1989* (Cambridge: Cambridge University Press, 1998), 77–78.

4. Ibid., 78.

5. Ibid., 78.

6. The Spanish Matador aircraft were based on the British Hawker Siddeley Harrier short take-off and vertical landing (STOVL)

aircraft. The Spanish version is almost identical to the U.S. Marine Corps' AV-8A Harrier.

7. Ministerio de Defensa, Secretaría General Técnica, *Defense White Paper 2000* (Madrid: Centro de Publicaciones, 2000), 193.

8. The Group of 8 was an international forum of the world's most highly industrialized states. After the annexation of Crimea, Russia was expelled from the G-8, resulting in the G-7.

9. Ministerio de Defensa, *Defense White Paper 2000,* 57. "Within the geostrategic unity of the Mediterranean, where problems and tension spread easily, Spain considers that its western basin requires much attention as a nearby area with specific characteristics." Ibid., 65.

10. Spain hast the second-highest unemployment rate among all EU members. Almost 20 percent of its working population is out of a job, many of them young adults. See: "Unemployment Rates, Seasonally Adjusted, July 2016.png."

11. Prézelin, *Combat Fleets,* xv.

12. Íñigo Puente, "Plan Alta Mar: ¿sueño de lo que pudo ser o anticipo de lo que será?" *Revista Naval* (December 1997).

13. Camil Busquets i Vilanova, "The Spanish F-100 Frigates," *Naval Forces,* 17, no. 5 (1996): 26.

14. It is likely that Spanish naval forces would have provided support to NATO operations in the case of a military confrontation with the Soviet Union. The Spanish are described as specifically looking to the Americans for help. See F. J. West Jr. et al., "Sea Plan 2000," in *U.S. Naval Strategy in the 1970s—Selected Documents,* ed. John Hattendorf (Newport, RI: Naval War College Press, 2007), 113. By the 1980s Spain's maritime role within NATO was clearly laid out. See Watkins, "Strategy 1984," 76.

15. "'Grupo Alfa'—the Spanish Navy's Main Fighting Force," *Naval Forces* 12, no. 5 (1991): 20.

16. For more information see Christopher Chant, *Ships,* 474–75.

17. A more detailed description of these ships can be found in both Prézelin, *Combat Fleets,* 803–806, and Norman Polmar,

The Naval Institute Guide to the Ships and Aircraft of the U.S. Fleet, 15th Edition (Annapolis, MD: Naval Institute Press, 1993), 143–46.

18. Prézelin, *Combat Fleets*, 473.

19. Ibid., 472.

20. Ibid., xv.

21. In the original: "La situación de la Flotilla de Submarinos de la Armada a principio de los 90 era magnífica, la mejor, sin duda, desde el advenimiento de la II República en 1931 (o quizá, incluso, la mejor de su historia). Se hallaban en servicio 8 submarinos pertenecientes a dos series, cuatro del tipo Delfín (S-60), construidos en torno a 1970, y cuatro Galerna (S-70), construidos diez años después." Puente, "Plan Alta Mar," n.p.

22. Bundesministerium der Verteidigung, *Weißbuch 2006, Zur Sicherheitspolitik Deutschlands und zur Zukunft der Bundeswehr* (Berlin, 2006), 122.

23. Ministerio de Defensa, *Defense White Paper 2000,* 193.

24. Ministerio de Defensa, Secretaría General Técnica, *Strategic Defence Review,* (Madrid: Imprenta Ministerio de Defensa, 2003), 107.

25. Ministerio de Defensa, Directive 001/2000 Admiral Chief of Staff of the Navy: "GRUFLOT Is Created."

26. Baker expands on the ships' impressive features: "[These amphibious warfare ships] can carry up to 6 helicopters in the hangars. [They] have 1,010m² internal vehicle parking space and can use 885m² docking . . . for additional vehicles; further vehicles can be carried on the helicopter deck and in the helicopter hangar." Baker, *Combat Fleets,* 723.

27. "The three partners were able to agree on practically identical operational requirements, establishing the basis for a cooperation programme [in 1994]." Michael Herwig, "Trilateral Cooperation for a Frigate Programme—Spain, the Netherlands, and Germany," *Naval Forces,* 15, no. 5 (1994): 35.

28. Busquets i Vilanova, "F-100," 25. For more detailed information on the capabilities see Wertheim, *Combat Fleets,* 672.

29. "Built to Spain's Juan Carlos I design, the ships' hulls were fabricated by Navantia at Ferrol Spain prior to being transported by heavy lift vessels to Williamstown near Melbourne for installation of their island structure and final fitting out by BAE Systems." Conrad Waters, "Regional Review—Asia and the Pacific," in *Seaforth World Naval Review 2015,* ed. Conrad Waters (South Yorkshire, U.K.: Seaforth Publishing, 2013), 28.

30. Massimo Annati, "European Aircraft Carrier Programmes," *Military Technology,* 29, no. 10 (2005): 44. For more information, also see article of Europe's amphibious vessels by: Christina MacKenzie and Andy Nativi, "Mission Ready: Amphibious Ship Designs Meet Diverse Operational Needs," *Defense Technology International* 3, no. 3 (2009): 34–35.

31. The CODLAG (combined diesel-electric and gas turbine) in the Juan Carlos creates a thrust of 30,500 hp allowing speeds up to 21 knots, while the nuclear reactor on U.S. carriers can produce over 280,000 hp giving the ships' sustained speed of over 30 knots.

32. Annati, "European Programme," 44.

33. "A major ongoing concern is the troubled S-80 submarine programme, which envisages completion of four boats to replace Spain's existing underwater flotilla. Construction work has effectively been suspended until major weight and buoyancy problems identified in the first submarine, *Isaac Peral* in May 2013 are resolved. General Dynamics Electric Boat of the USA has been brought in to assist a major re-design, which will involve lengthening the submarines into a S-80 Plus configuration." Conrad Waters, "Regional Review—Europe and Russia," in *Seaforth World Naval Review 2015,* ed. Conrad Waters (South Yorkshire, U.K.: Seaforth Publishing, 2014), 65. The following quote is from Bryan McGrath, "NATO Trends," fn 38. See Jose Alberto Gonzalez, "La Armada da de Baja el 'Siroco' y Centra Sus Esfuerzos en Los Submarines S-80" [The Navy Withdraws the 'Sirocco' and Focuses Its Efforts on the Submarine S-80], *La Verdad* (5 August 2012).

34. McGrath, "NATO Trends," n.p.

35. "NATO/WEU: Operation Sharp Guard," NATO (2 October 1996).
36. NATO, "Operation Active Endeavour" (3 March 2015).
37. John R. Ballard et al., *From Kabul to Baghdad and Back: The U.S. at War in Afghanistan and Iraq* (Annapolis MD: Naval Institute Press, 2012), 137.
38. Ibid. As of 2013 Spain had 856 troops deployed to the relatively stable Badghsi province in the northwest. This is a small number when compared to other countries' troop levels: Romania 1,077, Italy 2,825, and Germany 4,400. See Council on Foreign Relations, "U.S. War in Afghanistan, 1999–Present."
39. Departamento De Seguridad National, Presidencia Del Gobierno, *The National Maritime Security Strategy 2013: Sharing a Common Project* (Madrid, 2013), 35.
40. Larrabee, *Austerity,* 45–46.
41. Ibid., 49–50.
42. Larrabee, *Austerity,* 49. The sources vary between 0.9 percent and 1.2 percent of GDP, depending on what is included under the term "defense."
43. Cernuschi, "Marina Militare," 89.
44. Larrabee, *Austerity,* 51.
45. David Ing and Fenella McGerty, "Update: Spain to Increase Defence Spending," Janes.com (1 October 2014). Also David Ing and Fenella McGerty, "Spanish Defense Spending Increases 40% in 2015." Janes.com (20 April 2016).
46. Conrad Waters, "Regional Review—Europe and Russia," in *Seaforth World Naval Review 2014,* ed. Conrad Waters (South Yorkshire, U.K.: Seaforth Publishing, 2013), 65.
47. As of early 2013 the navy only had two submarines operating, with an average age of twenty-seven years, the *Galerna* and the *Tramuntana*, since the *Mistral* was under repair until the spring of 2013. If delays occur in the delivery of the S-80, the complexity of the construction that will take it beyond 2016, the armed forces would be operating only one submarine. It would be the *Mistral*, which as of early 2013 was passing its last major review. Later in

2013 *Tramuntana*, the most modern in the series, entered over-haul. The *Tramuntana* ends its operational life in 2018. See "Series 70 Galerna-type Submarines," globalsecurity.org.

48. Departamento De Seguridad, *National Maritime,* 21.

49. Department of Defense: Africa Command, "African Partnership Station," http://www.africom.mil/what-we-do/security-cooperation -programs/africa-partnership-station.

Chapter 8. Turkey and Greece

1. Christos Kollias and Gülay Günlük-Şenesen, *Greece and Turkey in the 21st Century: Conflict or Cooperation. A Political Economy Perspective,* eds. Christos Kollias and Gülay Günlük-Şenesen (New York: Nova Science, 2003), 1.

2. Turkish Ministry of Defense, *White Paper 2000,* Section Five, n.p.

3. Ibid., Section Five, Section Three, n.p.

4. Littoral disputes have also included Israel, with which Turkey froze its diplomatic ties for several years. See Burak Ege Bekdil and Umit Enginsoy, "Mediterranean Littoral Dispute Challenges Turkish Navy," *Defense News* (9 January 2012), 10.

5. Turkish Ministry of Defense, *White Paper 2000,* Section Two, n.p. Also see Hellenic Ministry of National Defense, *White Paper for the Armed Forces 1996–1997,* chapter 1, n.p.

6. The Russian *Zubr*-class air cushion vehicle landing craft are the largest in the world. See Wertheim, *Combat Fleets,* 253–54.

7. For the up-and-coming naval ship industry in the 1990s, see "Turkish Navy—Reasons to Celebrate" *Naval Forces,* 15, no. 4 (1994): 23–24.

8. "A Forecast for the 21st Century: George Friedman. ANU," min. 46:40.

9. Aaron Stein quoted in Humeyra Pamuk and Gareth Jones, "Turkish Military a Fractured Force After Attempted Coup," *Reuters* (26 July 2016).

10. "The primary Soviet thrust would be in *Central Europe*. Smaller attack would also occur to attempt to seize *Northern Norway*

and the *Turkish Straits.* A limited offensive is also possible in *Eastern Turkey,* to try to draw off forces defending the straits [italics in the original]." Watkins, "Strategy 1984," 78.

11. Ibid., 76.
12. The Black Sea has a size of roughly 436,000 km and its average depth is 1,200 meters, The Baltic Sea is of similar size, 377,000 km, but is much shallower, with an average depth of 55 meters.
13. Prézelin, *Combat Fleets,* 533–52.
14. "Celebrate," 24.
15. Ibid.
16. Two units were built by Blohm & Voss in Hamburg, two by the Gölcük shipyards.
17. These were somewhat larger and more capable than the Type 209/1200 already in service.
18. Wertheim, *Combat Fleets*, 802.
19. Gencer Özcan, "The Military and the Making of Foreign Policy in Turkey," in *Turkey in World Politics: An Emerging Multiregional Power*, eds. Barry M Rubin and Kemal Kirişci (London: Lynne Rienner Publishers, 2001), 24.
20. Turkish Ministry of Defense, *White Paper 2000,* Section Three, n.p.
21. Amphibious forces are only mentioned in the list of Turkish forces assigned to NATO: "The number of forces presently assigned to NATO by the Turkish Armed Forces is as follows: . . . 15 Frigates, 2 LSTs, 17 Patrol Boats, 9 Helicopters, 11 Minesweepers/hunters, 1 Logistic Support Ship, 7 Submarines and 1 Amphibious Infantry Battalion." Ibid., Part Two, n.p.
22. Mohamed Abdiwahab, "Turkey's Largest Military Base Oversea to be Opened in Somalia in April," sputniknews (17 March 2017). Turkish Naval Forces, *Turkish Naval Strategy* (Istanbul: Printing Office of the Turkish Naval Forces, 2016).
23. Wertheim, *Combat Fleets,* 751.
24. Turkish Ministry of Defense, *White Paper 2000,* Section Three, n.p.
25. Waters, "Europe 2010," 99.
26. Ibid.

27. An early outline of shipbuilding for the first decade of the twenty-first century is provided in "Ship Construction and New Projects," *Naval Forces* 18, no. 4 (1997): 27. More recent developments found in Umit Enginsoy and Burak Ege Bekdil, "Turkey Seeks Full Littoral Defense Architecture," *Defense News* (10 January 2011), 13.

28. Micha'el Tanchum, "Turkey Vulnerable to Rising Russian Power in the Black Sea," The Turkey ANALYST. A Biweekly Briefing on Current Affairs (9 April 2014), n.p.

29. Ibid.

30. Adnan Caglayan quoted in Umit Enginsoy and Burak Ege Bekdil, "Does Turkey Need an Aircraft Carrier?" *Defense News* (7 May 2012), 13.

31. Stockholm International Peace Research Institute, "Military Expenditure Database."

32. Ibid.

33. Thanos P. Dokos and Panayotis J. Tsakonas, "Greek-Turkish Relations in the Post-Cold War Era," in *Greece and Turkey in the 21st Century: Conflict or Cooperation. A Political Economy Perspective,* eds. Christos Kollias and Gülay Günlük-Şenesen (New York: Nova Science, 2003), 10.

34. Kollias, *Greece and Turkey,* 10.

35. Ibid.

36. Ibid., 37–48.

37. Faruk Sönmezoğlu and Gülden Ayman, "The Roots of Conflict and the Dynamics of Change in Turkish-Greek Relations," in *Greece and Turkey in the 21st Century: Conflict or Cooperation. A Political Economy Perspective,* eds. Christos Kollias and Gülay Günlük-Şenesen (New York: Nova Science, 2003), 39.

38. Ibid., 39.

39. Ibid., 30.

40. Hellenic Ministry of National Defense, *White Paper for the Armed Forces 1996–1997* (Athens, 1997), n.p.

41. Ibid.

42. Ibid.

43. Chant, *Ships,* 126.

44. Waters, "Europe 2010," 98.

45. Stergios Tsilikas, "Greek Military Strategy: The Doctrine of Deterrence and Its Implications on Greek-Turkish Relations" (Master thesis, U.S. Navy: Naval Postgraduate School, Monterey, 2001).

46. Wertheim, *Combat Fleets*, 248.

47. Waters, "Europe 2014," 70.

48. Stelios Alifantis and Christos Kollias, "Greece," in *Arms Procurement Decision Making Volume II: Chile, Greece, Malaysia, Poland, South Africa and Taiwan*, ed. Ravinder Pal Singh (Oxford: University Press, 2000), 39–66.

49. Hellenic Ministry of Defense, *White Paper 2014*, 18.

50. Ibid., 42.

51. For more information on the development of Hellenic naval strategy see thesis by Tsilikas, "Military Strategy."

52. Hellenic Ministry of Defense, *White Paper 2014*, 42.

53. Waters, "Europe 2014," 69.

Chapter 9. Germany

1. See William J. Lewis, *The Warsaw Pact: Arms, Doctrine, and Strategy* (London: McGraw-Hill, 1982), 180.

2. See Dieter Krüger and Felix Schneider (eds.), *Die Alpen im Krieg: Historischer Raum, Strategie und Sicherheitspolitik* (Munich: Oldenburg Verlag, 2012), 123, 243, 256, 269.

3. The naval strategy documents states that America's allies would deploy their forces according to plan. "The West German Navy would move to conduct forward operations in the Baltic, and the Turkish Navy, especially its submarines would do the same in the Black Sea." James D. Watkins, "The Maritime Strategy, 1984," in *U.S. Naval Strategy in the 1980s, Selected Documents*, ed. John B. Hattendorf and Peter M. Swartz (Newport, RI: Naval War College Press, 2008), 76.

4. For description of German naval forces between 1980 and 1995, see Christian Jentzsch, "Von der Escort-Navy zur

Expeditionary-Navy?" (presentation at the 16. Maritime Sicherheitskolloquiums, Rostock, October 20, 2016), https://dmkn. de/escort-navy-expeditionary-navy/. German mine inventory countered roughly 10,000 mines. See Arthur Moreau, "Maritime Strategy Presentation (for the Secretary of the Navy, 4 November 1982)," in *U.S. Naval Strategy in the 1980s, Selected Documents,* ed. John B. Hattendorf and Peter M. Swartz (Newport, RI: Naval War College Press, 2008), 38.

5. Grant, *Ships,* 41–46.

6. "In a significant increase to the Indonesia Navy a total of 39 ships have been procured from Germany covering ships of the former East German Navy." See Ezio Bonsignore et al., "Indonesia," *The World Defense Almanac 1992–1993,* 17, Issue 1 (1993): 190.

7. McGrath, "NATO Trends," n.p.

8. Gray, *Leverage,* 225.

9. The term "out of area" is explained by the Oxford dictionary as follows: "(Of a military operation) conducted away from the place of origin or expected place of action of the force concerned." In the case of Germany it can be explained as, "NATO Alliance operations and non-NATO coalition operations in which the United States and other NATO allies participate and that occur outside or on the periphery of Alliance territory." Myron Hury et al., *Interoperability: A Continuing Challenge in Coalition Air Operations* (Santa Monica: RAND Corporation, 2000), chapter 1, 1.

10. "[Die Marine wird] in die Lage versetzt sein, dauerhaft auch in großer Entfernung, im multinationalen Rahmen und unter Bedrohung vor fremden Küsten operieren zu können.... Deutsche maritime Kräfte können ungehindert und frühzeitig in weit entfernte Regionen vorausstationiert werden und diplomatische Aktivitäten flankieren. Neben ihrer Befähigung zum bewaffneten Einsatz auf See können sie wirkungsvoll zu Operationen an Land beitragen." Bundesministerium der Verteidigung, *Weißbuch 2006: Zur Sicherheitspolitik Deutschlands und zur Zukunft der Bundeswehr* (Berlin, 2006), 112–15.

11. Ulf Kaak, *Die Schiffe der Deutschen Marine: 1990 bis heute* (München: GeraMond Verlag, 2013), 6–7.

12. See, for example, Thorsten Jungholt and Simon Meyer, "Der Marine könnte es bald an Schiffen mangeln," Welt.de (6 April 2013) or Rainer Brinkmann, "Befehlshaber der Flotte: 'Deutsche Marine am Limit,'" shz.de (9 April 2017).

13. Larrabee, *Austerity*, 33.

14. Sebastian Bruns, "Elements of Twenty-First-Century German Naval Strategy," in *Routledge Handbook of Naval Strategy and Security*, ed. Joachim Krause and Sebastian Bruns (Abingdon, U.K.: Routledge, 2016). See also Heinz Dieter Jopp, "Maritime Abhängigkeiten und Schlussfolgerungen. Die Sicherheitspolitischen Rahmenbedingungen der Bundesrepublik Deutschland," *MarineForum*, Nr. 1–2 (2004), 3–7. Heinz Dieter Jopp, "Rückbesinnung," *MarineForum*, Nr. 7–8 (2017), 1.

15. Despite being outlined in earlier white papers the term was only used in the 2006 defense white paper. See Bundesministerium der Verteidigung, *Weißbuch 2006*, 112.

16. "[Die Neuausrichtung zu einer Marine, die] im Bündnisrahmen einen eigenständigen und sichtbaren Beitrag zur Aufrechterhaltung des Prinzips der 'Freiheit der Meere,' insbesondere jedoch für maritime Maßnahmen in der internationalen Krisenbewältigung [leistet]." German *Weißbuch 1994* quoted in Berthold Meyer, "Von der Entgrenzung nationaler deutscher Interessen. Die politische Legitimation weltweiter Militäreinsätze," in *HSFK-Report 10/2007* (Frankfurt a. M., 2007), 16.

17. See Jürgen Rhades, "The German Navy Faces the Future," *Naval Forces 13*, no. 6 (1992): 18–22.

18. Ibid., 20.

19. Ibid.

20. Ibid.

21. See Sigurd Hess, "Die konzeptionelle Planung der Marine 1989–2002," in *Die Wende. Die Deutsche Marine auf dem Weg in die Einheit*, eds. Stephan Huck and Hartmut Klüver (Bochum: Dieter Winkler Verlag, 2007), 21–30.

22. Parry, *Super Highway,* 185–87.
23. "Submarines with diesel-electric propulsion generally have to surface every couple of days to run the charging generator and recharge the batteries. However, with a special fuel cell system, subs can remain under water for longer. The present record—set by an HDW Type 212A submarine—is 14 days. If a submarine is unable to surface, the regulations require that the crew is able to survive for at least six days." Stefan Nitschke and Stephen Elliott, "Under Water," *Naval Forces* (January 2015).
24. Waters, "Type 212A," 152.
25. Ibid., 151.
26. The final two Type 212As for the German navy entered service by 2017. There are plans to add two further units to join the fleet by the mid-2020s.
27. Waters, "Type 212A," 152.
28. Chris Chant, *Kriegsschiffe Heute* (Stuttgart: Motorbuch Verlag, 2006), 75.
29. Herwig, "Trilateral," 35.
30. Ibid.
31. Ibid.
32. An interesting article regarding the German and Dutch AAW frigates can be found in Massimo Annati, "German and Dutch AAW Frigates at Sea," *Military Technology,* 26, no. 3–4 (2002), 102–108.
33. "The programme was aimed at the realisation of a very advanced multi-function radar, in some way comparable to the US SPY-1 and able to offer adequate performance to control both SM-2 and ESSM missiles, but at the same time remain well below the size, weight and power characteristics of its US counterpart." Ibid., 103.
34. The SMART-L and APAR were developed by the Dutch Signaal company, now Thales.
35. RIM-166 for low-tier AAW, ESSM for medium-tier, and SM-2 Block IIIA for high-tier air defense.
36. See Norman Friedman, "Technology Review. Ballistic Missile Defense and the USN," in *Seaforth World Naval Review 2013,* ed.

Conrad Waters (South Yorkshire, U.K.: Seaforth Publishing, 2012), 191 fn5.

37. "Vom Flugzeugträgerverband verabschiedet—Fregatte 'Hamburg' macht Heimatumdrehungen!" *Presseportal* (18 May 2013).

38. "NATO/WEU Operation Sharp Guard," *IFOR Final Factsheet* (2 October 1996).

39. Conrad Waters, "Regional Review—Europe and Russia," in *Seaforth World Naval Review 2010,* ed. Conrad Waters (South Yorkshire, U.K.: Seaforth Publishing, 2009), 96.

40. For general information see "Die Operation Enduring Freedom," *Bundeswehr* (4 December 2013). For criticism see Bündis 90 Die Grünen, "Operation Active Endeavour, Einsatz muss beendet werden," 29 January 2014.

41. Pierre Schubjé, "UNIFIL: Deutsch-libanesische Kooperation— Ein Zwischenbericht," *MarineForum* 1–2 (2014): 14–16.

42. Guy Toremans, "Significant Ships—Braunschweig Class Corvettes. Eagerly Awaited by the German Navy," in *Seaforth World Naval Review 2013,* ed. Conrad Waters (South Yorkshire, U.K.: Seaforth Publishing, 2012), 129.

43. Ibid., 146.

44. Ibid., 147.

45. Sebastian Bruns, quoted in Albrecht Müller, "New Frigate Underscores Germany's Shift from Cold War Naval Combat," *Defense News* (13 January 2014).

46. Bundesministerium, *Weißbuch 2006,* 122.

47. Wertheim, *Combat Fleets,* 233.

48. Ibid., 117.

49. Larrabee, *Austerity,* 30–34.

50. Bonsignore, "Germany," 131.

51. Larrabee, *Austerity,* 98.

52. Hans-Rudolf Boehmer, "Today, the Navy Is Better and More Capable Than Ever Before," *Naval Forces,* Special Issue 5 (1996): 10.

53. Bundesministerium der Verteidigung, *Weißbuch 2016: On German Security Policy and the Future of the Bundeswehr* (Berlin, 2016), 112–15.

54. McGrath, "NATO Trends," n.p.
55. Ibid.
56. Ibid.

Chapter 10. Denmark and the Netherlands

1. The Danish-Norwegian personal union included territorial possessions in the High North, the African West coast, India, and the Caribbean. Its power was surpassed by the Dutch, whose East India Trading Company propelled it to the forefront of political power during the seventeenth and eighteenth centuries.
2. Mahan quoted in Till, *Strategy,* 57.
3. See Parry, *Super Highway,* 57. For more information see "Port of Rotterdam," homepage, http://www.portofrotterdam.com/en/Port/port-in-general/Pages/default.aspx.
4. See Parry, *Super Highway,* 52–53.
5. Ibid., 54.
6. Mahan discusses Holland's dependence on the sea: "If England was drawn to the sea, Holland was driven to it; without the sea England languished, but Holland died. In the height of her greatness, when she was one of the chief factors in European politics, a competent native authority estimated that the soil of Holland could not support more than one eighth of her inhabitants." When the disastrous war with England in 1653–54 drew to a close it had turned the Dutch harbors into "a forest of masts; the country was full of beggars; grass grew in the streets, and in Amsterdam fifteen hundred houses were untenanted." Mahan, *Naval Warfare,* 32–34.
7. Although it only had a relatively small navy the Danes had heavy mechanized forces stationed in Germany.
8. The Royal Danish Navy had an inventory of roughly 6,600 mines. See Moreau, "Maritime Strategy," 38.
9. Prézelin, *Combat Fleets,* 104–14.
10. In fact, the icebreakers were "civilian-manned and subordinate to the Ministry of Trade and Shipping." See ibid., 113.

11. Parry, *Super Highway,* 186.

12. Hans Harboe-Hansen, "The Royal Danish Navy's Modernisation Programme," *Naval Forces,* 18, no. 6 (1997): 93.

13. For a description of Flyvefisken see Grant, *Kriegsschiffe,* 104. Initially, swapping StanFlex containers took forty-eight hours, but this time has been significantly reduced. See Guy Toremans, "Significant Ships. Iver Huitfeldt Class Frigates: Spearhead of the Royal Danish Navy," in *Seaforth World Naval Review 2014,* ed. Conrad Waters (South Yorkshire, U.K.: Seaforth Publishing, 2013), 108.

14. Parry, *Super Highway,* 186.

15. Harboe-Hansen, "Modernisation," 92–93.

16. Ibid., 92.

17. See Baker, *Combat Fleets,* 738.

18. See Harboe-Hansen, "Modernisation," 95.

19. Ibid., 94.

20. Wertheim, *Combat Fleets,* 158.

21. Ibid., 158. The *Absalon*'s speed is inherently limited—ca. twenty-two knots.

22. Danish Parliament, *The Danish Defense Agreement 2005–2009, Preliminary* translation, June (Copenhagen, 2004), 2.

23. Søren Nørby, "Fleet Review: The Royal Danish Navy," in *Seaforth World Naval Review 2017,* ed. Conrad Waters (South Yorkshire, U.K.: Seaforth Publishing, 2016), 83.

24. Danish Parliament, *Preliminary,* 7.

25. Of the 18,000 troops deployed over the course of 11 years—around 750 deployed at any given time—43 were killed. See "Operation Enduring Freedom," iCasualties.org.

26. See Combined Maritime Forces, "CTF-151: Counter-piracy."

27. Denmark will provide 700 million kroner in aid annually. See "Norway Cuts Afghan Aid over Lack of Progress on Women's Rights," TOLOnews (5 October 2013).

28. Cernuschi, "Marina Militare," 85.

29. Danish Parliament, *Danish Defense Agreement 2010–2014* (Copenhagen, 2009), 2, 7.

30. Ibid., 2.

31. Ibid., 3.

32. Ibid., 9.

33. Department of Defense, "Remarks by Secretary Hagel and Gen. Dempsey on the Fiscal Year 2015 Budget, Preview in the Pentagon Briefing Room, Transcript" (24 February 2014).

34. See T. X. Hammes, "Getting Our Money's Worth: LCS VS Iver Huitfeldt–class," *War on the Rocks* (6 August 2013). Also Steven Wills, "LCS Versus the Danish Strawman," Center for International Maritime Security (19 February 2015), and Sam LaGrone, "Navy Asks Industry for Input for Follow-on to Littoral Combat Ship," *USNI News* (30 April 2014).

35. Toremans, "Huitfeldt," 105–19.

36. Ibid., 105.

37. Ibid., 107.

38. See Friedman, "Missile Defense," 191 footnotes, and Friedman, "Ballistic Missile Defense," 191. The discussion concerning the possible expansion of the navy's air-defense capability can be found as early as 2007. Both SM-3 and SM-6 missiles were proposed in Joris Janssen Lok's article; neither system has been procured. See Joris Janssen Lok, "Danish Decision," *Defense Technology International* (April 2007): 17.

39. Adam Withnall, "Russia Threatens Denmark with Nuclear Weapons if It Tries to Join NATO Defence Shield," *Independent,* (22 March 2015).

40. Frank Trojahn, "The Commanders Response: Royal Danish Navy," *Naval Institute Proceedings* (March 2015).

41. Parliament, *Danish Defense,* 14.

42. Quoted in Toremans, "Huitfeldt," 115.

43. Christopher Cavas, "Aboard Danish Frigate, Clean Lines and Room to Grow," *Defense News,* (17 November 2014): 11.

44. Toremans, "Huitfeldt," 115.

45. Cavas, "Frigate," 11.

46. Nørby, "Danish Navy," 83.

47. Prézelin, *Combat Fleets,* xvi.

48. Ibid., 377–91.
49. An interesting article from the president of Thales Nederland can be found in Arno Peels, "New Thinking in Netherlands Defense," *Military Technology*, 25, no. 12 (2001): 93–96.
50. Harboe-Hansen, "Modernisation," 93.
51. Waters, "Europe 2010," 98.
52. Ibid.
53. The *Karel Doorman* class is described in more detail in Chant, *Kriegsschiffe*, 79.
54. Two units of these ships were ordered by the Spanish government as the *Galicia* class. Up to 611 marines and their equipment can be embarked. See ibid., 88.
55. Luuk Kroon, "Roles, Missions and Force Structure of the Royal Netherlands Navy," *Naval Forces*, Special Issue (1996): 4.
56. Ibid., 6.
57. Ministry of Defence, *Summary of the Defence White Paper 2000* (The Hague, 2000), 1.
58. Ibid., 18.
59. Ministry of Defence [Netherlands], *Paper 2000*, 1–24.
60. Marcial Hernandez, "Dutch Hard Power: Choosing Decline," American Enterprise Institute (3 April 2013), n.p.
61. Bonsignore, "Finland," *Military Technology. The World Defense Almanac 1990*, Issue 1 (1990): 116–17 "Finland is Buying Dutch Leopards for €200 Million," *DefenseUpdate* (19 January 2014).
62. Hernandez, "Dutch Power," n.p.
63. The defense agreement was established in July 1994 between the two states. The Belgian naval staff is integrated with the Dutch staff at Den Helder (NL). Although a commendable effort between two European neighbors, despite this closer cooperation, the crux remains that ultimately "command of each nation's ships, however, remains with their respective national government. Each government reserves the right to deploy their ships independently, for instance for operations in former colonies. Dutch warships remain homeported in Zeebrugge and den Helder, respectively and the Belgian Navy will keep a command

centre in Zeebrugge for its own national tasks." See Guy A. H. Toremans, "Belgian-Dutch Naval Cooperation," *Naval Forces* 15, no. 6 (1994): 18–24.

64. Wertheim, *Combat Fleets,* 475–76.

65. Ministry of Defence, *Netherlands Defence Doctrine* (The Hague: Defense Staff, 2005), 6, 39, fn 25.

66. Waters, "Europe 2015," 70.

67. Joris Janssen Lok, "On the Beat: Robust Ocean Patrol Vessels Maintain Law and Order on the Seas," *Defense Technology International* (November 2007): 33–39.

68. Operational environment includes the North Sea, Atlantic, Caribbean, and waters near their former colonies.

69. See Wertheim, *Combat Fleets,* 476.

70. Theodore Hughes-Riley, "Fleet Review: The Royal Netherlands Navy," in *Seaforth World Naval Review 2017,* ed. Conrad Waters (South Yorkshire, U.K.: Seaforth Publishing, 2016), 93.

71. Hernandez, "Dutch Power," n.p.

72. Only Luxemburg, Norway, Ireland, and Switzerland have a higher per capita GDP. See The World Bank, "GDP per Capita."

73. Hernandez, "Dutch Power," n.p.

Chapter 11. Sweden and Norway

1. Armed neutrality has a long history in Sweden. In particular, during the Cold War, the Swedish government often portrayed itself as a beacon of peace between the belligerents. However, secret political reassurances were made with NATO for the case of war. "In Sweden's case, the official interpretation of the Cold War is not the whole story. Official armed neutrality was complemented by secret bilateral cooperation with the United States and select NATO countries that guaranteed Western support in case of a war with the Soviet Union. That duality worked for a long time, and Sweden's political elites has been comfortable seeking security through informal bilateral ties to the United States and other European countries, rather than

through official membership in NATO." Jan Joel Andersson, "Nordic NATO. Why It's Time for Finland and Sweden to Join the Alliance," *Foreign Affairs* (30 April 2012).

2. Adm. Peter Nordbeck interviewed by Naval Forces, "Preparing the Navy for the Next Century," *Naval Forces,* Special Issue: The Royal Swedish Navy—Today and Tomorrow 2 (1996): 5.

3. Ibid.

4. For more information see Harboe-Hansen, "Trends," 20–24. Also see Torbjörn Hultman, "Reforming the Swedish Navy," *Military Technology: Special Supplement: Defence Procurement in Sweden—FMV: The Swedish Defence Materiel Administration* (1993): 62–71.

5. Hans Harboe-Hansen, "Swedish Naval Trends and Programmes," *Military Technology,* 17, no. 12 (1993): 20.

6. Chris Bishop (ed.), *The Encyclopedia of World Sea Power: A Comprehensive Encyclopedia of the World's Navies and Their Warships* (London: Guild Publishing, 1988), 52.

7. Nordbeck, "Next Century," 5–6.

8. Explained in more detail in Bishop, *Encyclopedia,* 239.

9. Parry, *Super Highway,* 47.

10. Unsurprisingly, other northern European states close to Russia and Kaliningrad Oblast operate such vessels. Germany has three ships, while Norway has one.

11. Guy Toremans, "Significant Ships: Sweden's Visby Class Corvettes: Stealth at All Levels," in *Seaforth World Naval Review 2012,* ed. Conrad Waters (South Yorkshire, U.K.: Seaforth Publishing, 2011), 161.

12. Leon Engelbrecht, "Fact File: Denel Dynamics Umkhonto Naval Short-Range Surface-to-Air Missile," defenseWeb (3 November 2008).

13. Loic Burton, "Bubble Trouble: Russia's A2/AD Capabilities," Foreign Policy Association (25 October 2016).

14. Guy Toremans, "Sweden's High Speed Stealthy V-Force," *Warships International Fleet Review* (January 2014): 31.

15. Commander Erik Uhren quoted in Ibid., 30.

16. Quote from the official website: "The Basics about NORDEFCO," *Nordic Defense Cooperation.*

17. Government Offices of Sweden, *Swedish Government Bill 2004/05:5, Our Future Defence—The Focus of Swedish Defence Policy 2005–2007* (2004), 13.

18. Ibid., 14.

19. "Interview Karin Enström. Sweden's Defense Minister," *Defence News* (18 August 2014), 22.

20. Viribus Unitis, "Nordic NATO Nominees," Center for International Maritime Security (9 May 2014).

21. In fact, Sweden was the only country that was not part of the Arab League or NATO to participate in enforcing the no-fly zone over Libya in 2011. "Sweden Sends Eight Fighter Jets to Libya," Swedish Wire (29 March 2011).

22. Andersson, "Nordic NATO," n.p.

23. Ibid., n.p.

24. Gerard O'Dwyer, "Norway, Sweden Spending Billions to Secure Surrounding Seas," *Defence News* (17 October 2011), 19.

25. Gerard O'Dwyer, "Russian Aggression Drives Swedish Defense Spending," *Defence News* (17 February 2016).

26. See Watkins, "Strategy 1984," 69–85.

27. Greenland-Iceland-United Kingdom.

28. Moreau, "Presentation," 29.

29. Chant, *Ships,* 166.

30. Prézelin, *Combat Fleets,* 401–10. For a more detailed description of the program see the article in *Naval Forces*: "MICOS—The New Mine Countermeasure Systems for the Royal Norwegian Navy," *Naval Forces,* Special Issue: Norwegian Naval Forces Today and Tomorrow (1995): 38–42.

31. Torolf Rein, "The Quality of Our Forces Remains a Primary Condition," *Naval Forces,* Special Issue: Norwegian Naval Forces Today and Tomorrow (1995): 4.

32. Ibid.

33. Ibid.

34. During the Cold War many Norwegian forces were at a constant alert readiness of less than thirty minutes. See Kjell Amund Prytz interviewed by *Naval Forces*: "The Way Ahead," *Naval Forces*, Special Issue: Norwegian Naval Forces Today and Tomorrow (1995): 18.

35. Rein, "Quality," 4.

36. Baker, *Combat Fleets*, 503.

37. See "General Dynamics Awarded $18 Billion by U.S. Navy for 10 Virginia-Class Submarines," General Dynamics (28 April 2014).

38. Eivind Hauger-Johanessen, "The Navy Materiel Command Norway: Facing a Historic Challenge," *Military Technology* 21, no. 12 (1997): 37.

39. RIMPAC is hosted by the United States annually and constitutes the largest naval exercises in the world.

40. "Frigate Berthed for Its Spare Parts," NEWS in ENGLISH.no (30 September 2013).

41. Guy Toremans, "Significant Ships: Skjold Class FACs: Norway's Fighting Cats: Stealth Reigns Supreme," in *Seaforth World Naval Review 2015,* ed. Conrad Waters (South Yorkshire, U.K.: Seaforth Publishing, 2014), 126–27.

42. Ibid.,129.

43. Ibid., 139. Note that these ships have been included in Figure 12-4. Norway therefore has a total of eleven capable surface combatants.

44. Ibid.

45. Norwegian Ministry of Defense, *Norwegian Defence* (2006), 3–4.

46. Norwegian Ministry of Defense, *Norwegian Defence* (2004), 7.

47. Norwegian Ministry of Defense, *Norwegian Defence* (2008), 5.

48. See Ezio Bonsignore et al., "Norway," *Military Technology: The World Defense Almanac 2004,* 1 (2004): 149.

49. See Norwegian Armed Forces website home page: "Norwegian Joint Headquarters." Also Gerard O'Dwyer, "Norway Maintains Littoral Focus on High North," *Defence News* (10 January 2011), 12.

50. See Doug Stanglin, "Sweden Reinstates Military Draft over Concerns about Russian Aggression," *USAToday* (2 March 2017).

Also Elisabeth Braw, "Norway's Gender-Neutral Draft," War on the Rocks (23 June 2016).

51. Svein Efjestad, "IV. Norway and the North Atlantic: Defence of the Northern Flank," in *RUSI Whitehall Paper 87, NATO and the North Atlantic, Revitalising Collective Defense,* ed. John Andreas Olsen (Abingdon, U.K.: Taylor & Francis, 2017), 59–74.

52. John Richardson, "Chief of Naval Operations' White Paper: The Future Navy," *USNI News* (16 May 2017), 1.

53. Sloggett, "Norway Leads," 23.

Chapter 12. Analysis and Observations

1. Etienne de Durand, "NATO in an Era of Global Competition, Defending Borders," min: 52:00.

2. Waters, "Europe 2012," 93.

3. Gerard O'Dwyer, "Nordic Support for Baltic Littoral Defenses," *Defense News* (9 January 2012), 11. More recently in Iain Ballantyne, "NATO Boss Make Vow TO PROTECT BALTIC," *Warships International Fleet Review* (January 2015): 2.

4. Conrad Waters, "Regional Review—Europe and Russia," in *Seaforth World Naval Review 2017,* ed. Conrad Waters (South Yorkshire, U.K.: Seaforth Publishing, 2016), 73.

5. Ibid.

6. Parry, *Super Highway,* 329.

7. J. B. Haldane and Sam J. Tangredi quoted in Geoffrey Till, "A Global Survey of Naval Trends: The British Approach," in *Oslo Files on Defence and Security: The Rise of Naval Powers in Asia and Europe's Decline,* eds. Bjørn Terjesen and Øystein Tunsjø (Oslo: n.p., 2012), 17.

8. Ibid., 103.

9. Larrabee, *Austerity,* 106.

10. Chris Pagenkopf, "Cooperation Is the Key to NATO's Future," *Naval Institute Proceedings* (September 2014): n.p.

11. A brief illustration of the malaise India's naval sector finds itself in can be found in Dave Sloggett, "India's Navy Falters," *Warships International Fleet Review* (July 2014): 12–13.

12. It is worth noting that the respective Asian navies already operated relatively large fleets in 1990. However, many of the vessels at the time were obsolete while today these fleets are largely composed of modern warships.

13. See John Andreas Olsen, ed., *Whitehall Papers 87: NATO and the North Atlantic, Revitalising Collective Defense* (Abingdon, U.K.: Taylor & Francis, 2017).

14. Larrabee, *Austerity,* 7. Also in Benitez, "Alliance," n.p.

15. Ibid., 86.

16. Nearly every air campaign since the end of the Cold War has shown that Europe's arsenal of precision ammunition was quickly depleted. Karen DeYoung and Greg Jaffe, "NATO Runs Short on Some Munitions in Libya," *Washington Post* (15 April 2011).

17. In 2013 the U.S. spent a total of $735 million on the NATO defense budget compared to a total of $288 million of all other allies. See Pagenkopf, "Cooperation," n.p.

Conclusion

1. NATO, *Wales Summit Declaration* (5 September 2014), n.p.

2. Ibid., n.p.

3. The current problem of financing NATO operations in the Baltic States and Poland is discussed in detail in De Durand, "NATO," min: 14:00.

4. Gray, *Leverage,* Prologue.

5. Bobbitt, *Consent,* 537.

6. Parry, *Super Highway,* 215.

7. Seidler, "Europe's Role," n.p.

8. Ibid.

9. A navigable Northeast Passage, plausible in the coming decades, would reduce the distance between China's production sites and the European market by roughly ten thousand kilometers. According to various predictions, vessels traveling on these routes will, however, continue to be dependent on the assistance

of icebreakers. Currently, "Russia maintains a decided advantage in Arctic operations in its ownership of seven nuclear-powered civilian vessels and nineteen diesel-powered variants, with six more planned in the near future." Parry, *Super Highway*, 146–47.

10. Note that in 2017, Poland published a comprehensive naval strategy. Meanwhile efforts to procure a range of more capable naval platforms continue. Seidler, "NATO's Pivot," n.p.

11. European Commission, Press Release Database: "Explaining the Treaty of Lisbon" (1 December 2009).

12. Parry, *Highway*, 33.

BIBLIOGRAPHY

Primary Sources

Official Publications and White Papers

Bundesministerium der Verteidigung. *Defense Policy Guidelines for the Responsibility of the Federal Minister of Defense.* Berlin, 2003.

———. *Defense Policy Guidelines: Safeguarding National Interests— Assuming International Responsibility—Shaping Security Together.* Berlin, 2011.

———. *Weißbuch zur Sicherheit der Bundesrepublik Deutschland und zur Lage und Zukunft der Bundeswehr.* Berlin, 1994.

———. *Weißbuch 2006: Zur Sicherheitspolitik Deutschlands und zur Zukunft der Bundeswehr.* Berlin, 2006.

———. *Weißbuch 2016: On German Security Policy and the Future of the Bundeswehr.* Berlin, 2016.

Bundeswehr. "Die Operation Enduring Freedom." 4 December 2013. http://www.einsatz.bundeswehr.de/portal/a/einsatzbw.

Combined Maritime Forces. "CTF-151: Counter-piracy." https:// combinedmaritimeforces.com/ctf-151-counter-piracy/.

Danish Parliament. *Danish Defense Agreement 2010–2014.* Copenhagen, 2009.

———. *The Danish Defense Agreement 2005–2009, Preliminary translation.* Copenhagen, 2004.

Departamento De Seguridad National, Presidencia Del Gobierno. *The National Maritime Security Strategy 2013: Sharing a Common Project.* Madrid, 2013.

Department of Defense. *Africa Command.* "African Partnership Station." http://www.africom.mil/tags/africa-partnership -station.

————. *Annual Report to Congress, Military and Security Developments Involving the People's Republic of China 2014.* Washington, DC: GPO, 2014.

————. *Defense Strategic Guidance: Sustaining U.S. Global Leadership, Priorities for 21st Century Defense.* Washington, DC: GPO, 2012.

————. *Military and Security Developments Involving the People's Republic of China—2010.* Washington, DC: GPO, 2010.

————. *Military and Security Developments Involving the People's Republic of China—2011.* Washington, DC: GPO, 2011.

———— *Military and Security Developments Involving the People's Republic of China—2014.* Washington, DC: GPO, 2014.

————. *Military Power of the People's Republic of China.* Washington, DC: GPO, 2009.

Department of the Navy. *A Cooperative Strategy for 21st Century Sea Power.* Washington, DC: GPO, 2007.

————. *A Cooperative Strategy for the 21st Century Sea Power. Forward, Engaged, Ready.* Washington, DC: GPO, 2015.

Department for Transport. *Statistical Release—Shipping Fleet Statistics 2014.* 18 February 2015.

European Commission. Press Release Database. "Explaining the Treaty of Lisbon." 1 December 2009. http://europa.eu/rapid/press-release_MEMO-09–531_de.htm?locale=en.

EU External Action. *A Global Strategy for the European Union's Foreign and Security Policy: Shared Vision, Common Action: A Stronger Europe.* Brussels, 2016.

Finnish government. *Finnish Security and Defence Policy 2001: Report by the Government to Parliament,* 2001.

Government Offices of Sweden. *Swedish Government Bill 2004/05:5, Our Future Defence—The Focus of Swedish Defence Policy 2005–2007.* Stockholm, 2004.

Hellenic Ministry of Defense. *White Paper 2014.* Athens, Directorate of National Defense Policy, 2015.

Hellenic Ministry of National Defense. *White Paper for the Armed Forces 1996–1997.* Athens, 1997.

HM Ministry of Defence. *British Maritime Doctrine* (BR 1806). 2nd ed. London: The Stationery Office, 1999.

———. *Delivering Security in a Changing World, Defense White Paper.* London, 2003.

———. *A Secure and Prosperous United Kingdom, National Strategy and Strategic Defence and Security Review 2015.* London: The Stationery Office, 2015.

———. *Securing Britain in an Age of Uncertainty, The Strategic Defence and Security Review.* London: The Stationery Office, 2010.

———. *Strategic Defence Review.* London, 1998.

HM Ministry of Defence, FJS. *Combined Joint Expeditionary Force (CJEF) User Guide.* Swindon and Paris: The Development, Concepts and Doctrine Centre and Centre Interarmées de Concepts, de Doctrine et d'Expérimentations, 2012.

Kelley, P. X., and James D. Watkins. "Amphibious Strategy." In *U.S. Naval Strategy in the 1980s, Selected Documents,* edited by John B. Hattendorf and Peter M. Swartz, 105–36. Newport, RI: Naval War College Press, 2008.

Lehmann, John F. "The 600-Ship Navy." In *U.S. Naval Strategy in the 1980s, Selected Documents,* edited by John B. Hattendorf and Peter M. Swartz, 246–58. Newport, RI: Naval War College Press, 2008.

Ministère de la Défense. *Defense Key Figures, 2015 Edition.* Paris: 2015.

———. *French White Paper, Defense and National Security 2013.* Paris: 2013.

———. *The French White Paper on Defence and National Security.* Paris: 2008.

———. *Livre Blanc sur la Défense 1994.* Paris: 1994.

Ministerio de Defensa, Secretaría General Técnica. *Defense White Paper 2000.* Madrid: Centro de Publicaciones, 2000.

———. *Strategic Defence Review.* Madrid: Imprenta Ministerio de Defensa, 2003.

Ministerio di Defensa. Directive 001/2000 Admiral Chief of Staff of the Navy: "GRUFLOT Is Created." http://www.armada.

mde.es/ArmadaPortal/page/Portal/ArmadaEspannola/
conocenos_organizacion/prefLang_en/03_Flota—02_Flota
-Fuerza-Accion-Naval—023_COMGRUP2—02_historia_
grup2_es.

Ministry for Foreign Affairs of Finland. "Finland and NATO–FAQ."
http://formin.finland.fi/public/defaultaspx?contentid=
115832&contentlan=2&culture=en-US.

Ministry of Defence. *Netherlands Defence Doctrine.* The Hague,
Defense Staff, 2005.

———. *Summary of the Defence White Paper 2000.* The Hague, 2000.

Moreau, Arthur. "Maritime Strategy Presentation (for the Secretary
of the Navy, 4 November 1982)." In *U.S. Naval Strategy in
the 1980s, Selected Documents,* edited by John B. Hattendorf
and Peter M. Swartz, 19–44. Newport, RI: Naval War College
Press, 2008.

NATO. *Alliance Maritime Strategy.* 2011. http://www.nato.int/cps/on/
natohq/official_texts_75615.htm.

———. "NATO's Relations with Finland." http://www.nato.int/cps/
en/natohq/topics_49594.htm.

———. *Strategic Concept for the Defence and Security of the Members
of the North Atlantic Treaty Organization: Active Engagement,
Modern Defense.* Brussels: NATO Public Diplomacy
Division, 2015.

———. *Wales Summit Declaration.* 2014. http://www.nato.int/cps/
ic/natohq/official_texts_112964.htm.

———. "NATO/WEU: Operation Sharp Guard." 2 October 1996.
http://www.nato.int/ifor/general/shrp-grd.htm.

———. "NATO/WEU Operation Sharp Guard, IFOR Final Factsheet." 1996. http://www.nato.int/ifor/general/shrp-grd
.htm.

Nordic Defense Cooperation. "The Basics about NORDEFCO."
http://www.nordefco.org/The-basics-about-NORDEFCO.

Norwegian Armed Forces. "Norwegian Joint Headquarters." http://
mil.no/organisation/about/norwegianjointheadquarters/
Pages/default.aspx.

Norwegian Ministry of Defence. *Norwegian Defence.* Oslo, 2004.

———. *Norwegian Defence.* Oslo, 2006.

———. *Norwegian Defence.* Oslo, 2008.

Prime Minister's Office. *Finnish Security and Defence Policy 2004: Government Report 6/2004.* Helsinki: Prime Minister's Office Publications, 2004.

———. *Finnish Security and Defence Policy 2009: Government Report.* Helsinki: Prime Minister's Office Publications, 2009.

Richardson, John. "Chief of Naval Operations' White Paper: The Future Navy." *USNI News,* 16 May 2017.

Royal Navy. "Cougar 14." http://www.royalnavy.mod.uk/news-and -latest-activity/operations/mediterranean-and-black-sea/ cougar.

Taylor, Claire. *A Brief Guide to Previous Defence Reviews.* House of Commons Library, 2010. www.parliament.uk/briefing-papers/ SN05714.pdf.

Trost, Carlisle A. H. "Looking Beyond the Maritime Strategy." In *U.S. Naval Strategy in the 1980s, Selected Documents,* edited by John B. Hattendorf and Peter M. Swartz, 259–67. Newport, RI: Naval War College Press, 2008.

Turkish Ministry of Defense. *White Paper 2000.* Ankara, 2000.

Turkish Naval Forces, *Turkish Naval Strategy.* Istanbul: Printing Office of the Turkish Naval Forces, 2016.

Watkins, James D. "The Maritime Strategy, 1984." In *U.S. Naval Strategy in the 1980s, Selected Documents,* edited by John B. Hattendorf and Peter M. Swartz. 45–104. Newport, RI: Naval War College Press, 2008.

West Jr., F. J., et al. "Sea Plan 2000." In *U.S. Naval Strategy in the 1970s—Selected Documents,* edited by John Hattendorf, 103–24. Newport, RI: Naval War College Press, 2007.

Interviews and Official Statements (Listed Chronologically)

Bayazit, Vural. "A Secure Turkey—A Secure Alliance." *Naval Forces.* Special Supplement: Turkish Naval Forces Today and Tomorrow (1992): 2–8.

Bathurst, Benjamin. "The Royal Navy in the 1990s." *Naval Forces* 14, no. 4 (1993): 14–21.

Hultman, Torbjörn. "Reforming the Swedish Navy." *Military Technology*. Special Supplement: Defence Procurement in Sweden—FMV: The Swedish Defence Materiel Administration (1993): 62–71.

Prytz, Kjell Amund. "The Way Ahead." By Naval Forces. *Naval Forces*. Special Issue: Norwegian Naval Forces Today and Tomorrow (1995): 18–23.

Rein, Torolf. "The Quality of Our Forces Remains a Primary Condition." *Naval Forces*. Special Issue: Norwegian Naval Forces Today and Tomorrow (1995): 4.

Boehmer, Hans-Rudolf. "Today, the Navy Is Better and More Capable Than Ever Before." *Naval Forces*. Special Issue 5 (1996): 6–10.

Kroon, Luuk. "Roles, Missions and Force Structure of the Royal Netherlands Navy." *Naval Forces*. Special Issue (1996): 4–7.

Nordbeck, Peter. "Preparing the Navy for the Next Century." *Naval Forces*. Special Issue: The Royal Swedish Navy—Today and Tomorrow 2 (1996): 4–8.

Guarnieri, Umberto. "Roles, Missions and the Force Structure of the Italian Fleet." By Naval Forces. *Naval Forces*. Special Issue 1 (1997): 10–16.

Hauger-Johanessen, Eivind. "The Navy Materiel Command Norway: Facing a Historic Challenge." *Military Technology* 21, no. 12 (1997): 32–40.

Mariani, Angelo. "A Strategic View of the Italian Navy." *Naval Forces*, Special Issue 1 (1997): 6–8.

Lavonen, Eero. "Finland's International Cooperation for Defence Material." *Military Technology*. Special Supplement: Defence in Finland 22, no. 6 (1998): 6–8.

Taina, Anneli. "National Defence Vitally Important to Finland." *Military Technology*. Special Supplement: Defence in Finland 22, no. 6 (1998): 3.

Hinden, Alan. "La Fayette Ship Profile (I)." *Naval Forces* 19, no. 2 (1999): 45–47.

Di Paolo, Giampaolo. "Il Concetto Stregico del Capoi die Stato Maggiore dell Difesa, 2005." https://www.difesa.it/SMD_/CaSMD/ConcettoStrategico/Pagine/default.aspx.

Bangar, Manohar K. "Nobody Asked Me but . . . The Royal Navy: Whither Goes Thou?" *Naval Institute Proceedings* (March 2008). http://www.usni.org/magazines/proceedings/2008-03/nobody-asked-me.

Branciforte, Bruno. "The Commanders Respond: Italian Navy." *Naval Institute Proceedings* (March 2012). http://www.usni.org/magazines/proceedings/2012–03/commanders-respond-italian-navy.

Di Paola, Giampaolo. "L'evoluzione della Difesa italiana negli ultimi trent'anni." Ministerio della Difesa (28 September 2012). http://www.difesa.it/Il_Ministro/Articoli/Pagine/LEVOLUZIONEDELLADIFESAITALIANA.aspx.

Department of Defense. "Remarks by Secretary Hagel and Gen. Dempsey on the Fiscal Year 2015 Budget, Preview in the Pentagon Briefing Room, Transcript" (24 February 2014). http://www.defense.gov/Transcripts/Transcript.aspx?TranscriptID=5377.

"Interview Karin Enström. Sweden's Defense Minister." *Defence News* (18 August 2014), 22.

"SPIEGEL Interview with Henry Kissinger: 'Europeans Hide Behind the Unpopularity of President Bush.'" *Spiegel Online International* (18 February 2008). http://www.spiegel.de/international/world/0,1518,535964,00.html.

Trojahn, Frank. "The Commanders Response: Royal Danish Navy." *Naval Institute Proceedings* (March 2015). http://www.usni.org/magazines/proceedings/2015–03/commanders-respond-royal-danish-navy.

Secondary Sources

Monographs and Reference Works

Alifantis, Stelios, and Christos Kollias. "Greece." In *Arms Procurement Decision Making Volume II: Chile, Greece, Malaysia,*

Poland, South Africa and Taiwan, edited by Ravinder Pal Singh, 39–66. Oxford: University Press, 2000.

Baker III, A. D. *The Naval Institute Guide to Combat Fleets of the World 2000–2001: Their Ships, Aircraft, and Systems.* Annapolis, MD: Naval Institute Press, 2000.

Ballard, John R., et al. *From Kabul to Baghdad and Back: The U.S. at War in Afghanistan and Iraq.* Annapolis, MD: Naval Institute Press, 2012.

Beedall, Richard. "The Royal Navy: Mind the Gaps." In *Seaforth World Naval Review 2014,* edited by Conrad Waters, 77–87. South Yorkshire, U.K.: Seaforth Publishing, 2013.

Bernard, Prézelin. *The Naval Institute Guide to Combat Fleets of the World, 1992–93: Their Ships, Aircraft, and Systems.* Annapolis, MD: Naval Institute Press, 1992.

Bishop, Chris, ed. *The Encyclopedia of World Sea Power. A Comprehensive Encyclopedia of the World's Navies and Their Warships.* London: Guild Publishing, 1988.

Bobbitt, Philip. *Terror and Consent, The Wars for the Twenty-First Century.* New York: Anchor Books, 2009.

Bruns, Sebastian. "Elements of Twenty-First-Century Germany Naval Strategy." In *Routledge Handbook of Naval Strategy and Security,* edited by Joachim Krause and Sebastian Bruns, 283–82. Abingdon, U.K.: Routledge, 2016.

Bush, Steve. *British Warships & Auxiliaries.* Liskeard, Cornwall: Maritime Books, 2013.

Cassidy, Robert M. *Counterinsurgency and the Global War on Terror: Military Culture and Irregular War.* Westport, CT: Praeger Security International, 2006.

Cernuschi, Enrico, and Vincent P. O'Hara. "Fleet Review—Italy: The Marina Militare: A Well-balanced Force in Time of Crisis." In *Seaforth World Naval Review 2013,* edited by Conrad Waters, 79–89. South Yorkshire, U.K.: Seaforth Publishing, 2012.

———. "Significant Ships—The Aircraft Carrier Cavour: Doctrine and Sea Power in the Italian Navy." In *Seaforth World Naval*

Review 2010, edited by Conrad Waters, 116–31. South York-shire, U.K.: Seaforth Publishing, 2009.

Chant, Chris. *Kriegsschiffe Heute.* Stuttgart: Motorbuch Verlag, 2006.

———. *Ships of the World's Navies.* London: Brain Trodd Publishing House, 1990.

Childs, Nick. *Britain's Future Navy.* Rev. ed. Barnsley, U.K. Pen & Sword Maritime, 2014.

Corbett, Julian S. *Some Principles of Maritime Strategy.* Mineola, NY: Dover Publications, 2004 (1911).

Coticchia, Fabrizio. "Il Lungo Sentiero sul Lago di Ghiaccio: L'Evoluzione della Politica di Difesa Italiana dalla Fine della Guerra Fredda all'Operazione Leonte." PhD diss., Lucca: IMT Institute for Advanced Studies, 2009.

Dokos, Thanos P., and Panayotis J. Tsakonas. "Greek-Turkish Rela-tions in the Post-Cold War Era." In *Greece and Turkey in the 21st Century: Conflict or Cooperation. A political Economy Perspective,* edited by Christos Kollias and Gülay Gün-lük-Şenesen, 10–35. New York: Nova Science, 2003.

Efjestad, Svein. "IV. Norway and the North Atlantic: Defence of the Northern Flank." In *RUSI Whitehall Paper 87: NATO and the North Atlantic, Revitalising Collective Defense,* edited by John Andreas Olsen, 59–74. Abingdon, U.K.: Taylor & Francis, 2017.

Ferguson, Niall. *Civilization: The West and the Rest.* New York: Penguin Books, 2011.

Friedman, Norman. *The Fifty Year War: Conflict and Strategy in the Cold War.* London: Chatham Publishing, 2000.

———. "Technology Review. Ballistic Missile Defense and the USN." In *Seaforth World Naval Review 2013,* edited by Conrad Waters, 184–91. South Yorkshire, U.K.: Seaforth Publishing, 2012.

———. "Technological Reviews—Naval Sensors and Weapons." In *Seaforth World Naval Review 2010,* edited by Conrad Waters, 167–76. South Yorkshire, U.K.: Seaforth, 2009.

Gascoyne-Cecil, Robert (Marquis of Salisbury). "Letter to Robert Bulwer-Lytton, 1st Earl of Lytton. 15 June (1877)." In Lady

Gwendolen Cecil. *Life of Robert Marquis of Salisbury.* London: Hodder and Stoughton Limited, 1921.

Grant, R. G. *Battle at Sea: 3,000 Years of Naval Warfare.* London: Dorling Kindersley Limited, 2008.

Gray, Colin S. *The Leverage of Sea Power, The Strategic Advantage of Navies in War.* New York: The Free Press, 1992.

Haynes, Peter D. *Towards a New Maritime Strategy: American Naval Thinking in the Post-Cold War Era.* Annapolis, MD: Naval Institute Press, 2015.

Hess, Sigurd. "Die konzeptionelle Planung der Marine 1989–2002." In *Die Wende. Die Deutsche Marine auf dem Weg in die Einheit,* edited by Stephan Huck, Hartmut Klüver, 21–30. Bochum: Dieter Winkler Verlag, 2007.

Holsti, Kalevi J. *Peace and War: Armed Conflicts and International Order 1648–1989.* Cambridge: Cambridge University Press, 1998.

Hudson, Peter, and Peter Roberts. "The UK and the North Atlantic: A British Military Perspective." In *RUSI Whitehall Paper 87: NATO and the North Atlantic. Revitalising Collective Defense,* edited by John Andreas Olsen, 75–91. Abingdon, U.K.: Taylor & Francis, 2017.

Hughes-Riley, Theodore. "Fleet Review: The Royal Netherlands Navy." In *Seaforth World Naval Review 2017,* edited by Conrad Waters, 92–103. South Yorkshire, U.K.: Seaforth Publishing, 2016.

Hury, Myron, et al. *Interoperability: A Continuing Challenge in Coalition Air Operations.* Santa Monica: RAND Corp., 2000.

Kaak, Ulf. *Die Schiffe der Deutschen Marine: 1990 bis heute.* München: GeraMond Verlag, 2013.

Koda, Yoji. "Naval Developments in Japan." In *Olso Files on Defense and Security: The Rise of Naval Powers in Asia and Europe's Decline,* edited by Bjørn Terjesen and Øystein Tunsjø, 53–66. Oslo: December 2012.

Kollias, Christos, and Gülay Günlük-Şenesen, eds. *Greece and Turkey in the 21st Century: Conflict or Cooperation. A Political Economy Perspective.* New York: Nova Science, 2003.

Krüger, Dieter, and Felix Schneider, eds. *Die Alpen im Krieg: Historischer Raum, Strategie und Sicherheitspolitik.* Munich: Oldenburg Verlag, 2012.

Larrabee, F. Stephen, et al. *NATO and the Challenges of Austerity.* Santa Monica: RAND Corp., 2012.

Lewis, William J. *The Warsaw Pact: Arms, Doctrine, and Strategy.* London: McGraw-Hill, 1982.

Mahan, Alfred Thayer. *The Influence of Sea Power upon History.* 1890. Reprint, Mineola, NY: Dover Publications, 1988. https://archive.org/details/seanpowerinf00maha.

———. *Mahan on Naval Warfare. Selections from the Writing of Rear Admiral Alfred T. Mahan.* 1941. Edited by Allan Westcott. Reprint, Mineola, NY: Dover Publications, 1999.

Meyer, Berthold. "Von der Entgrenzung nationaler deutscher Interessen. Die politische Legitimation weltweiter Militäreinsätze." *HSFK-Report 10/2007.* Frankfurt: n.p., 2007.

Moulin, Jean. "France: The Marine Nationale: The Bare Minimum for the Job." In *Seaforth World Naval Review 2015,* edited by Conrad Waters, 76–87. South Yorkshire, U.K.: Seaforth Publishing, 2014.

Nørby, Søren. "Fleet Review: The Royal Danish Navy." In *Seaforth World Naval Review 2017,* edited by Conrad Waters, 83–91. South Yorkshire, U.K.: Seaforth Publishing, 2016.

Nye Jr., Joseph S. *Soft Power: The Means to Success in World Politics.* New York: Public Affairs, 2004.

Olsen, John Andreas, ed. *Whitehall Papers 87: NATO and the North Atlantic, Revitalising Collective Defense.* Abingdon, U.K.: Taylor & Francis, 2017.

Øystein Tunsjø. "Maritime Developments in Asia: Implications for Norway." In *Olso Files on Defense and Security: The Rise of Naval Powers in Asia and Europe's Decline.* Edited by Bjørn Terjesen and Øystein Tunsjø Tunsjø, 93–104. Oslo: December 2012.

Parry, Chris. *Super Highway: Sea Power in the 21st Century.* London: Elliot and Thompson Limited, 2014.

Polmar, Norman. *The Naval Institute Guide to the Ships and Aircraft of the U.S. Fleet,* 15th Edition. Annapolis, MD: Naval Institute Press, 1993.

———. *The Naval Institute Guide to the Ships and Aircraft of the U.S. Fleet,* 19th Edition. Annapolis, MD: Naval Institute Press, 2013.

Potter, Elmar B., Chester W. Nimitz, and Jürgen Rohwer, eds. *Seemacht. Eine Seekriegsgeschichte von der Antike bis zur Gegenwart.* München: Pawlak Verlag, 1986.

Reynolds, Clark G. *Command of the Sea. The History and Strategy of Maritime Empires.* 1974. Reprint, Malabar: Krieger Publishing, 1985.

Roberts, John. *Safeguarding the Nation: The Story of the Modern Royal Navy.* Barnsley, U.K.: Seaforth Publishing, 2009.

Rommetveit, Karl, and Bjørn Terjesen. "Introduction." In *Oslo Files on Defense: The Rise of Naval Power in Asia and Europe's Decline,* edited by Bjørn Terjesen and Øystein Tunsjø, 9–16. Oslo: December 2012.

Olsen, John Andreas, ed. *RUSI Whitehall Paper 87. NATO and the North Atlantic, Revitalising Collective Defense.* Abingdon, U.K.: Taylor & Francis, 2017.

Özcan, Gencer. "The Military and the Making of Foreign Policy in Turkey." In *Turkey in World Politics: An Emerging Multiregional Power,* edited by Barry M Rubin and Kemal Kirişci, 13–30. London: Lynne Rienner Publishers, 2001.

Smith, Rupert. *The Utility of Force. The Art of War in the Modern World.* London: Penguin, 2005.

Sönmezoğlu, Faruk, and Gülden Ayman. "The Roots of Conflict and the Dynamics of Change in Turkish-Greek Relations." In *Greece and Turkey in the 21st Century: Conflict or Cooperation. A Political Economy Perspective,* edited by Christos Kollias and Gülay Günlük-Şenesen, 37–48. New York: Nova Science, 2003.

Tangredi, Sam J. *Anti-Access Warfare, Countering A2/AD Strategies.* Annapolis: Naval Institute Press, 2013.

Till, Geoffrey. "A Global Survey of Naval Trends: The British Approach." In *Oslo Files on Defence and Security: The Rise of Naval Powers in Asia and Europe's Decline,* edited by Bjørn Terjesen and Øystein Tunsjø, 17–28. Oslo: December 2012.

———. *Seapower. A Guide for the Twenty-First Century.* Revised 3rd ed. New York: Routledge, 2013.

Toremans, Guy. "Significant Ships—Braunschweig Class Corvettes. Eagerly Awaited by the German Navy." In *Seaforth World Naval Review 2013,* edited by Conrad Waters, 128–47. South Yorkshire, U.K.: Seaforth Publishing, 2012.

———. "Significant Ships—Iver Huitfeldt Class Frigates: Spearhead of the Royal Danish Navy." In *Seaforth World Naval Review 2014,* edited by Conrad Waters, 104–19. South Yorkshire, U.K.: Seaforth Publishing, 2013.

———. "Significant Ships—Skjold Class FACs: Norway's Fighting Cats: Stealth Reigns Supreme." In *Seaforth World Naval Review 2015,* edited by Conrad Waters, 124–39. South Yorkshire, U.K.: Seaforth Publishing, 2014.

———. "Significant Ships—Sweden's Visby Class Corvettes: Stealth at All Levels." In *Seaforth World Naval Review 2012,* edited by Conrad Waters, 148–65. South Yorkshire, U.K.: Seaforth Publishing, 2011.

Tsilikas, Stergios. "Greek Military Strategy: The Doctrine of Deterrence and Its Implications on Greek-Turkish Relations." Master's thesis, Monterey: U.S. Navy: Naval Postgraduate School, 2001. www.dtic.mil/dtic/tr/fulltext/u2/a397555.pdf.

Tsypkin, Mikhail. "The Challenge of Understanding the Russian Navy." In *Olso Files on Defense and Security: The Rise of Naval Powers in Asia and Europe's Decline,* edited by Bjørn Terjesen and Øystein Tunsjø, 79–92. Oslo: December 2012.

Conrad Waters. "Regional Review—Asia and the Pacific." In *Seaforth World Naval Review 2014,* edited by Conrad Waters, 62–76. South Yorkshire, U.K.: Seaforth Publishing, 2013.

———. "Regional Review—Europe and Russia." In *Seaforth World Naval Review 2010,* edited by Conrad Waters, 86–106. South Yorkshire, U.K.: Seaforth Publishing, 2009.

———. "Regional Review—Europe and Russia." In *Seaforth World Naval Review 2014,* edited by Conrad Waters, 62–76. South Yorkshire, U.K.: Seaforth Publishing, 2013.

———. "Regional Review—Europe and Russia." In *Seaforth World Naval Review 2015,* edited by Conrad Waters, 60–75. South Yorkshire, U.K.: Seaforth Publishing, 2014.

———. "Regional Review—Europe and Russia." In *Seaforth World Naval Review 2017,* edited by Conrad Waters, 64–81. South Yorkshire, U.K.: Seaforth Publishing, 2016.

———. "Significant Ships—France's Aquitaine: First French FREMM Heralds a Renaissance for Its Surface Fleet." In *Seaforth World Naval Review 2013,* edited by Conrad Waters, 90–107. South Yorkshire, U.K.: Seaforth Publishing, 2012.

———. "Significant Ships—Germany's Type 212A Submarines: Cutting-Edge Technology Drives German Maritime Transformation." In *Seaforth World Naval Review 2014,* edited by Conrad Waters, 137–154. South Yorkshire, U.K.: Seaforth Publishing, 2013.

———. "Significant Ships—HMS Daring: The Royal Navy's Type 45 Air-Defence Destroyer." In *Seaforth World Naval Review 2010,* edited by Conrad Waters, 132–49. South Yorkshire, U.K.: Seaforth Publishing, 2009.

———. "Significant Ships—Italian Fremms: Carlo Bergamini (General Purpose) and Virginio Fasan (Anti-Submarine) Frigates." In *Seaforth World Naval Review 2015,* edited by Conrad Waters, 88–107. South Yorkshire, U.K.: Seaforth Publishing, 2014.

Wertheim, Eric. *The Naval Institute Guide to Combat Fleets of the World, 16th Edition: Their Ships, Aircraft, and Systems.* Annapolis, MD: Naval Institute Press, 2013.

Xia, Dawei. "China—The People's Liberation Army Navy." In *Seaforth World Naval Review 2010,* edited by Conrad Waters, 56–65. South Yorkshire, U.K.: Seaforth Publishing, 2009.

Journals and Newspapers

Annati, Massimo. "European Aircraft Carrier Programmes." *Military Technology* 29, no. 10 (2005): 42–49.

———. "German and Dutch AAW Frigates at Sea." *Military Technology* 26, no. 3–4 (2002): 102–108.

Ballantyne, Iain. "The Big Interview, First Sea Lord of the RN." *Warships International Fleet Review* (September 2009): 4–7, 32–33.

———. "NATO Boss Make Vow TO PROTECT BALTIC." *Warships International Fleet Review* (January 2015): 2.

Beaufort, Francis. "French Chiefs 'In Revolt.'" *Warships International Fleet Review* (July 2014): 3.

———. "Today's RN Frigate & Destroyer Force Is 'Woefully' Inadequate." *Warships International Fleet Review* (January 2017): 5.

Bekdil, Burak Ege, and Umit Enginsoy. "Mediterranean Littoral Dispute Challenges Turkish Navy." *Defense News* (9 January 2012), 10.

Bonsignore, Ezio, et al. "Finland." *Military Technology. The World Defence Almanac 1990,* Issue 1 (1990): 116–17.

Bonsignore, Ezio, et al. "Germany." *Military Technology. The World Defence Almanac 2014 ,* Issue 1 (2014): 125–36.

Bonsignore, Ezio, et al. "Indonesia." *Military Technology. The World Defence Almanac 1992–1993 ,* Issue 1 (1993): 189–91.

Bonsignore, Ezio, et al. "Norway." *Military Technology. World Defence Almanac 2004,* Issue 1 (2004): 147–49.

Bonsignore, Ezio, et al. "United Kingdom." *Military Technology. The World Defence Almanac 1995–96,* Issue 1 (1996): 167–71.

Bonsignore, Ezio, et al. "United States of America." *Military Technology. The World Defence Almanac 2014,* Issue 1 (2014): 28–44.

Busquets i Vilanova, Camil. "The Spanish F-100 Frigates." *Naval Forces* 17, no. 5 (1996): 24–30.

Cavas, Christopher. "Aboard Danish Frigate, Clean Lines and Room to Grow." *Defense News* (17 November 2014), 11.

Dudney, Robert S. "Verbatim." *Air Force Magazine* (July 2013): 45.

Eberle, James. "Maritime Strategy," *Naval Forces* 8, no. 2 (1987): 38–49.

Enginsoy, Umit, and Burak Ege Bekdil. "Does Turkey Need an Aircraft Carrier?" *Defense News* (7 May 2012), 13.

———. "Turkey Seeks Full Littoral Defense Architecture." *Defense News* (10 January 2011), 13.

"France and Italy Launch Joint Frigate Programme." *Military Technology* 27, no. 2 (2003): 64–68.

Freeman, Sam Perlo, et al. "Trends in World Military Expenditure, 2012." In *SIPRI Fact Sheet* (April 2013).

Giorgerini, Giorgio. "The Italian Navy in the 1990s." *Military Technology* 14, no. 5 (1990): 47–54.

Grolleau Henri-Pierre. "RAFALE Demonstrates Interoperability." *Military Technology* 32, no. 10 (2008): 94.

"'Grupo Alfa'—the Spanish Navy's Main Fighting Force." *Naval Forces* 12, no. 5 (1991): 16–28.

Guarnieri, Umberto. "Roles, Missions and the Force Structure of the Italian Fleet." *Naval Forces.* Special Issue 1 (1997): 10–16.

Harboe-Hansen, Hans. "The Royal Danish Navy's Modernisation Programme." *Naval Forces* 18, no. 6 (1997): 92–95.

———. "Swedish Naval Trends And Programmes." *Military Technology* 17, no. 12 (1993): 20.

Herwig, Michael. "Trilateral Cooperation for a Frigate Programme—Spain, the Netherlands, and Germany." *Naval Forces* 15, no. 5 (1994): 35–38.

Hooton, E. R. "Britain's Strategic Defence Review: Smiles All Around." *Military Technology* 22, no. 9 (1998): 32–36.

———. "Britain's Type 45 Destroyers Advantage." *Military Technology* 25, no. 6 (2001): 57–60.

———. "'Delivering Security in a Changing World': UK Defence White Paper 2003." *Military Technology* 28, no. 2 (2004): 76–78.

Ikenberry, John G. "The Illusion of Geopolitics. The Enduring Power of Liberal Order." *Foreign Affairs* (May/June 2014): 80–91.

Jopp, Heinz Dieter. "Maritime Abhängigkeiten und Schlussfol-gerungen. Die Sicherheitspolitischen Rahmenbedingungen der Bundesrepublik Deutschland." *MarineForum,* 1–2 (2004): 3–7.

———."Rückbesinnung." *MarineForum,* 7–8 (2017): 1.

Kopp, Carlo. "COIN Reorientation—Too Far or Not Far Enough." *Defence Today* 9, no. 2 (2011): 24–27.

"La Fayette Frigate Programme: A Major Success." *Naval Forces.* Special Issue: French Naval Technology (1994): 21–22.

Lefebvre, Jean-Charles. "The French Navy in a Phase of Transition." *Naval Forces* 13, no. 5 (1992): 37–41.

Lok, Joris Janssen. "Danish Decision." *Defense Technology International* (April 2007): 17.

———. "On the Beat: Robust Ocean Patrol Vessels Maintain Law and Order on the Seas." *Defense Technology International* (November 2007): 33–39.

MacKenzie, Christina, and Andy Nativi. "Mission Ready: Amphibious Ship Designs Meet Diverse Operational Needs." *Defense Technology International* 3, no. 3 (2009): 34–35.

Maninger, Stephan. "Der Schattenkrieg—Ergänzungen zur 'Counterinsurgency'—Debatte," *Österreichische Militärische Zeitschrift* 3 (2013): 301–306.

"Mare Nostrum: Commando e Controllo e Operazioni Aeronavali." *Foto X-tra'gli speciali di Revista Italiana Difesa* 10 (2014).

Mead, Walter Russel. "The Return of Geopolitics: The Revenge of Revisionist Power." *Foreign Affairs* (May/June 2014): 69–79.

Michael J. Boyle, "Do Counterterrorism and Counterinsurgency Go Together?" *International Affairs* 86, no. 2 (2010): 333–53.

"MICOS—The New Mine Countermeasure Systems for the Royal Norwegian Navy." *Naval Forces.* Special Issue: Norwegian Naval Forces Today and Tomorrow (1995): 38–42.

Nativi, Andy. "Mission Ready: Italy's New Carrier Has Multiple Roles." *Defense Technology International* 2, no. 8 (2008): 19–20.

O'Dwyer, Gerard. "Nordic Support for Baltic Littoral Defenses." *Defence News* (9 January 2012), 11.

———. "Norway Maintains Littoral Focus on High North." *Defence News* (10 January 2011), 12.

———. "Norway, Sweden Spending Billions to Secure Surrounding Seas." *Defence News* (17 October 2011), 19.

Peels, Arno. "New Thinking in Netherlands Defense." *Military Technology* 25, no. 12 (2001): 93–96.

Philippe, Jean-Paul. "The CHARLES DE GAULLE Takes Shape." *Military Technology* 16, no. 10 (1992): 44–52.

Preston, Antony. "France's Naval Industry in the 1990s." *Naval Forces* 13, no. 5 (1992): 14–24.

———. "The Italian Navy Today." *Naval Forces* 14, no. 6 (1993): 28–32.

———. "Warship Design for the French Navy." *Naval Forces* 13, no. 1 (1992): 16–22.

Promé, Jean-Louis. "The French 1992–94 Military Programme Law: A Case of 'Let's Wait and See' While Adapting." *Military Technology* 16, no. 9 (1992): 42–43.

———. "'Optimar 95' For The French Navy." *Military Technology* 16, no. 9 (1992): 51–56.

Rhades, Jürgen. "The German Navy Faces the Future." *Naval Forces* 13, no. 6 (1992): 18–22.

Rubel, Robert C. "Straight Talk on Forward Presence." *Naval Institute Proceedings* (March 2015): 24–29.

Sadlowski, Manfred. "What Is different from Finland." *Military Technology.* Special Supplement: Defence in Finland 22, no. 6 (1998): 2.

Scholik, Nikolaus. "Mahan oder Corbett: Das maritim-strategische Dilemma, Chinamerika' im indo-pazifischen Raum." *Österreichische Militärische Zeitschrift* 2 (2013): 140–51.

Schubjé, Pierre. "UNIFIL: Deutsch-libanesische Kooperation—Ein Zwischenbericht." *MarineForum* 1–2 (2014): 14–16.

"Ship Construction and New Projects." *Naval Forces* 18, no. 4 (1997): 27.

Sloggett, Dave. "India's Navy Falters," *Warships International Fleet Review* (July 2014): 12–13.

———. "Norway Leads Where Others Should Follow." *Warships International Fleet Review* (May 2009): 22–23.

Sloggett, Dave, and Ian Ballantyne. "Charting a New Course for the 'Special Relationship' at Sea." *Warships International Fleet Review* (March 2015): 18–19.

———. "Franco Russian Carrier Saga." *Warships International Fleet Review* (January 2015): 13–14.

Stöhs, Jeremy. "Intelligence and Deterrence at Sea: The Role of US Naval Information Technology During the 1980s and Today." *JIPSS* 8, no. 2 (2014): 73–91.

———. "US Defense Policy Since the End of the Cold War: The Difficulty of Establishing a Balanced Force Structure." *JIPSS* 8, no. 1 (2014): 139–41.

Thalassocrates, Alcibiades. "A Fateful Name—Horizon." *Naval Forces* 18, no. 2 (1997): 14–15.

———. "Glimmer on the HORIZON." *Military Technology* 19, no. 7 (1995): 10–17.

Toremans, Guy. "Belgian-Dutch Naval Cooperation." *Naval Forces* 15, no. 6 (1994): 18–24.

———. "Sweden's High-Speed Stealthy V-Force." *Warships International Fleet Review* (January 2014), 29–31.

"Turkish Navy—Reasons to Celebrate." *Naval Forces* 15, no. 4 (1994): 23–24.

Articles and General Information from Digital Sources

Abdiwahab, Mohamed. "Turkey's Largest Military Base Oversea to Be Opened in Somalia in April." sputniknews (17 March 2017). https://sputniknews.com/africa/201703 171051688402-turkey-somalia-base/.

Agence France-Presse. "Italy Removes Aircraft Carrier from Libya Campaign." *Defense News* (7 July 2011). http://archive.defensenews.com/article/20110707/DEFSECT05/ 107070311Italy-Removes-Aircraft-Carrier-from-Libya-Campaign.

Andersson, Jan Joel. "Nordic NATO. Why It's Time for Finland and Sweden to Join the Alliance." *Foreign Affairs* (30 April 2012). http://www.foreignaffairs.com/articles/141377/jan-joel-andersson/nordic-nato.

"Austrian Jagdkommandos to Embark German Tender for EU Mission Sophia." Navaltoday.com (1 March 2017). http://navaltoday.com/2017/03/01/austrian-jagdkommandos-to-embark-german-tender-for-eu-mission-sophia/.

"Baltische Länder erhöhen Militärausgaben." news.ORF.at (13 April 2015). http://orf.at/stories/2273071/2273070/.

Benitez, Jorge. "Alliance at Risk." *Atlantic Council* (26 February 2016). http://www.atlanticcouncil.org/publications/reports/alliance-at-risk.

Braw, Elisabeth. "How Migrants Rescued the Italian Navy." *Foreign Policy* (31 May 2016). http://foreignpolicy.com/2016/05/31/how-migrants-rescued-the-italian-navy/.

———. "Norway's Gender-Neutral Draft." War on the Rocks (23 June 2016). https://warontherocks.com/2016/06/norways-gender-neutral-draft/.

Brinkmann, Rainer. "Befehlshaber der Flotte: 'Deutsche Marine am Limit.'" shz.de (9 April 2017). https://www.shz.de/regionales/schleswig-holstein/befehlshaber-der-flotte-deutsche-marine-am-limit-id16551266.html.

Bündis 90 Die Grünen. "Operation Active Endeavor, Einsatz muss beendet werden." (29 January 2014). https://www.gruene-bundestag.de/themen/sicherheitspolitik/einsatz-muss-beendet-werden-29–01–2014.html.

Burton, Loic. "Bubble Trouble: Russia's A2/AD Capabilities." Foreign Policy Association (25 October 2016). https://foreignpolicyblogs.com/2016/10/25/bubble-trouble-russia-a2-ad/.

Cavas, Christopher P. "US NAVY Deploys Most Carrier Groups since 2012." *Defense News* (6 June 2016). http://www.defensenews.com/story/defense-news/2016/06/06/navy-aircraft-carrier-strike-groups-deployed-china-russia-operations/85526820/.

Churchill, Robin R. "Law of the Sea." *Encyclopedia Britannica.* https://www.britannica.com/topic/Law-of- the-Sea#ref913546.

Chuter, Andrew. "Cameron: UK Will Operate 2 Aircraft Carriers." *Defense News* (5 September 2014). http://archive.defense-news.com/article/20140905/DEFREG01/309050019/Cameron-UK-Will-Operate-2-Aircraft-Carrier.

Council on Foreign Relations. "U.S. War in Afghanistan, 1999–Present." http://www.cfr.org/afghanistan/us-war-afghanistan/p20018.

Davies, Lizzy, and Arthur Neslen. "Italy: End of Ongoing Sea Rescue Mission 'Puts Thousands at Risk.'" *Guardian* (31 October 2014). http://www.theguardian.com/world/2014/oct/31/italy-sea-mission-thousands-risk.

Department of the Navy. "The Amphibs." http://www.navy.mil/navydata/ships/amphibs/amphib.asp.

DeYoung, Karen, and Greg Jaffe. "NATO Runs Short on Some Munitions in Libya." *Washington Post* (15 April 2011). http://www.washingtonpost.com/world/nato-runs-short-on-some-munitions-in-libya/2011/04/15/AF3O7ElD_story.html.

Duxbury, Charlie. "Sweden Plans to Increase Military Spending." *Wall Street Journal* (12 March 2015). http://www.wsj.com/articles/sweden-plans-to-increase-military-spending-1426198507.

"Egypt Close to Buying 22 Rafale Fighters, 2 FREMM Frigates Worth Euro 6 Billion." Defenseworld.net (16 January 2015). https://www.defenseworld.net/news/11936/Egypt_Close_To_Buying_22_Rafale_Fighters__2_FREMM_Frigates_Worth_Euro_6_Billion#.VTTqZZMaZew.

Engelbrecht, Leon. "Fact File: Denel Dynamics Umkhonto Naval Short-Range Surface-to-Air missile." defenceWeb (3 November 2008). http://www.defenceweb.co.za/index.php? option=com_content&view=article&id=610.

"Fincantieri and Finmeccanica Will Renew the Italian Navy Fleet." defense-aerospace.com (7 May 2015). http://www.defense-aerospace.com/articles-view/release/3/163456/italy-launches-%E2%82%AC5.8bn-naval-plan.html.

"Finland Is Buying Dutch Leopards for €200 Million." Defense Update (19 January 2014). http://defense-update.com/20140119_finland_buys_dutch_leopards.html#.VQSkpuFY5ew.

"France Deploys Aircraft Carrier in Arabian Gulf for ISIL Fight." National (23 February 2015). http://www.thenational.ae/world/middle-east/france-deploys-aircraft-carrier-in-arabian-gulf-for-isil-fight.

"Frigate Berthed for Its Spare Parts." NEWS in ENGLISH.no (30 September 2013). http://www.newsinenglish.no/2013/09/30/frigate-berthed-for-spare-parts/.

Frisk, Corporal. "Where Are the Finnish Submarines?" Corporal Frisk Wordpress (3 January 2015). https://corporalfrisk.wordpress.com/2015/01/03/where-are-the-finnish-submarines/.

"General Dynamics Awarded $18 Billion by U.S. Navy for 10 Virginia-Class Submarines." General Dynamics.com (28 April 2014). http://www.generaldynamics.com/news/press-releases/detail.cfm?customel_dataPageID_1811=19222.

Gonzáles, Miguel. "España intervendrá con cuatro cazas F-18, una fragata F-100, un submarino y un avión de vigilancia maritime." El País International (19 March 2011). http://internacional.elpais.com/internacional/2011/03/19/actualidad/1300489214_850215.html.

Gonzalez, Jose Alberto. "La Armada da de Baja el 'Siroco' y Centra Sus Esfuerzos en Los Submarines S-80 [The Navy Withdraws the 'Sirocco' and Focuses Its Efforts on the Submarine S-80]." La Verdad (8 May 2012). http://www.laverdad.es/murcia/v/20120508/cartagena/armada-baja-siroco-centra-20120508.html.

Hammes, T. X. "Getting Our Money's Worth: LCS vs Iver Huitfeldt-class." War on the Rocks (6 August 2013). http://warontherocks.com/2013/08/getting-our-moneys-worth-lcs-vs-iver-huitfeldt-class/.

Hernandez, Marcial. "Dutch Hard Power: Choosing Decline." American Enterprise Institute (3 April 2013). http://www.aei.org/publication/dutch-hard-power-choosing-decline/.

Ing, David, and Fenella McGerty. "Spanish Defence Spending Increases 40% in 2015." IHS Jane's 360 (20 April 2016). http://www.janes.com/article/59663/spanish-defence-spending-increases-40-in-2015.

———. "Update: Spain to Increase Defence Spending." IHS Jane's 360 (1 October 2014). http://www.janes.com/article/43968/update-spain-to-increase-defence-spending.

Jentzsch, Christian. "Von der Escort-Navy zur Expeditionary-Navy?" (Presentation, 16. Maritime Sicherheitskolloquium, Rostock, October 20, 2016). https://dmkn.de/escort-navy-expeditionary-navy/.

Jones, Ben. "Franco-British military Cooperation a New Engine for European Defence?" Occasional Paper 88 (February 2011). https://www.iss.europa.eu/content/franco-british-military-cooperation-new-engine-european-defence.

Jungholt, Thorsten, and Simon Meyer. "Der Marine könnte es bald an Schiffen mangeln." Welt.de (6 April 2013). https://www.welt.de/politik/deutschland/article115056737/Der-Marine-koennte-es-bald-an-Schiffen-mangeln.html.

Kingston, Tom. "Italy Closing in on Patrol Vessel Deal." *Defense News* (26 October 2014). http://archive.defensenews.com/article/20141026/DEFREG01/310260018/Italy-Closing-Major-Patrol-Vessel-Deal.

LaGrone, Sam. "Navy Asks Industry for Input for Follow-on to Littoral Combat Ship." *USNI News* (30 April 2014). http://news.usni.org/2014/04/30/navy-asks-industry-input-follow-littoral-combat-ship.

Lert, Frédéric. "Egypt to Acquire FREMM Frigate." IHS Jane's 360 (23 February 2015). http://www.janes.com/article/49163/egypt-to-acquire-fremm-frigate.

Lowe, Joch. "EU Migration: Why Has the Home Office Opposed Rescuing Migrants?" *Prospect* (28 October 2014). http://www.prospectmagazine.co.uk/blogs/prospector-blog/eu-migration-why-has-the-home-office-opposed-rescuing-migrants.

McGrath, Bryan. "NATO at Sea: Trends in Allied Naval Firepower." American Enterprise Institute (18 September 2013). http://www.aei.org/publication/nato-at-sea-trends-in-allied-naval-power/.

Merrill, Jamie. "MoD Asks for American Help in Searching for Russian Submarine Near Scotland." *Independent* (1 April 2014). http://www.independent.co.uk/news/uk/politics/mod-asks-for-american-help-in-searching-for-russian-submarine-near-scotland-9966080.html.

Müller, Albrecht. "New Frigate Underscores Germany's Shift from Cold War Naval Combat." *Defense News* (13 January 2014). http://archive.defensenews.com/article/20140113/DEFREG01/301130031/New-Frigate-Underscores-Germany-s-Shift-From-Cold-War-Naval-Combat.

Nitschke, Stefan, and Stephen Elliott. "Under Water." *Naval Forces* (January 2015), http://www.nafomag.com/2015/01/under-water-faq-on-submarines.html.

"Norway Cuts Afghan Aid over Lack of Progress on Women's Rights." TOLOnews (5 October 2013). http://www.tolonews.com/en/afghanistan/12168-norway-cuts-afghan-aid-over-lack-of-progress-on-womens-rights.

O'Dwyer, Gerard. "Russian Aggression Drives Swedish Defense Spending." *Defense News* (17 February 2016). http://www.defensenews.com/story/defense/policy-budget/warfare/2016/02/07/russian-aggression-drives-swedish-defense-spending/79841348/.

———. "Sweden Plans Defense Spending Boost." *Defense News* (15 October 2013). http://archive.defensenews.com/article/20131015/DEFREG01/310150017/Sweden-Plans-Defense-Spending-Boost.

"Operation Enduring Freedom." iCasualties.org. http://icasualties.org/oef/Nationality.aspx?hndQry=Denmark.

Pagenkopf, Chris. "Cooperation Is the Key to NATO's Future." *Naval Institute Proceedings* (September 2014). http://www.usni.org/magazines/proceedings/2014–09/cooperation-key-natos-future.

Pamuk, Humeyra, and Gareth Jones. "Turkish Military a Fractured Force After Attempted Coup." Reuters (26 July 2016). http://www.reuters.com/article/us-turkey-security-military-insight-idUSKCN10619L.

"Port of Rotterdam." http://www.portofrotterdam.com/en/Port/port-in-general/Pages/default.aspx.

Puente, Íñigo. "Plan Alta Mar: ¿sueño de lo que pudo ser o anticipo de lo que será?" Revista Naval (December 1997). http://www.revistanaval.com/www-alojados/armada/especial/planalta.htm.

RUSI eds. "Accidental Heroes. Britain, France and the Libya Operation—An Interim RUSI Campaign Report." *RUSI.org* (11 September 2011). https://rusi.org/rusi-news/accidental-heroes-britain-france-and-libya-operation-rusi-interim-libya-campaign-report.

Schmitt, Gary J. "Italian Hard Power: Ambitions and Fiscal Realities." American Enterprise Institute (1 November 2012). http://www.aei.org/publication/italian-hard-power-ambitions-and-fiscal-realities/.

Seidler, Felix. "Europe's Role in an East Asian War." Center for International Maritime Security (11 June 2014). http://cimsec.org/europes-role-east-asian-war/11576.

———. "NATO's Pivot to Russia: Cold War 2.0 at Sea?" Center for International Maritime Security (25 April 2014). http://cimsec.org/natos-pivot-russia-cold-war-2–0-sea/10723.

"Series 70 Galerna-type Submarines." globalsecurity.org. http://www.globalsecurity.org/military/world/europe/s-70.htm.

Stanglin, Doug. "Sweden Reinstates Military Draft over Concerns about Russian Aggression." *USA Today* (2 March 2017). https://www.usatoday.com/story/news/2017/03/02/sweden-reinstates-draft-over-concerns-russia/98641010/.

Stockholm International Peace Research Institute. "Military Expenditure Database." https://www.sipri.org/databases/milex.

"Sweden Sends Eight Fighter Jets to Libya." Swedish Wire (29 March 2011). http://www.swedishwire.com/politics/9146-sweden-sends-eight-fighter-jets-to-libya.

Tanchum, Micha'el. "Turkey Vulnerable to Rising Russian Power in the Black Sea." The Turkey ANALYST. A Biweekly Briefing on Current Affairs (9 April 2014). http://www.turkeyanalyst. org/publications/turkey-analyst-articles/item/101-turkey-vulnerable-to-rising-russian-power-in-the-black-sea.html.

"UK: BAE Systems Secures $1.92 Bln Submarine Deal." Navaltoday. com (11 December 2012). http://navaltoday.com/2012/12/11/uk-bae-systems-secures-1-92-bln-submarine-deal/.

"Unemployment Rates, Seasonally Adjusted, July 2016.png." Euro-stat.http://ec.europa.eu/eurostat/statistics-explained/index. php/File:Unemployment_rates,_seasonally_adjusted,_ July_2016.png.Unitis, Viribus. "Nordic NATO Nominees." Center for International Maritime Security (9 May 2014). http://cimsec.org/nordic-nato-nominees/11192.

US Naval War College. "EMC Chair Symposium: Maritime Strategy." Symposium took place in Newport, RI on 23–24 March 2016. https://www.usnwc.edu/maritime-2016.

"Vom Flugzeugträgerverband verabschiedet—Fregatte "Hamburg" macht Heimatumdrehungen!" Presseportal (18 June 2013). http://www.presseportal.de/pm/67428/2495613/vom -flugzeugtr-gerverband-verabschiedet-fregatte-hamburg -macht-heimatumdrehungen.

Wee, Sui-Lee. "China Explains Why It's Building Islands in the South China Sea." Business Insider UK (9 April 2015). http:// uk.businessinsider.com/china-explains-why-its-building-islands-in-the-south-china-sea-2015–4?r=US.

Wills, Steven. "LCS Versus the Danish Strawman." Center for International Maritime Security (19 February 2015). http://cimsec. org/lcs-versus-danish-strawman/14974.

Withnall, Adam. "Russia Threatens Denmark with Nuclear Weapons if It Tries to Join NATO Defence Shield." *Independent* (22 March 2015). http://www.independent.co.uk/news/world/ europe/russia-threatens-denmark-with-nuclear-weapons-if-it-tries-to-join-nato-defence-shield-10125529.html.

World Bank. "GDP per capita." http://data.worldbank.org/indicator/ NY.GDP.PCAP.CD.

Videos

De Durand, Etienne. "NATO in an ERA of Global Competition, Defending Borders." https://www.youtube.com/watch?v= VLZSQjBpHNk.

Friedman, George. "A Forecast for the 21st Century: George Friedman. ANU." https://www.youtube.com/watch?v=RiMRAhupqE0.

Mearsheimer, John. "Imperial by Design." http://www.youtube.com/ watch?v=sKFHe0Y6c_0.

Posen, Barry. "Panel Discussion: A Moment of Transition." https:// www.youtube.com/watch?v=MIg_ZDHeoJg.

RUSI. "Debating Continuous-at-Sea Deterrence: Britain's Nuclear Security." https://www.youtube.com/watch?v=jC3-TPRnXhM &list=PLFAgO2TZWpwBH9t3LB4CJscyDOo5M3dt9

Willett, Lee. "The Strategic Defence and Security Review, a Preliminary RUSI Assessment." https://www.youtube.com/watch? v=yt0NOuFL_Ss.

INDEX

137; Article 5, 182; Cold War naval doctrine and mission, 16; French rejoining of, 68; Greek membership, 117–18; as guarantor of equilibrium in western hemisphere, 186–87; Mine Countermeasure Group, 101, 137; naval doctrine, 15; operational challenges to, 190; Partnership for Peace (PfP), 168; as pillar of European sea power, 186; pivot to Russia, 198; role in Mediterranean, 114, 134, 137; role in reducing redundancy, 187; sea-based theater ballistic missile system, 133–34; Sharp Guard, 101, 114, 147; Standing Maritime Groups, 85, 101, 114, 121, 137, 147, 152, 187, 197; Standing Naval Force Mediterranean, 134; unease regarding situation in Iraq, 48; U.S. obligation to, 23

North Sea, 58, 138, 170; Bundesmarine, Cold War role in, 126; collective defense in, 176; Dutch and Danish shift away from operations in, 144; German planning for operations in, 136; Kongelige Danske Marine Cold War role in, 143; Koninklijke Marine role in, 153; Swedish naval operations in, 164

Norway: 35; Armed Forces Joint Headquarters Bod, 176; cooperation with Nordic and Baltic partners, 176; cooperation with U.S. and U.K., 176; defense against amphibious assault, 171; growing security concerns of, 176; importance of SLOC to, 173; preeminent role of territorial defense, 170, 176, 184; reduction in defense budget during 1990s, 171; reintroduction of conscription, 176; role during Cold War, 169–70; role of territorial defense in, 161, 163, 170, 176; shift in defense policy, 176

nuclear-powered attack submarines (SSN), 41, 43, 54, 60

Ocean, Indian, 5, 22, 48, 72–73, 80, 88, 129, 152, 192

Ocean amphibious assault ship (U.K.), 46

Ocean Shield, Operation, 147

offshore patrol vessels (OPV), 33, 53, 60–61, 63, 105–6, 142, 158, 185

O'Hara, Vincent P., 80

Oliver Hazard Perry class, 96, 101, 106, 111, 184

On Naval Warfare, 13

Orion intelligence gathering vessel (Sweden), 166, 168

Oslo-class frigate (F-300), 170, 173

OTO Melara, 96, 174

Ouragan-class LPD (France), 60

out-of-area operations, 93, 97, 109, 128, 132, 144, 175, 186

Oyashio-class submarine (Japan), 60

P-3: B Orion maritime patrol aircraft, 122, 153; C, 156

P-8 Poseidon maritime patrol aircraft, 38, 87, 176

Pacific Ocean, 8, 22, 24, 92, 170; Chinese defense strategy for, 25–26; EU irrelevance in, 197; French deployment in, 58; U.S. shift from Atlantic to, 5, 24, 36, 40, 88, 192–93. *See also* Asia-Pacific Region (APR)

Pagenkopf, Chris, 188

Parry, Chris, 5, 11, 18, 77, 141, 185, 196

Pattugliatore Polivalente d'Altura (PPA) frigate (Italy), 84

peace: dividend, xi, 39, 42, 130, 183, 185, 194; enforcement, 7

Penguin Mk 2 SSM, 165, 171

Persian Gulf, 23, 68, 72, 80, 134, 198

Phalanx CIWS, 44

piracy. *See* anti-piracy operations

Poland, 184: role in Baltic Sea, 184; role of territorial defense in, 184

Polish navy, 184

Portugal, 32

Posen, Barry R., 21

post-heroic societies, xiii

post-modern navies, 7, 185

power distribution: oceans as medium of, 4; shift to multipolar, 21

power-projection: British attempts to reassert capabilities, 35, 54–55; British lack of capabilities, 48, 57, 183; Danish increase in capabilities, 152; Dutch efforts to sustain capability, 156, 158; German lack of, 137, 139, 183; Greek capabilities, 108, 118; Italian capabilities, 60, 75–76, 84, 183; Japanese lack of capabilities, 41; platform, 84, 93; shift toward, 108; Spanish capabilities, 93, 99; Turkish capabilities, 108, 113–14; U.S. ability to, 15

Prézelin, Bernard, 77, 97, 153

Prince of Wales carrier (U.K.), 54

Principe de Asturias carrier (Spain), 59, 94–97, 101, 104, 170

Principle Anti-Air Missile System (PAAMS), 45, 82–83

Promé, Jean-Louis, 61

Puente, Íñigo, 97

ABOUT THE AUTHOR

Jeremy Stöhs is an Austrian American defense analyst at the Institute for Security Policy at Kiel University (ISPK) and its adjunct Center for Maritime Strategy & Security. He is also a non-resident fellow of the Austrian Center for Intelligence, Propaganda & Security Studies. Jeremy has studied in Austria, Germany, and the United States and holds a master's degree in history and English. Prior to his studies, he worked in law enforcement with the Austrian Federal Police.

The **Naval Institute Press** is the book-publishing arm of the U.S. Naval Institute, a private, nonprofit, membership society for sea service professionals and others who share an interest in naval and maritime affairs. Established in 1873 at the U.S. Naval Academy in Annapolis, Maryland, where its offices remain today, the Naval Institute has members worldwide.

Members of the Naval Institute support the education programs of the society and receive the influential monthly magazine *Proceedings* or the colorful bimonthly magazine *Naval History* and discounts on fine nautical prints and on ship and aircraft photos. They also have access to the transcripts of the Institute's Oral History Program and get discounted admission to any of the Institute-sponsored seminars offered around the country.

The Naval Institute's book-publishing program, begun in 1898 with basic guides to naval practices, has broadened its scope to include books of more general interest. Now the Naval Institute Press publishes about seventy titles each year, ranging from how-to books on boating and navigation to battle histories, biographies, ship and aircraft guides, and novels. Institute members receive significant discounts on the Press' more than eight hundred books in print.

Full-time students are eligible for special half-price membership rates. Life memberships are also available.

For a free catalog describing Naval Institute Press books currently available, and for further information about joining the U.S. Naval Institute, please write to:

Member Services
U.S. Naval Institute
291 Wood Road
Annapolis, MD 21402-5034
Telephone: (800) 233-8764
Fax: (410) 571-1703
Web address: www.usni.org